eXtreme Investor

eXtreme Investor

RANDY RODMAN
with Don Logay

A Lark Production

Entrepreneur Press
2445 McCabe Way, Irvine, CA 92614

Managing Editor: Marla Markman
Book Design: Sylvia H. Lee
Copy Editor: Lynn Pomije
Proofreader: Megan Reilly
Cover Design: Mark Kozak
Production Designers: Mia H. Ko, Marlene Natal
Indexer: Ken DellaPenta

Library of Congress Cataloging-in-Publication Data

Rodman, Randy.
    Extreme investor: intelligent information from the edge/by Randy Rodman with Don Logay.
        p. cm.
    Includes index.
    ISBN 1-891984-16-0
    1. Investments 2. Speculation. 3. Day trading (Securities) I. Logay, Don.
II. Title.
    HG4521 .R6658 2000
    332.63'2--dc21

                                             00-044259

Printed in Canada

09 08 07 06 05 04 03 02 01 00   10 9 8 7 6 5 4 3 2 1

Acknowledgements

First, to the extreme investors who shared their stories, but who, for privacy reasons, have elected not to be fully identified: You know who you are, and thank you.

The authors are also grateful for the assistance of professional day traders Landon Ray, Vladamir Efros, Alexis Zanone and Michael Ray; other professionals from within the day trading community, including John O'Donnell (On Line Trading Academy), Merrick Okamoto (Trade Portal), David Marion (Daystocks, Inc.), Matthew Ostrowski, Jim Sugarman, and Tim Borquin (On Line Trading Expo).

From others quarters of the world of finance we thank Jay De Bradley (Fox Inc./Asset Manager), Linda Tors (stock options trader), Willy Hauptman (World Currency Trading), and David Saito-Chung and Jed Graham (*Investors Business Daily*).

Also the many experts who made valiant efforts to cooperate with our extreme requests, including Jerome Schneider (*Complete Guide to Offshore Money Havens*), Marc Friedfertig (*The Electronic Day Trader*), Jack Segner (*SAMS e-Real Estate*), Ira Eptsein (commodities and option broker), Clifford Goldstein (Niche Mutual Funds), Jeff Horowitz (financial planner), Mike McMahon (daytrader/training instructor), and John Saunders (London Coin Galleries).

Personal thanks to Ulla Rodman, Steven Viscusi, Catherine Sundin and Tim Sims. And thanks Karen Watts and those nice folks at Lark, who break all records for bringing up the rear.

Table Of
Contents

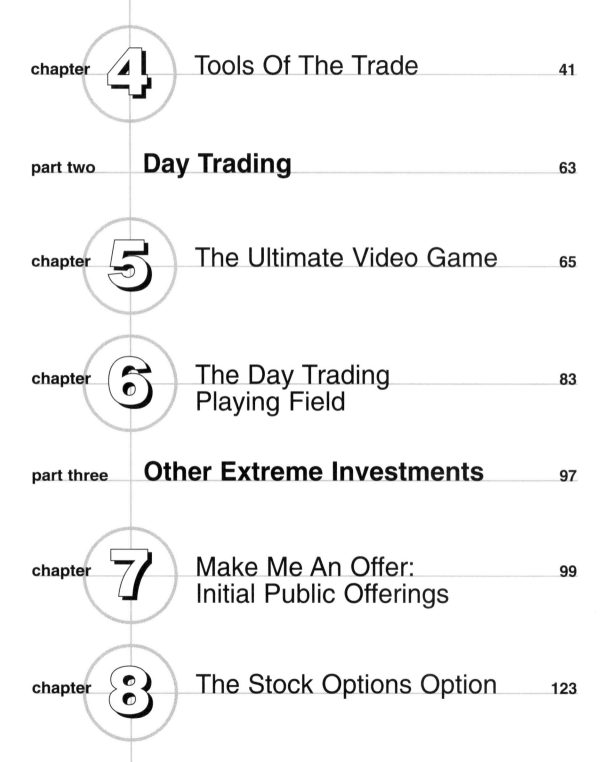

Preface

So you want to make a killing in the stock market. Who doesn't? My grandmother wants to make a killing in the stock market!

You spotted *Extreme Investor* nestled among a number of investment books. Why were you drawn to pick it up? This is not *Dollars for Dimwits* or *Money for Morons*. Nor is it a step-by-step tutorial on building wealth. Rather, it is a challenge.

You obviously have something ticking away at some level in your brain that makes this concept worth investigating. But is it for you? In the pages that follow, we will help you make that determination. And step one lies in fully understanding what you may be venturing into.

By definition, *investing* is "putting money to use, by purchase or expenditure, in something offering potential profitable returns, such as interest, income or value appreciation." Yawn. If this does it for you, we suggest one of the *Dimwits* or *Morons* titles close at hand.

But when you add the word "extreme" to the equation, mundane goes out the window. By definition, *extreme* investing becomes everything from "farthest removed from the ordinary or average" to "maximum in degree or intensity" and "exceeding the bounds of moderation." Other words and phrases, like "utmost," "far beyond" and "way the heck out there," come to mind.

Now, if reading that made you imagine little Johnny's college fund going up in a cloud of smoke, put this book down immediately—before someone gets hurt. However, if it piqued your interest and upped your pulse a beat or two, read on. This book *may* be for you.

In the following pages, we will look at some of the latest trends and many of the new and creative investing concepts being used by those who qualify as extreme investors. Come along as we venture down the (super) highways and (mental) byways of those who live the life and reap the rewards. Yes, they're the ones you've heard about. The waiter who makes a killing as a day trader. The housewife who buys and sells options from home. Those who profit big from minor fluctuations in foreign currency, hot real estate trends and emerging investment vehicles, such as rare coins and collectibles.

A peek into their worlds offers invaluable insights vs. step-by-step road maps to wealth and riches. Come along as we investigate the process rather than the procedure that makes up the extreme investor, and you will quickly learn that a keen awareness of looming opportunity and the ability to rapidly adapt to new technologies are key ingredients of success that "exceeds the bounds of moderation."

We will also help you determine which, if any, of these extreme investing concepts, techniques and/or opportunities may right for you. Much of this book centers on using the Internet and personal computers, as they are the tools du jour of the financially fleet-footed. However, this can change in the blink of an eye, as new technology emerges. And when it does, you can be assured that the extreme among the investment community will be first to embrace and capitalize on new and improved tools.

This may be a good time to stop and ask yourself "Am I a new technology junkie?" If you always keep up with the latest developments in TV, audio and computer technology, score one point. If you're usually the first on your block to actually go out and buy it, score two points. If you seek it out, buy it immediately and stay up all night using it, score three points, and consider yourself having made the first cut as an extreme investor.

However, if you're still using an 8-track tape player because the tapes are still good and you want to get your money's worth, well, deduct two points and read this book for edu-tainment purposes only.

A big trend we'll take a close look at is the day trading phenomenon—an extreme form of investing that is evolving as fast as the explosive Internet itself. Nearly all the vehicles and techniques visited in this book revolve around computers, the Internet and current opportunities in the stock market or other related financial instruments, as well as some uniquely new and exciting derivatives.

In addition to getting a glimpse of regular everyday people with heart-pounding success stories, as you read this book you will learn about buying and selling stocks from a unique perspective, and see how and why trading has become one of the most popular wealth-building vehicles available today. More important, we'll investigate (and share) the elements, techniques and concepts that take ordinary and mundane to the extreme.

Obviously, it helps if you have already done some actual investing and stock trading, and know basics like what a commodity futures contract is and what an IPO is. And while you may not know *how* a short sale is transacted, it helps to know that "shorting" is an alternative to "going long." With us so far?

For our purposes, your knowledge of investment lingo and the markets need not be extensive, but it will help if you know the fundamental concepts behind investment instruments and the vehicles companies use to obtain money with which they expand their businesses, i.e. stocks and bonds. Options are a derivative of stocks and are also players in today's hotbed of financial activity. *Extreme Investor* will help show you what's behind these instruments and why they represent one of the ultimate pursuits in today's arena of rapidly changing investment opportunities.

Perhaps you've considered trading stocks or options but are uncertain of the risks, rewards and strategies. *Extreme Investor* offers a simple explanation of how things work and some strategies that can speed up your learning curve on various forms of extreme investing.

Junk bonds—what's the deal with them? And did your jaw drop when you heard Martha Stewart's IPO made her an instant billionaire—on its first day of trading? Why didn't you get a piece of that? Better yet, why wasn't it *you* instead of her?

Had you read *Extreme Investor* earlier, perhaps you could have joined the fun (past tense). Now, you can (present and future). In other words, this book is a portal for those who have a basic understanding of what's out there but need greater insight into successful concepts that weigh opportunity and risk, and green-light extreme action when personal indicators are right.

This book works well for the casual investor who wants to know if today's investment models are opportunities worth considering or something to be avoided. In fact, *Extreme Investor* is written for a wide range of nonprofessional investors and traders.

○ Have you dabbled in the market with some success? Are you now ready for more challenge with greater returns, beyond just good pick recommendations?

○ Are you seeking new ideas, fresh concepts and better ways to dive in and maximize investment opportunities?

○ Have you always bought and held investments? Are you conservative in the traditional sense? Do you now see the rules and rewards of investment changing, and you don't want to miss the revolution?

○ Has the meteoric and historic success of entirely new realms and vehicles—like global, techs and dotcoms—got you thinking maybe it's time you stepped up to the plate, too?

Extreme Investor will help pave the way.

As such, P/E ratios, corporate earnings, stock charts and many other standard tricks and tools of the trade are covered from a different perspective—as they apply to extreme investing. But this is not intended to be a tutorial on available investment tools or how to master them. Rather, many of the trading tools mentioned herein have been used for years by not-so-extreme investors, but today we find they have new meaning and vastly different interpretations for those who venture into the exciting realm of extreme investing.

This book outlines the playing field and helps define the rules to play by, and it contains some strategic tips. But it is by no means all you will need to get started. Instead, *Extreme Investor* offers a foundation upon which to build and move forward.

As we've said, the majority of extreme investments, and the research that precedes them, involve the Internet. Therefore, we assume online access and basic computer proficiency. You will also find a fair amount of information about—and references to—Web sites, software products and online investment tools, including stock trading order execution systems. And while a section of this book briefly delves into what type of computer setup and Internet connectivity speeds are best, you will find it minimal because technology changes at the speed of light.

Wanting to do something and being truly qualified to do it are two different things. Extreme investors are supremely confident (and you'll see why). Like a hawk that can spot a field mouse a mile away, extreme investors see and sense opportunities others often miss. And when they do, they pounce . . . and put it all on the line—without hesitation. They are the real movers and shakers—the leaders and winners—in today's fast-paced world of extreme investing.

Welcome to the world of the extreme investor.

Introduction

Most people work five days a week and look forward to playing and relaxing on weekends. Their jobs and careers are only a means to an end—a spouse, a house, 2.3 kids, a dog and extras that make life worth living.

The average American has long-range goals, short-term responsibilities and midrange vacation plans, and one day hopes to somehow alter the equation so they can relax and play *seven* days a week instead of just on weekends. For most people, buying stocks, trading in the market and making financial investments are another means to that end.

While this type of investing is perfect for those who want to follow the traditional retirement route, there are those among us who have begun turning this secondary interest into a parallel universe that is wildly exciting and richly rewarding.

On the surface, things may look pretty much the same on your street. But take a closer look. Neighbor Bob now rushes home to day-trade his burgeoning stock portfolio. That nice Mr. Phillips on the next block? Haven't seen him much lately? He's holed up trading foreign currencies—having fun and making a good buck, too. The busy soccer mom across the way? She trades stock options for two hours every day after she puts her kids on the school bus. She's turned a $5,000 savings account into a $35,000 war chest in just five months.

These ordinary, extraordinary people have stepped up the pace, broadened horizons and made success and adventure a new hobby. While many continue to plow discretionary income into old standbys like savings accounts, insurance policies, conventional bonds and traditional real estate, others roam worldwide and cyber-search new continents seeking new investment horizons and emerging opportunity.

They are a new breed. All are extreme investors in their own right.

Taking The Plunge

Rita looks ordinary on the outside—she's petite, tan and fit, a typical California girl. But on the inside, she's an adrenaline junkie—an avid skydiver and licensed parachute jump instructor who is often asked why she does it. Why *does* someone enjoy jumping out of airplanes, anyway?

Her answer goes right to the point. "It makes me feel powerful and vulnerable at the same time. It's a mixture of confrontation, intense humility, wild exhilaration and a feeling of mastery, all wrapped in a 45-second free fall and a five-minute total jump." For her, an exhilarating hobby provides extreme recreation.

Extreme investors at all levels realize much the same exhilaration through dedicated pursuit of a *secondary* vocation. For most, extreme investing provides both successful financial results and extreme recreation.

Are you willing to risk a little more in making a jump to the next level of financial freedom? Want to make ordinary, mundane investment routines an exhilarating and lucrative hobby? Should you become an extreme investor in your own right? Maybe.

Coulda, Shoulda, Woulda

It is often said that "He who hesitates is lost." However, a blind leap of faith isn't always the best idea, either.

Extreme Investor not only covers many of the key investment vehicles available today but also helps you determine if the psychological intrigue in the fast-track world of raising the stakes, quick-draw investments and living on (or near) the edge is right for you.

Extreme investing involves seeking out the most radical financial vehicles—and most radical *approaches* to existing financial vehicles—and mastering how they are traded and/or executed. Extreme investing involves taking a calculated, speculative risk in expectation of significant short-term profit—and having a blast doing it.

It all revolves around keen awareness and catching a trend early, then moving on it quickly, using the most advanced tools and latest technologies in concert with heightened instinct and your own personalized approach to make more money. Hopefully, lots more money.

Extreme investing is also far more risky than its more moderate counterparts and is certainly not recommended for the meek or tentative.

You need to determine whether this form of speculating fits your personality, budget and expectations. In this book, you'll find an arsenal of information on day trading and other extreme investment vehicles, any one of which may open the door to a new vocation for you.

Even if you are already familiar with some of the extreme trading and investment approaches contained in this book, *Extreme Investor* still offers many new ideas, concepts and techniques that will serve to expand your thinking and enhance your current investment style.

The World At Your Fingertips

The Internet puts the world at your fingertips. Figuratively and literally.

Stockwise, it offers a new way to reach out and get market advice and opinions from countless investment groups—from anywhere in the world. It's all there, almost anything you could possibly want to know, just for the asking.

Today's incredible Internet provides the infrastructure to instantaneously collect voluminous information on numerous financial products and allows easy side-by-side, point-by-point comparison. You can also set up a personalized electronic profile of your investment preferences through one of many online investment companies and then have your computer at work 24 hours a day seeking out any products that meet your criteria, ranked in order from perfect match to those with near suitability.

You then execute buy or sell commands with the click of a mouse. *That's* power. If you've already traded online, you have experienced the exhilaration of stock trading. To make a profit is a rush. Extreme investing steps it up a notch. Are you ready?

Junk bonds are still risky, and they represent an extreme investment that can pay big dividends. The savings and loan crisis in the late 1980s, along with Drexel Burnham Lambert and Michael Milken, are all things of the past. Thus, junk bonds are really not that junky at all when you are careful to diversify and follow other sound investment strategies. Options trading is easier than ever, thanks to all the new information and analytical tools now available. While options trading has not yet caught fire like day trading, it may soon be on its way due to the errant and experimental nature of traders and their affinity for increased risk and leverage. We'll take a closer look at this sleeping giant, too.

Thanks to the Internet, investing in real estate has gotten more interesting, too. Virtual tours, countless Web sites (for everything from cities and states to niche realty experts), and the endless volumes of statistical and comparative research available today have souped up traditional buy-and-wait investment techniques.

Want to get in on the land boom of the moment? Where is it? Las Vegas? Hmmm. Hit the city's Web site, ferret out local land experts, peruse county records, check listings and review recent sales, match up comparables for properties being offered, shop mortgages and financing, make offers—and see just how fast you might become a wheelin'-and-dealin' land baron of major proportions.

As you see, thanks to the Internet—and extreme thinking—even real estate ain't Dad's old tired Buick anymore. It's a hold-on, pedal-to-the-metal, fast track to success for those making the decision to drive, those who buckle up and then hit the pavement running at high speed.

Trading Stocks Like A Pro

Technological advancements such as personal computers and the Internet—along with a drop in trading commissions, new services offered by brokerage firms and changes in the rules of trading—all came together at this point in time to make day trading a viable reality for hundreds of thousands of average folks.

It has put awesome power at our fingertips, allowing us to step in and out of stocks as easily as one might change shoes. These days, anyone with a few thousand dollars can buy and sell stocks using many of the high-powered trading tools used by professionals.

Day trading—at almost any level—represents a most lucrative and extreme tactic for taking advantage of our new and rapidly expanding global economy. Why? A few years ago, the Internet was too slow to enable successful trading. For stock trades, execution speed was sluggish because PCs and connectivity channels were too slow. Traders really needed to go to one of those infamous day trading shops to rent time on a pepped up PC to successfully execute extremely time-sensitive day trades.

But today's PCs are much faster, and 15-minute delayed quotes are pretty much a thing of the past. Internet connections are now cheap and fast by virtue of products such as DSL (digital subscriber line). DSL uses your current phone line to make an Internet connection far faster than a normal modem connection. According to Pioneer Consulting, the number of DSL subscribers will grow from 760,000 in 1999 to more than 12 million in the year 2003. And the cost to execute a trade has dropped so much that it is no longer a deterrent to fast, in-and-out trading.

Discount brokers popped up overnight, and the trend spread quickly to the big brokers. Some offer trades for less than $5, and others charge an annual fee for unlimited trades. Some creative brokerage house may suddenly decide to let you trade for free in exchange for allowing them to feature on-screen banner advertising, or if you subscribe to an investment newsletter or buy products through its online bookstore affiliations.

Today, the rules of stock trading have changed so that the individual investor can play with greater success. Brokers and clearinghouses now offer all kinds of free or low-cost stock analysis tools that level the playing field. Day trading is now an any time, anywhere reality, and you, too, can conduct business on a major exchange seamlessly and directly.

Easy Access—A Roll Of The Dice?

Ask the man on the street his opinion of IPOs, stock options or day trading on the Internet, and he will likely suggest it's just another form of gambling. And it seems to be a rather *easy* form of gambling, too.

Buy stocks and then hope you sell them for more than you paid. The odds seem random, depending on the business climate and a few other factors, and that sounds a lot like gambling. At least that's the way it appears to the novice on the street.

Gambling, speculating and investing all involve risking capital and taking a chance to varying degrees. To better differentiate, let us first delve into the mind of the long-term investor. They are the least extreme of all. Looking for security, they put their risk capital to work in investment-grade bonds offered by huge corporate giants like DuPont and General Electric. They never put money into junk bonds. When they invest in the stock market, they put their money behind well-established companies with the expectation of getting back a reasonable and regular return on their money through dividends and price appreciation of the stock.

The problem is that in exchange for safety, they sacrifice the gratification of immediate profit and only anticipate modest gains. The long-term investor is patient, never extreme.

Speculators (extreme investors) and gamblers (also extreme, but not the subject of this book) thrive on the *short-term* view. They don't care about dividends, for example, and they are primarily interested in a quick and/or substantial profit. They also take larger risks in the process.

Speculation is a natural part of life. When confronted with alternatives you can't avoid, you are forced to speculate based on the information at hand. Choosing which employee to hire, which form of transportation to use on a business trip, or how much inventory you should carry in your warehouse are all based on speculation combined with your own data and personal experience. This type of speculation is a necessity in all facets of everyday life, including work and conducting business.

On the other hand, gambling is optional. It is taking a risk that you don't have to take, and that elective risk is not based upon reason, but on chance. Gamblers depend on luck, often with only a 50/50 chance of success. In gaming meccas like Las Vegas and Atlantic City, it's even less than a 50/50 prospect. Generally, *way* less. Still, they come and wager.

While it is certainly possible to approach investing and day trading from the perspective of a gambler, this would qualify as extreme foolishness, not extreme investing. The lottery is a form of gambling. It's a risk nobody has to take, yet many ignore the horrendous odds against winning and freely plunk down hard-earned money with predictable results.

Conversely, the speculator's money follows intelligent forethought based on statistical and analytical research that takes into consideration the hazards that lie ahead and the associated risk/reward ratios. And while some gamblers know their craft extremely well and can say the same thing, most gamblers depend on chance to a greater degree than upon intelligent forecasting and hard information that better the odds.

In big-time casinos, the card games and slot machines work so that the buttered side of the toast invariably lands face up at least 52 times out of 100, and face down on the azure blue carpet the remaining 48 times—giving the house a predictable and consistent edge over the long haul. Thus, even if you fully understand blackjack, for example, and you double down on 11 and play every hand well, you're likely to lose in the long run. Roulette wheels are even worse in terms of who's got the odds in their favor.

The speculator/extreme investor consistently turns the proverbial house odds in his or her favor to the extent and degree that he or she is able to accumulate specialized trading tools and amass technical support and workable experience.

Maybe everybody knows the big, extravagant casinos exist only because they have the advantage, and everyone knows who pays. Still, they come. People who visit the tinsel and glitter of gaming towns see them as adult Disneylands and mostly wager for fun, with few actually expecting to profit.

Thus, we put this age-old inevitable comparison to rest. Investing is not gambling. Gambling is all chance and wagering, and just another form of entertainment from which (except for those who lose more than they can afford to) most benefit only in spirit.

On The Flip Side Of The Coin

Extreme investing is not entertainment; it's business. And in terms of the value it creates, extreme investing offers something far more beneficial than entertainment. The stock market is directly related to providing working capital for new business ventures. It is the mechanism by which a person can be part of a company, its products and management. Through its stock, investors buy and own a piece of a company.

Most important, without publicly traded stock, companies would lack the capital to expand. Without bond issues, many good companies might not be as successful as they are today. Without stock options and futures as hedge instruments, the economies of the world might be less stable. And without the liquidity provided by the stock market, fewer brilliant businesspeople would risk developing new technology.

Thus, Amazon.com would not be selling books, eBay would not be the auction capital of the world, and you might not even have an e-mail address if it weren't for the stock market providing the incentive to all those visionaries who dream up new and interesting businesses.

The greater the number of traders, the more likely it is that a company's stock will accurately reflect its fair value at any given moment. Day traders make the stock market more liquid (liquidity being directly related to the number of buyers and sellers) by aggressively taking advantage of the fact that it is easier to enter or exit a stock trade, and therefore executing more trades. The volume of trading on Wall Street isn't breaking records for nothing, you know!

In the long run, this benefits everyone through rapid development of new technology, new and improved products, and expanded services. The stock market attracts money that represents new opportunities. Some investor/traders will win. Others will lose.

Still, gamblers will always have the poorest chance of winning because they have an inherent inability to resist the urge to bet. Knowledgeable investors have control over this urge and can easily stay out of a market that is not providing a clear signal based on finely tuned trading criteria.

If you are a buy-and-hold investor, this book will be fun reading, and you should be content to protect your nerves and stick with your tried-and-true investing techniques. If you are a gambler, please don't read this book at all, as it will inspire you to pursue irrational exuberance and a pratfall to match. But if you are willing to combine the psychological factors mentioned above with the general approaches outlined in this book, then you are ready to move the throttle forward on your way to potentially lucrative extreme endeavors.

Like A Hawk

While there are many books on the psychology of trading, even more on stock market analysis and trading strategies, and scores of books on commodities, options, futures and day trading—and books on how markets work—few (if any) provide accurate, valuable and workable insight on the advantages and disadvantages of extreme investment tactics and opportunities.

This book is not intended to be a "how to become extreme" primer. You will not find easy-to-follow steps telling you to: 1) pick up the phone and 2) tell the nice man you want . . .

Rather, you will garner insights into the edgy world of sharp thinking, quick action and (more often than not) enviable results that are the hallmark of the true extreme investor.

They are out there everywhere, often in unlikely quarters, wisely profiting in a unique and personal fashion. Once you've met them and applied some of their thinking to your world, chances are you'll find yourself being a bit more extreme, too.

One thing is for sure: After reading extreme investor cover to cover, you'll never read the business section, scan real estate listings or listen to news in the same way again. You'll start seeing every bit of news and information you come across as a possible lead on an opportunity. You'll begin feeling like the hawk looking for the field mouse, with a sharpened awareness, poised for action, ready to swoop in at a moment's notice.

What you make of your newly heightened senses is what separates the extreme from the mild. *That's* the challenge.

part one

Have **You** Got What It Takes To Be An **Extreme** Investor?

There is a wide range of must-haves when it comes to extreme investing. Some things are very tangible—like start-up money, a computer and access to information that will help you make investment decisions. Others are less tangible, like the techniques and strategies that form your approach to extreme investing. Still others are downright abstract—you can't really measure them because they're traits and characteristics that enable extreme investors to do what they do. Filling you in on these must-haves is what Part One of this book is all about.

Do You Qualify?

chapter one

To succeed at extreme investing, you must have a burning desire to master the rules and strategy of the game. This is essential if you want to develop a trading system or skill set that will work for you in the pursuit of extreme investing. Extreme investing demands significant discipline—which means you must possess Zen-like control while trading and adhere to strict risk management techniques. But the first step is to determine if your financial situation allows for this extreme adventure.

Taking Your Financial Temperature

To be an extreme investor, you need extra capital—money you can live without comfortably, both in terms of continuing lifestyle and peace of mind. This strictly excludes retirement money or the kids' college fund! Many investors start with money that's simply idle and not already earmarked for a specific purpose. Some investors divide their existing stock account into two separate accounts: one for long-term investing, the other for playing options and day trading.

The point is that money used for extreme investing must be extra money, not money you need to live on, and not money you are diverting from other vital accounts. If you have the slightest doubt about whether your financial status will allow for any extreme activity, you need to produce an overall financial plan—a snapshot, if you will, of your financial status—for you and your family.

Establishing a definitive financial plan isn't the goal of this book. And if you've been out there dancing around the edges of the extreme, we trust you've already mapped out your financial status. But if you haven't, you must understand that without a financial plan, you can't know how prudent extreme investing is for you. Part of the extreme investing concept involves implementing risk management techniques, but just in case you flub up on the risk management stuff—or if the risk itself overwhelms all your best-laid risk management plans—you'll have an automatic backup system in place. If you trade with money

Get With The Plan

Even if you don't pursue extreme investing, it's a good idea to have a financial plan. Princeton Survey Research Associates recently queried U.S. households about their financial goals and strategies for saving and investing. Two-thirds of the households surveyed had set aside money for emergencies and for their retirement. That's good, but 43 percent who expect to put their kids through college hadn't figured out where that money was going to come from, and 66 percent who plan to buy their first home within the next 10 years had no money set aside for a down payment. As for putting Mom into Shady Pines when she gets old, less than 20 percent had any savings or investments set aside for that purpose. The take-home message? If you've never done a financial plan, create one *now*.

you can afford to live without, you'll not only protect yourself from financial pitfalls, but you'll also approach investing without desperation or fear—two emotions that don't mix well in the world of extreme investing.

Plan Particulars

The following are simple guidelines for making a personal financial plan. In practice, although the term is common, it's not "plan" at all—it's a snapshot of your financial status and goals that enables you to make a plan. For our purposes, it's also a means to figure out if you're in the right league to pursue extreme investing. Your financial plan will not indicate how much you should allocate for extreme investing, but it will help you get somewhere in the ballpark of that figure.

To get a finger on the pulse of your financial world, start by taking inventory of what you have (your net worth). Then figure out what you need to live on and what you can put aside (your working financial picture). Next, identify your financial goals (goal-setting) and estimate the cost of achieving them. If this were a golf course, your net worth is everything you've done in advance of teeing off, and your working financial picture is everything you do between the first hole and the final putt. Goal-setting is deciding how many strokes under par you want to be at the end of 18 holes and which beer you're going to order in the clubhouse. Fore!

> If you **trade** with **money** you **can afford** to **live without**, you'll not only **protect yourself** from **financial pitfalls**, but you'll also **approach** investing without **desperation** or **fear**.

Your Net Worth

The first step in making your personal financial plan is figuring out your net worth. The following checklist will help make sure you don't leave anything out.

Starting with your assets, put dollar amounts next to each category below:

○ **Cash:** checking, savings or credit union accounts, money market accounts, CDs, and other money on hand $_____

It Ain't Over Till It's Over

You will feel very accomplished when you first map out your financial status and goals, as if you've finally taken care of something really important that you've been putting off, like your will. But be aware that writing a financial plan is a job that's never finished. It is critical to revisit your entire financial status on paper regularly—anywhere from every month (or more often) to every four months, depending on how active you are as an investor or a consumer. It's easy to lose sight of your precise status in the rough-and-tumble of everyday life, and when you're extreme investing, it's vital to keep a clear and precise picture of where you are at all times. This is more than an exercise—it's a safeguard against operating with a false perception of your financial situation. Think of it as the financial equivalent of flossing—it's not glamorous or fun, but in the long run, you'll be mighty glad you did it.

○ **Stocks and bonds:** include mutual funds and any other fixed income securities you have $_____

○ **Insurance:** cash value and the surrender value of annuities
$_____

○ **Real estate:** current value of your home, second home, that island you just bought, rental property, rental partnerships, and any other form of real estate $_____

○ **Personal property:** cars and other vehicles, boats, jewelry, household furnishings, antiques, collectibles (coins, gold, stamps, maybe even your kid's Pokèmon cards), artwork, and any other stuff you have that's worth mentioning in terms of valuation $_____

○ **Retirement accounts:** 401(k)s, IRAs, pension plans, company stock options (these are iffy, but assign a value as best you can), and anything else related to retirement $_____

Your Total Assets: $_____

Now add up all your liabilities, including:

○ **Your primary residence:** mortgage, second mortgage, vacation home mortgage, investment property loans $_____

○ **Vehicle loans:** $_____

○ **Credit card debt:** $_____

○ **Tuition debt:** $_____

○ **Taxes owed (property and/or income tax):** $_____

○ **Other miscellaneous debt:** $_____

Your Total Liabilities: $_____

Now, subtract your liabilities from your assets and you have . . .

Your Net Worth: $_____

Your Working Financial Picture

Now let's deal with the daily living stuff—how much money you need for basic living expenses and how much disposable income you have left over. To determine this working financial picture, you need to add up how much you make annually and then subtract how much you spend over the course of the year.

Starting with income, add up all the money that comes in each year:

○ **Your yearly salary:** (net, after withholding taxes, insurance and retirement) and/or business income, along with your spouse's, including tips/commissions/bonuses $_____

○ **Interest:** earned each year from dividends, trusts, alimony, social security, pensions $_____

○ **Rents collected:** $_____

○ **Other money received during the year:** $_____

Your Total Income: $_____

Now for expenses—add up all your annual expenses (this list is usually long compared to the income list):

○ **Household expenses:** mortgage or rent, utilities (gas/electricity/trash), cable TV (a write-off for the extreme investor who watches CNBC all the time), telephone, property taxes and insurance, maintenance for yard/pool/housekeeping, in-home child care or baby-sitting; if you rent furniture or appliances, throw those expenses in here too $_____

○ **Living expenses:** everything you buy at the grocery store; clothes and shoes; cosmetics: dry cleaning; health stuff including vitamins, your health club, medical bills and medicine not covered by insurance; any monthly insurance premiums, dental care and insurance, and any other insurance expenses (life and/or disability) $_____

○ **Education and entertainment:** club memberships, soccer equipment for your kid, ballet lessons for your other kid, presents for all of them on holidays and birthdays, current education costs for you and your family $_____

○ **Transportation:** includes everything you need to get around in your daily routine, including car/SUV/motorcycle and all associated lease and loan payments; tune-ups and tires; insurance, gas, and registration; if you travel to work by train or bus or subway or airplane, those go in this category, too $_____

○ **Leisure:** vacations (hotels, flights, miscellaneous), golf or tennis club memberships, season tickets to the theater, all your dining out expenses $_____

○ **Everything else not covered:** any additional expenses you have, including charitable or political contributions, legal and accounting services, and SEP/IRA contributions at the end of the year. Check your credit card bills to remind yourself of those surprise or noncategoriz-able expenses that sneak up $_____

Your Total Expenses: $_____

Stocking Up?

It's true that most people pay a huge amount of interest over the life of their home loan, sometimes more than twice the original amount borrowed for a typical 30-year, fixed-rate mortgage. Prepaying an extra month's mortgage just prior to the year-end is one approach to minimizing the mortgage interest chokehold. Another is to voluntarily increase your monthly payment to reduce debt and accelerate your payback period. But this path to building wealth is slow, and under most circumstances, it's more prudent to invest in the stock market than to prepay your mortgage. Here's why:

First, the interest you pay on your mortgage is usually tax-deductible. So even if you decide to use your extra money to prepay debt, start with debt that's not tax-deductible, like credit card debt. Now back to your mortgage. It's important to compare apples to apples here, so you need to compare the after-tax cost of the interest against your potential returns in the stock market. Even if your interest rate is fixed at 8.5 percent, if you are in a 28 percent tax bracket, your actual interest rate is just over 6 percent (calculated by reducing your 8.5 percent interest rate by 28 percent). So, if you can make more than 6 percent annually in the stock market (the stock market has historically shown an annual pretax return of more than 13 percent), then prepaying your mortgage might be a goof. Naturally, you will have to pay taxes on the sale of your stock, but if you hold it longer than a year, you'll pay the capital gains rate of 20 percent, leaving your after-tax profit on stocks at more than 10 percent.

Now it's time to subtract your total expenses from your total income. This figure is what's called . . .

Your Disposable Income: $\$$_____

Let's assume it's a positive number. This amount tells you how much money you have left over for purposes other than your annual expenses, including your future plans—and possibly extreme investing.

Goal-Tending

You've looked the cold, hard facts square in the eye—you've itemized all your assets and liabilities, you've compared your earnings and your expenses—and you're staring at the snapshot of where you are now. It's time to look at what lies ahead. You may have a college tuition or two looming in the not-too-distant future, or you may soon be facing special care for an aging parent. Whatever the challenge, now is the moment to look to the future and visualize your own personal goals.

"how can I get there from here?"

So take a moment and dream. Not "if only" dreams or "what if I won the lottery" dreams but real, quantifiable "how can I get there from here" dreams. These dreams should include your specific vision of a comfortable retirement, but they might also include enjoying some extreme entertainment along the way.

Here is a checklist for planning the future. (If only it were that easy!) It takes into account your retirement picture and the expenses associated with keeping your family happy and healthy. There are four very general areas that need to be addressed. Each requires some thinking and some math, so sharpen that pencil.

1. **Identify your ideal image of retirement.** Itemize each aspect of your retirement dreams (like, say, you want to travel twice a year or be able to help with your grandkids' education), visualize the details, place target dates on getting there, and put a price tag on the bundle. $\$$_____

2. **Set up a fund that allows you to pay for unplanned necessities and emergencies without going into debt.** You may fall short of having

The Opposite Of Extreme

When manufacturing executive Jim Q. and wife Cathy envisioned their future when they were young marrieds, they imagined a house full of healthy children (who would all attend college), yearly family vacations, and a retirement spent in the garden and seeing the world. Forty years, five children, 10 jobs and little financial planning later, Jim and Cathy realized their vision of retirement hadn't been exact enough, at least not in terms of how to get from A to B. They'd saved a little, invested a little, and fielded life's foul balls well enough, but in the end, the math didn't come out in their favor. They'd never quantified their goals, never made an aggressive plan, and therefore never enabled the achievement of those goals. Their retirement is pleasant, but it's spent entirely in the garden, not all over the world. The moral? Plan for your dreams, every single day. A smart financial plan can be your road map—your Rx—for the future.

the full amount if that time comes, but it's important to have some money set aside for emergencies. (No, you can't use this money for extreme investing.) $_____

3. **Determine and plan for health insurance, and life and disability insurance.** Insurance is a powerful and important tool. Always have insurance. $_____

4. **Figure out how much you need for college tuition, a down payment for a home, and other family responsibilities.** How much time do you have before you'll need to pay for these expenses? $_____

Total Cost Of Your Future Plans: $_____

The Envelope, Please

It's time to put all the financial puzzle pieces together and see if you have money that isn't earmarked for some vital or looming expense—money that you might put aside for extreme investing.

○ **Look at your net worth.** Take into consideration how long it took you to get where you are and how far you are from achieving your retirement goals. What must your net worth be for you to feel secure in retirement? What's the difference between your net worth and the cost of your future plans?

○ **Consider your current income-and-expense picture.** If you pursue extreme investing at any level, will your current income source be affected at all?

○ **If you have extra money, should that money be safely invested for future expenses that you've identified in your financial plan?** If you have extra capital but pending expenses, don't risk that capital on extreme investing.

You now have all the data you need to ascertain whether you have the extra capital to risk on extreme investing. Because some of your measurement tools are subjective variables, your number may not be an "X-equals" sort of figure but rather a range that makes clear to you whether you're an extreme investor prospect or an extreme investor wanna-be. If you still have doubts, talk to a financial consultant. Give him all the information you've put together above. That's pretty much all he'll need.

Start Me Up

Several forms of extreme investing are explored in this book, and each requires a different level of capital to get started. Extreme investing in initial public offerings (IPOs), for example, requires more time and less capital than other forms of extreme investing. Your time is spent researching your prospect and strategizing your timing. These days, you can invest as little as a few thousand dollars in an IPO and make a small fortune in a month—or you can lose it all in a day. Naturally, the more you put at risk, the greater your potential reward.

Trading options also requires little start-up capital. You can buy an option for a few hundred dollars and turn that into a few thousand within days or weeks, but the risk of losing every dollar you spent on that option is significantly greater than in other investment scenarios. That's because, unlike owning stock in a company, stock options can expire worthless. More on this extreme sport later.

> **These** days, **you** can **invest** as **little** as a **few thousand** dollars in an **IPO** and **make** a **small fortune** in a **month**—or you can **lose it** all in a **day.**

Whether you hope to pursue extreme investing two hours a day or 24/7, you need to treat this endeavor as a business. In fact, you need to think of yourself as a start-up, with a plan and seed capital and all the ifs and maybes and trial and error that characterize every start-up. This means that you may need to factor in a period of loss at the start, so you'll need to allow for a

A Cautionary Tale

While the common practice of margin borrowing has kept many an extreme investor in the game, it's important not to lean too hard on the margins. When April 14, 2000, dawned on day traders, many were crushed by their margin debt. On this wild day on Wall Street, the value of stocks plummeted, margin loans were called, and many were in the hole for millions. Learn from others' mistakes: The margin is no place to be on a dark day at the market. So don't go there until you've determined all the elements of your risk management plan and have a rock-solid exit strategy that protects you from the worst-case scenario.

sufficient start-up period and enough money to support yourself until you're generating income.

For day trading, the most common form of extreme investing, there are certain underlying expenses you can count on upfront. Your seed capital might range from $5,000 to $25,000, depending on how much time you intend to devote, as well as how vulnerable you can stand to feel at the start. Whatever amount you use as your trading capital, however, it's generally marginable, which means you will actually have twice that amount to trade with once you sign on with a trading firm. Using the equity in your account as collateral, they lend you money to trade with, and they usually don't charge you interest on that money if you liquidate your positions into cash again at the end of the trading day.

Nuts And Bolts (And RAMs And More)

Aside from investment capital, your new start-up business may call for additional operating expenses. And remember, this is a business, so you need to have a business plan that projects your expenses. It's likely you have some or all these already, but following is a list of some of the expenses you can anticipate:

○ computer system
○ Internet hookup and monthly fees
○ trade books and periodicals to learn the trade
○ data feed and software for market information
○ monthly fees for your data hookup

We will get into the gory details later, but expect to pay $150 a month for services and necessary research support sources. In any case, you will need to be online with a computer that doesn't make you tear your hair out because it's so slow. If you have an older Macintosh or a 486 PC, well, yikes, take it straight to your nearest charitable organization and be prepared to get new stuff (ka-ching!— that's another $3,000 or more).

rocket execution speed

There are ways to cut corners. One way to reduce some of your start-up costs is to go where you can rent computer time. The only such places that offer on-site assistance with extreme investing are day trading shops, which can provide you with exposure to the trading process. You rent a spot that comes equipped with a computer and all the required connections. It's a turnkey setup, and spending time with other day traders can be a good learning experience, but beware. Only the most professional day trading shops take a long-term view of you as a trader, and they may not take you under their wing with enthusiastic training and tutorials. So it's easy to lose your capital rather quickly.

Trading stock options, trading in junk bonds, and getting involved in IPOs requires a slightly less fancy computer setup. You don't need rocket execution speed, but you may want a bigger monitor to play with graphs. No matter where your extreme investing takes you, though, you do have to spend money to get up to speed. Books, newsletters, seminars and

Patience, Grasshopper

When you break into any form of extreme investing, your natural inclination will be to play the game to make money right away. This is a mistake. Instead, your immediate goal should be to learn how it all works. If you take things gradually, you can learn the required lessons without blowing your investment capital. But this means you must be willing to forego actually making money for a while, and instead spend time making smaller investments, and maybe even learning the art of taking a loss. It's all part of your education. The real investment is your time, and you must allocate lots of it to learning. You can keep your tuition costs down by being patient and sticking with tiny investments until you get the hang of it.

other educational opportunities are available for free and for a fee; most are available over the Internet.

At this point, you don't have all the information you'll need to begin extreme investing, but you have a rough idea of the costs involved in getting set up for this venture.

Time's The Thing

Even if you have the money required, you need to figure out how much time you're prepared to spend on extreme investing. If you pursue extreme investing as a part-time venture, it may take many months of preparation and "paper trading" (simulated investing that does not use real money) before you're ready to put your money at risk. After all, extreme investing often means you're going up against full-time pros— and you're entering as a novice. If you're only playing part time, your efforts will have to be even more focused.

Aside from the amount of time you'll need to spend each day pursuing your chosen form of extreme investing, you'll need to spend time getting up to speed—and staying there. One of the most time-consuming elements of getting started involves sifting through all the products and services available and determining the requirements for your particular investment environment. For day trading, you will need to choose a broker and an appropriate trading platform. Sometimes they come as a package, but you will need to know enough about day trading to discern which ones have the order execution speed you need for your style of trading.

Other forms of extreme investing require less setup time. Your current broker and trading platform may be quite suitable for the type of extreme investing you have in mind. While cumbersome and inefficient for day trading, most brokers offer what's required to invest in IPOs and stock options. Most of them offer plenty of trading tools to get started. If you don't have a broker or a trading firm, and you choose to get involved in IPOs or options—or some form of stock trading—you'll need to interview brokerage firms. You'll need to speak with their customer service people to see if

> **Even** if **you** have the **money required**, you **need** to **figure** out **how** much **time** you're **prepared** to spend on **extreme investing.**

they're available when you need them, and to determine whether you think they're knowledgeable and pleasant to deal with. You will need to investigate issues that involve data integrity and stability. (You may have heard about some of the online brokers having servers crash, leaving traders hanging for hours.)

The point is, there is a lot to learn in terms of setting up the game board and figuring out the playing field. Once you have done that, then you have to learn the game—how your chosen investment market works. The learning curve for any form of extreme investing is slower if you work at it part time. Part-time investors will be better off paper trading for a few months and may want to veer toward longer-term and less hectic forms of investing that are more suitable for part-time involvement—although holding stocks for days, weeks, or maybe longer can be an intense experience, too.

If you decide to pursue extreme investing on a part-time basis, you'll still need the same tools of the trade as if you were involved full time. We'll point you toward lots of hot resources for furthering your education later in this book, but there is no substitute for exposure to—and hands-on practice with—the markets themselves. The more you play, the better you'll get. It's really as simple as that.

In addition to just spending time learning, there is the "time of day" issue to consider, too. Extreme investors need to determine what particular part of their day they're able to devote to executing and monitoring investments. Stock, bond and option traders, for example, need to dedicate specific hours of the day to trading. The stock market opens at 9:30 a.m. and closes at 4 p.m. Eastern Standard Time (of course if you live on the West Coast, that's 6:30 a.m. to 1 p.m. Pacific Standard Time). That's when you need to be working.

The recent introduction of after-hours trading makes it possible to trade when the normal market is closed, but there are too few people trading then, which results in very erratic price fluctuations. The only real advantage to trading during after hours occurs as the result of news, like an exaggerated earnings report that sends a particular stock rocketing up or plummeting down. This is a branch of extreme investing all on its own. During

Open All Night

After-hours trading is accomplished a little differently than trades made during normal market hours. Your broker has access to one or more electronic communications networks (ECNs) they use to display and execute limit orders for after-hours trading. ECNs are used during normal trading hours, too; an ECN is simply a service that matches buy orders with sell orders. But in after-hours trading, if you want to buy a stock, you may find that there aren't any sellers at the moment (all the traders are at home watching Ally McBeal), so you may have to wait awhile for a matching sell order to come in before your trade takes place.

In after-hours trading, you may experience weird delays, and some trades may not happen at all. On top of all that, quotes coming in from your broker's particular ECN are not consolidated with other ECNs to provide a single market quote that reflects the true market price. You may want to sell shares of a stock at $50 and some other guy wants to buy at $50, but the two of you may never know each other exists during after-hours trading sessions. (This is not the case during regular trading hours.) Plus, there may be other orders ahead of yours. Keep in mind, too, that some stocks simply don't trade in after hours. For now, after-hours trading is not a desirable forum for extreme investors, but it will be. With the rapid evolution of all things techno-economic, you can count on it. Follow after-hours trading and study it, but don't get in on it until the benefits are visible.

after hours, you can quickly take advantage of the move up or down before the major market has reacted. But after-hours trading sessions are a poor venue for learning how the market moves and reacts, so it's absolutely necessary for you to be at your computer during normal trading hours to obtain what you need to learn.

Within normal trading hours, there are specific trading periods when the market is either particularly active or inactive. During lunch time on the East Coast, the market volume tapers off. When trading volume is low, that means there is less volatility to exploit and usually no momentum to follow. There are rarely major moves during this time. The opposite is true of the market open and the close. There is often a lot of trading volume during these periods. The working day of an extreme investor involved in stocks generally starts about a half hour before the market opens, and ends after the market closes, but the most extreme investors are doing their homework at all hours in between.

Do You Have The Style?

Virtually every form of extreme investing covered in this book revolves around some form of trading, which means identifying an investment vehicle that's about to move in a certain direction, taking a position (buying it), waiting for the move to reach a target price, and then closing out your position at a profit. The rules are similar for all trading, but the pace and strategy depends on your trading style.

Many extreme investors buy and then sell within the same day (they often liquidate all their positions by the market close). This represents the most intense form of extreme investing and is not a good idea if you intend to do your investing on a part-time basis. When trading on a part-time basis, odds are the distinct advantage goes to the more experienced trader in the deal. This will be true even if the part-time trader owns the best and fastest trading tools and execution systems available. These fast-paced trading styles work best with full-time participation because they require rapid decision-making and equally rapid execution speed that can be mastered only with lots of experience.

Slower-paced trading methodologies are more forgiving for those just learning about extreme investing. The extended time horizon allows investors to more casually react to market changes or other factors that might indicate the wisdom of reversing a position. With a longer time horizon, you enter an investment with a plan to stick with it until your target price is reached, or until the conditions upon which you entered the trade change—and the faster the pace, the less forgiving. You can make money day trading part time, but there is a lot to learn, so start slowly. Once the slower forms are mastered, then it makes sense to rev up to the faster-paced forms of investing.

How About Homework?

All the research, hands-on practice and learning curve stuff we've talked about so far boils down to lots of homework. Homework before you get started, and homework every single day once you're on the investing highway. All traders, no matter what style of trading they pursue, need to be familiar with various forms of investment analysis, which is the most critical of the day-to-day homework. If you're trading soybeans, stock options, gold futures or actual stocks, there are two primary forms of analysis. One is called *technical analysis*, which is basically charting the movement of financial instruments using graphs to predict future movements. These days charting is computerized, and many software products are available that can make this happen in a flash. Most brokers provide such charts; the hard part is knowing how to interpret them.

Libraries of books are available on technical analysis to predict future movements. These charts are used to establish trend lines and levels of support and resistance, indicating when to get in or out of an investment. Traders use these tools to set up their entry points (the exact price to buy or short something) based on buying and selling crescendos—also called "peaks" and "pullbacks." Technical analysis is an interesting and complex science, and the more you know about it, the better.

> **If** you **are interested** in IPOs, **fundamental analysis is** a **must**.

The other primary form of analysis is called *fundamental analysis*. This means determining a stock's desirability based on the industry sector and specific health and growth potential of a company within that sector. You research a company's earnings, price-to-earnings ratios, corporate management, competition, product pipeline (a term used to describe new products that have yet to come to market), revenue growth, and a ton of other things about a company that lead you to an investment decision. This form of analysis doesn't typically lend itself to short-term trading. If you use only fundamental analysis, it's likely that you are more interested in a less edgy, less extreme form of investing. However, if you are interested in IPOs, fundamental analysis is a must, and we'll explore this in more depth later.

Both technical and fundamental analysis are ways investors study the markets using past performance and current information to determine future movement. But the markets have been behaving in such an unprecedented way lately that a third investment tool is gaining in popularity: *sentiment analysis*. Sentiment analysis is the study and application of mass psychology within the investment community. It measures investor sentiment by analyzing the underlying psychological criteria that affects market movement. Sentiment analysis is a little mushy—no software program can chart mass psychology, right? But books on the psychology of trading do a good job of explaining sentiment analysis and how you might factor it into your thinking.

Investors frequently use a combination of these tools. They may use tools employed by buy-and-hold traders mixed in with some of those used by short-term investors. Some traders watch market-maker screens (discussed later) to see what the bigger investors and dealers are trading. They might incorporate old-fashioned research on a company, and then use their computer to generate graphs that indicate a short-term trend. They know about sectors (for example the transportation sector, which includes American Airlines and FedEx, or the Internet sector, which includes eBay and Amazon), and they may look at momentum within a sector to ferret out individual stocks for trading. They choose stocks and sectors that they want to learn about, making the entire research process more fun. All this eventually leads to choosing an investment vehicle they want to pursue and finding the direction in which they think it's about to move.

Investors not only use a mixture of trading tools, but they often use more than one trading discipline. For example, they may choose different time horizons for different trades, depending on market conditions and sometimes even the time of day. No matter what tools or trading style they use, everything leads to the next decision—what price to get in at and at what price to exit. If traders choose to hold on to a position for a couple of days based on the movement of a stock over the past week or several months, they have a slightly higher tolerance for error. If they use intra-day charts that indicate the current momentum of a stock within the past few hours or minutes, their trading strategy may target a small move and their tolerance for error might be a minute fraction of a point. Longer-term trades might allow for tolerating a drop of several points, as in the case of stocks that cost $100 per share or more.

Whether or not traders liquidate their position at the end of the day or buy and hold for a longer

> No **matter** what **tools** or **trading style** they use, everything **leads** to the **next** decision— what **price** to **get in at** and at what price to **exit.**

period, all successful investors know what their entry and exit points are before they trade. If their trade goes against them, they know ahead of time how far they're willing to ride a trend that they've identified incorrectly—then they exit.

There are many strategies to consider, and we'll look at them all more closely as we move along the extreme ledge. The bottom line is that there is no preset formula that can tell you how much money you need to bring to the table, how much time you need to devote to trading each day, or what it takes to succeed at a particular style of extreme investing. The key to your enjoying—and profiting from—any form of extreme investing will come from your love of the sport, and your willingness to do what it takes to master it.

The Right Stuff

f you're with us so far, it's likely you've determined that you have the time and the money for extreme investing, so let's get started, eh? Not so fast. There's something else you've just gotta have. To survive as an extreme investor, you need to embody certain characteristics. You need patience, optimism, self-confidence, excellent judgment, focus and discipline. If you have all these qualities and you practice them routinely, you must be tired of people bowing down to you as you enter rooms with Buddha-like serenity. Go to a mountaintop, sit cross-legged and contemplate the meaning of the universe and report back immediately! As for the rest of us, developing these personality traits requires work, and honing them is of tremendous value for extreme investing. Those who accomplish this maturation will be superior investors and traders. And extreme investing will constantly put these characteristics to the test.

When you apply these characteristics to extreme investing, you will find yourself "in the zone"—like a professional athlete. You'll not only be confident in your strategy, but you'll develop an intuition for timing. You will be keen at sniffing out opportunities. On the other hand, if you are prone to debilitating emotions, they will most certainly arise at the worst time, sending your extreme investing experience into an extreme tailspin. Your computer may have the best tools and your brain may house a good strategy, but you *will* fail if you don't have the ability to control potentially devastating impulses and emotions.

Gotta Have It

People are not born with self-discipline and emotional control. These are mental skills we learn, and they're vital to the extreme investor. Establishing a game plan with entry and exit points, for example, is unworkable if the investor lacks the confidence to stick with his game plan when he hits the first speed bump.

Extreme investors must learn to tune out market noise and tune in the market trend. Otherwise, the investor is prone to hanging on to losing trades or taking profits too early. Extreme investors monitor their emotions with keen awareness. They're prepared for losses. One of the greatest obstacles in extreme investing is not being able to recognize when your decisions are based on intelligence and clear thinking as opposed to when they're based on emotions or wishful thinking. When upset, arrogant or afraid, you can't trade objectively. At the opposite end, investors sometimes experience euphoria after a winning trade, which isn't a bad thing, but it's hard to make your next trade a sound one when you're giddy.

Certain mental characteristics are common to all successful investors. They tend to be independent thinkers. They rarely have a 9-to-5 mentality. They enjoy putting their capital at risk. They love experimentation. And they recognize and work within their limitations. They don't overestimate their abilities.

> **Extreme** investors **must** learn to **tune** out **market noise** and **tune in** the **market** trend.

The extreme investor who does well at his or her game has a master scheme, a plan, a road map that has a beginning and a clearly defined end. To succeed at extreme investing, you need to know under what conditions you will unequivocally exit an investment. Carefully prepared plans may fail to work as predicted, and spontaneous decisions often lead to trading flops.

The Road Map Rules

When given the choice between an excellent system based on fundamental and/or technical knowledge and psychological control, the extreme investor will always choose psychological control because it's the hardest part of the game. It's generally accepted that the majority of all successful extreme investing is attributable to psychological factors, not systems or strategies.

With that said, it's absolutely imperative that you have a system. This system will be your road map for the minute-to-minute, hour-to-hour, day-to-day and so on. There are as many systems out there as there are extreme investors, and no matter how much you search for the perfect system, you are not going to find one. There is no perfect system. That's because the stock market is not perfect. The weather that affects wheat crops is not perfect. Companies' best efforts are imperfect. In fact, the financial, economic and stock markets are a montage of ambiguous technical indicators, changing business climates, and vague and contradictory market information, and all this comes into your sensory system, adding your personality to the bizarre mix. All investing systems are personal. Yours will be, too.

> The **majority** of **all** successful **extreme investing** is **attributable** to psychological **factors**, not **systems** or **strategies.**

Anatomy Of An Investing System

Your investing system consists of the tools (in your hands and in your head) and specific strategies that are the framework (and Checkpoint Charlies) for every investment decision you make. The tools in your hands (the hardware, software, support services, etc.) bring you the practical information you need to make decisions. The tools in your head are your predetermined gauges and levers used to decide how and when to proceed with an investment.

Here is the lowdown on investing systems: A system provides guidelines that confirm the viability of each decision you make. It begins with research and preparation and is followed by a series of "go/no-go" decisions. The preparation narrows down the field of investments you'll consider based on parameters you have established. You will ultimately know exactly what you want to trade and why you've chosen it. Your system will lead you to a precise entry point you patiently wait for. When you're there, you will tingle with confidence. But don't just sit there tingling. Remember that your system dictates how long you anticipate keeping the trade open and at what point you intend to take your profit. It also has determined what your maximum downside tolerance will be, as well as how many shares, options, contracts, bonds, etc., to trade based on a sound money-management program designed to maximize capital preservation.

Your system for investing will evolve over time. And it will be all yours—no two systems are alike because each person brings his or her own quirks and requirements to even the most standard investment approach. This book will help orient you to the types of tools at your disposal. With this knowledge, you can start gathering information, reading, studying the parts you like and rejecting the ones you don't. The more time you spend investigating, the better your system will be. Your system is your personal road map to extreme investing.

Working With A Net: Risk Management

Anyone who's ever written about or discussed risk management in the context of investing pretty much agrees on the same principals. Your decision on whether to pursue extreme investing should include an under-

The Ultimate In Personal Liquidity

Imagine a business that offers you the opportunity to liquidate for cash, at fair market value, virtually all your business assets at the end of each day. If you have a bagel shop, an accounting firm or a steel mill, your business is illiquid. You only cash out once, usually at the end of your career. Day traders cash out at the end of each day. In many ways, day trading can be construed as less of a gamble than that taken by the serious long-term investor. At least he knows where he stands every night when he climbs into bed!

standing that there is another discipline to be learned if you are to succeed. That discipline is risk management.

All extreme investors experience losses during the course of trading. Risk management strategies keep the astute trader in the game, even when up against a persistent losing streak. Mainstream investors (the buy-and-hold people) protect themselves using what they refer to as diversification. Extreme investors use this same concept but think more in terms of not risking everything at once. The more they risk as a percentage of their trading capital, the more intolerant of loss they become.

Robert W., an options trader in New York, failed because of poor risk management. At 28 years old, Robert had built a successful chain of laundromats and decided to sell his business to pursue something more interesting. He chose options trading. He loved everything about options. He spent all day and almost every night learning the trade. And he put $25,000 into his account to get started. But within three months, he had run out of money and was forced to remove himself from the game altogether.

never depend on a few big killings

When Robert studied options trading, he knew that he had to have an entry and exit strategy. He had worked out a viable system that included a plan for exiting a trade. But he lacked the discipline to act on that plan. Fear of a loss kept him in, along with his hope of recovery—the perfect formula for failure. Ironically, Robert's first few weeks went very well. He gained a respectable amount of confidence in his approach based on a series of winning trades in Cisco and America Online. Because of the relatively large leverage involved, he became rather enthusiastic about his success. But he gave it all back in a few losing transactions on the same companies. It's not unusual to make a string of good trades, especially in an up market. But if you don't have a risk management strategy in place for times of adversity—and the self-discipline to enforce it—you will be blasted right out of the market.

The solution is to know in advance how much you can afford to lose on any given trade and at what point you will absolutely cut your loss.

Beginning traders must learn to take small losses to survive. If the losses begin to stack up, you'll need to stop trading and reassess your trading approach. This concept of taking tiny losses also requires that you make profits slowly. You will need to get used to making a series of small wins and never depend on a few big killings. Taking small losses and taking modest profits is imperative to success.

Jim V. is an investor from Carson City, Nevada, who practices a "2 percent rule." This rule indicates that he can have no more than 2 percent loss of his equity on any one trade. If he had $100,000 in his account, for example, he wouldn't risk more than $2,000 on any one trade. Many professional investors believe this 2 percent rule is too high. Jim does a great deal of research and doesn't choose many stocks to invest in. And he is correct in his predictions most of the time. But he's a long-term investor, not a day trader. It's logical to extrapolate that shorter-term traders need to have even tighter limits.

Position traders (trades that take only a few days) often allow only 1 percent. If they have $100,000 in their account, the maximum loss they will endure is $1,000 before exiting a trade. Conservative operators often limit their trades to 0.5 percent of their equity as a downside limit.

Some traders specify a percentage of the actual trade amount. They use technical analysis to determine one exit point (an analytical loss threshold) and a percentage of their equity as another exit point (a risk management threshold). They check to see where both of these logical stops fall and avoid a trade altogether if their risk management threshold comes first.

Carl K. in El Segundo, California, allocates 10 percent of his investment portfolio to Internet IPOs. After doing his due diligence on Internet companies going public, he narrows the field down to four companies per month. He gets in based on a combination of trends and company fundamentals. He exits the investments that don't respond the way he wants them to, and he has a pre-defined loss threshold that he sticks to. His upside exit point is four times what his downside loss threshold is. So even though

> Taking **small losses** and taking **modest profits** is **imperative** to **success.**

he may be wrong on three out of four of his IPO picks, he cuts his losing positions early enough so that the total of those three losses is still significantly smaller than the total of his one gain. His approach to extreme investing would be very risky if he were not within the 10 percent allocation of his entire portfolio because prices can fall so quickly. Over the long haul, he has made incredible gains.

Carl also uses a running P&L to stay on top of his risk exposure, something extreme investors need to constantly consider. This factors in your gains and losses for all trades you have open as a means of judging your overall trading success ratio at any point in an investment period. Software programs can perform this task automatically.

Bottom line: All risk management methods involve a small tolerance for loss. If the losses happen consistently, quit trading until you rework your strategy. Test it without using real money; then implement the new plan with small trades. Successfully implementing rigid risk management plans means the difference between winning and losing at the extreme game. It's as simple as that.

Rules And Strategies Of The Game

To understand the rules and strategies of extreme investing, you must understand what drives the markets in the first place. That driving force is sometimes called mass market psychology, or market mentality. It is this market mentality that determines price and its subsequent movement.

The first step to understanding market mentality is to see past the glitter that's typically associated with a stock, bond, contract or some other financial instrument being traded. In reality, these pieces of paper are usually just that—pieces of paper. For example, take a futures contract for corn. Naturally, the corn has intrinsic value, but the paper you trade will most likely never be converted to a delivery of corn to your door.

The stock of a company may have assets and perhaps a dividend value, but just like the corn, it is not really worth anything beyond what someone else is willing to pay for the paper it represents. The things represented by the instruments being traded are less important than what's going on in the minds of those who are trading them.

Case in point: the crash of 1929. The market went up and then it tanked, leaving investors with their mouths hanging open in shock as they began to learn the fruitful lesson of market mentality. The important thing to note here is that the intrinsic value associated with a particular company's stock didn't change after the crash (or after any crash). The company's sales didn't go down, nor did management change, nor did its new product pipeline shrink or disappear. All that happened was that the

Tiptoe Through The Tulips

It's hard to believe that the tulip frenzy of the mid-1600s was the equivalent of the recent dotcom madness. The tulip story is a very timely lesson in how many goofy people are out there buying stuff at outrageous prices just because they think someone else will eventually pay more for it. The "greater fool" theory in spades.

> **The tulip story is a very timely lesson in how many goofy people are out there buying stuff at outrageous prices.**

People weren't just charmed by tulips in the 17th century—they were obsessed with them. The obsession started slowly. People from Holland began importing tulips from Turkey in the 1500s, and no one seemed overwhelmed with them at first. But as their popularity grew in the 1600s, so did people's preoccupation with owning them.

Hollanders began to pay more and more for tulips, and it soon turned into a frenzy. With each passing day, the price of tulips rose, further fueling the speculative bubble. Speculation in tulip bulbs reached outrageous levels in the Netherlands as demonstrated by one unenviable collector who paid 1,000 pounds of cheese, four oxen, eight pigs, 12 sheep, a bed, and a suit of clothes for a single bulb of the Viceroy tulip. That's no Honus Wagner card, baby. That was in 1634. The story ends in 1637, when Dutch tulip prices collapsed after years of wild speculation. Now tulips are just, well, tulips, worth no more than how nice they look in a vase. Go figure.

greater fool theory

herd mentality made a quantum shift, like the shift away from tulip bulbs in the 1600s (see "Tiptoe Through The Tulips" on the facing page) or Cabbage Patch Dolls in the 1980s. What a world.

All this relates to the "greater fool" theory, which basically revolves around the concept that as long as the music is still playing, and you're not the guy left standing when the music stops, a greater fool than yourself will allow you to execute a successful trade. This is not to say that trading is bad—it isn't. It's part of life. The lesson here is to recognize what's being valued and why, and more importantly, what's moving prices.

They Don't Call It A Mass Market For Nothing

Even after markets crash, there continue to be buyers for goods, no matter what the market. But after a crash, buyers and sellers tend to trade at more realistic prices. The lesson here has nothing to do with intrinsic value or what price we find realistic; it has to do with the importance of perceived value as indicated by mass market psychology at any given moment.

Market mentality has a few obvious postulates. Buyers want to pay as little as possible for what they're buying, and sellers want to get as much as possible for what they're selling. Simple stuff. But if buyers and sellers don't agree on an exact amount, no transaction takes place. If they agree on an amount, a trade is consummated. Otherwise, they all just wait until either the buyer comes around to the meet the seller's price, or the seller comes down to meet the buyer's offer. Then a trade takes place. Bear in mind that all this time, there is no real way to put a value on what's being traded, other than the fact that two people agreed on a price at some point in time.

When it comes to trading for profit, sellers believe the price of what they're selling is about to fall. Buyers think the price of what they're buying is about to rise. Somebody is about to goof, since the price can't go up and

> **There** is **no** real **way** to **put** a **value** on **what's** being **traded**, other **than** the **fact** that **two people** agreed **on** a **price** at **some point** in **time**.

down simultaneously. Markets are made up of people who attempt to acquire or get rid of something at the expense of the other party involved in the trade. Every extreme investor is on his own, against every other investor out there, each one attempting to finagle and outsmart the other.

While a few of the action-oriented players are trading, the vast majority remains on the sidelines watching and waiting for the right moment to get in or out. Naturally, all buyers know if they don't suck up that good deal staring them in the face, some other smart guy will. And if a seller thinks the market is drifting ever lower, he knows that some other trader may jump in front of him and try to sell his for even less. The sellers have an "ask" price. The buyers have a "bid" price. One is asking $10 for his Beanie Baby; the other is bidding $9 to buy it. No trade happens until they reach a single, agreed-upon price.

It is a common misconception that prices go up because there are more buyers than sellers on a particular day. In actuality, there has to be one buyer for each seller. The lines may seem longer on one side than the other, but there are never more buyers than sellers in terms of transactions completed. It is the daily tally of these completed transactions that paints a portrait of the market's history. It's a tug of war between the bullish buyers and the bearish sellers. One of these groups eventually loses its enthusiasm, and the market goes up or down accordingly.

While this may appear to be simple common sense, it's amazing how amateur investors frequently buy something based on their belief that a company, commodity or some other financial instrument or vehicle is of such paramount value that it's not possible for that company's stock, or that commodity future, to go down. Market mentality drives prices, and it's a weird beast. But the beast is simple-minded and unsophisticated, and it works in patterns that are characterized by crude repetition. Extreme investors can extract money from this beast when they recognize what they're dealing with and develop a clear trading strategy and a good game plan in advance.

Ticket To Ride

The market mentality that drives all buying and selling consists of players who bring different skills to the game. Many of the investors you'll be rubbing elbows with (figuratively speaking, of course) are professionals who buy and sell using big money provided by huge brokers who represent gigantic corporate clients. When an insurance company collects your homeowner's insurance premium, it uses that money to make more money, buying and selling stuff all over the place. Those people are usually your worst adversaries. And when some guy out there does that for a living, using other people's money, he can get very good at it, and he has the psychological advantage of not worrying about playing with his own money.

Your tremendous advantage lies in the fact that you don't have to trade at all. Extreme investors are not obliged to do anything—investing is *optional*. On the other hand, the professional investor *has* to trade. He may have limits on how much he can lose before he's sacked, but professional investors *have* to trade. Many amateurs lack the discipline to quit after one or more losing trades, at least until they adjust their game plans. So while financial institutions have to remain active in the bond market, hot dog companies have to remain active in the cattle market, and brokers have to remain active in the stock market, you don't have to be active in any market. You can pick and choose. You are free to wait until the opportunity is just right.

In addition to common-sense tips like "You don't have to trade until the setup is perfect," there's a lot of advice traders hear over and over that should be at the root of any sound game plan. Much of this advice comes in the form of chestnuts like these two, which are particularly useful, not to mention tried-and-true: "The trend is your friend" and "The market is always right." Corny, maybe, but for the extreme investor, market behavior is not to be argued with, and it's usually not wise to go against the trend.

identify the trend

There are no "canned" trading systems that can accurately tell you what and when to buy or what and when to sell. But there are certain principals that work in setting up a sound strategy. Here are some of the proven strategies used by successful traders:

○ **Identify the trend.** It's important to know the trend of the overall market, the sector in which you're trading and the trend of the individual instrument you choose to trade. Heating oil, Swiss francs, IBM, the S&P 500 index, whatever you're looking to buy or sell—you must know all about that market and its current trend.

- **Trade with the trend.** As simple as it sounds, one way to trade successfully is to ride on the coattails of the prevailing trend and not try to guess at the tops and bottoms. Things that are moving up generally tend to go even higher. Things moving lower tend to continue going lower. Buying in weakness and selling in strength works for the pros but not as well for the individual investor.

- **Work from a precise plan of action.** Trade with your road map, not in response to price changes. Know ahead of time under what precise conditions you will consider entering or exiting a trade and at what moment you'll actually go for it (these are your entry points and exit points). And use your own trading plan, not someone else's.

- **Assume responsibility for your trades.** The results of extreme investing are never accidental. Extreme investors recognize that every trade is their own doing and not the result of any external circumstance or condition. If you don't believe you are in total control of both your decisions and how they are reflected by the results, don't trade.

- **Make money slowly.** The majority of successful extreme investors understand the importance of not aiming for the fence with every swing. Along with accepting only small losses, they gladly accept small profits, too. Novice traders frequently think that some forms of investing are an easy way to get rich quick. Some actually do, but most do not. For you to reach the same level of trading success as a professional fund manager might be an admirable goal—and making 30 percent on your money in a year is nothing to sneeze at—but you need to rely on many small successes, not a few big killings. Irrationally exuberant expectations squash the hopes and dreams of many new traders.

When Newbies Screw Up

You have to love extreme investing and know it intimately to make it work. But even if you know the markets inside and out, and you've mastered the skills of the game, bad days still happen. Sometimes the obvious becomes apparent so slowly it hurts. Trial and error is an expensive approach to mastering extreme investing. Fortunately, every mistake you could possibly make has already been made by someone before you. Knowing the mistakes new traders commonly make may provide you with vicarious experience that will prevent a firsthand lesson.

exit strategy

○ **Poor risk management:** Extreme investors recognize that their losses can get away from them quickly. The potential exists for unlimited loss since the price of a stock can conceivably go down without any imposed limits. Therefore, trends that move unchecked against the trader can represent a cancerous scenario and spontaneous combustion. Use sound risk management. If you don't, it's the one mistake that can remove you from the game entirely.

○ **Not having a predefined exit strategy:** Every trader who executes a trade has expectations of success. But every seasoned trader knows that a fair percentage of trades, no matter how well-thought-out, are going to move against him. Having an exit strategy is crucial. If you're using charts to find your entry point, for example, it's important to use the same to find your exit point in a worst-case scenario. Exit points are clearly tied to your trading time frame and the size of your trade. When trading stocks, you can set your trade not to exceed or fall below a certain point (a stop order) so it trades automatically. But many extreme investors do not use programmed stop orders that execute the trade; instead, they have a clear mental picture and target price at which they know their trade did not work. Then they exit. These are mental stop orders.

○ **Averaging down:** Beginning traders have a tendency to average down in an attempt to take advantage of a falling stock price. If they buy a Russell 2000 index option at $100 and it drops to $90, they can buy another like number of contracts and bring their average price to $95. Then they frequently stay in the position and hope for the best. Huh? All this does is tie up even more trading capital, making an adverse turn even more devastating. This strategy can take you out of the game in a hurry.

○ **Staying with a loser or not taking a winner:** This is the most painful of all lessons. If you're like many extreme investors, losing on a bad trade generates greater dissatisfaction than winning on a good trade creates glee. This helps instill the discipline needed to exit according to plan. But even for emotionally grounded traders, the temptation is there to allow hope to enter the picture just as you reach your predetermined exit point. Hope doesn't fill the coffers, and successful extreme investors just don't allow this to happen.

Rules And Strategies Of The Game

John Ford, a novice day trader in San Diego, decided to trade Qualcomm Inc. (QCOM) over a one-week period. Qualcomm had just announced a 4-for-1 stock split—meaning the company increased the number of shares of stock by four so that the price per share was one quarter what it had been before the split—and the stock had already run up to new all-time highs, with several hundred percent gains. He did both fundamental and technical analysis on Qualcomm. His fundamental analysis indicated the company's growth was driven by a star product, its CDMA chipsets, and the company would receive huge royalties from manufacturers of wireless equipment that employ Qualcomm's patents. All things looked favorable, as the seer would say.

> **John** didn't **really have** an **exit strategy**—and a **"gut feeling"** doesn't count **as** a **viable** system.

Then John did his charting to find an entry point. What he found was that the charts were straight up, which gave him no historical data on this company's stock that would indicate how high or low the stock might go. This stock was going ballistic, and he wanted in, so he entered the trade planning to trade only 100 shares to be safe, although 100 shares of this stock cost almost $38,000 at the time ($380 per share). So even though his charting showed no limits yet to help him define his exit point, he jumped in anyway, without nailing down a clear exit strategy.

His timing was perfect, at least for a few hours, as the stock climbed to around $400. On his own hunch, John was prepared to follow this stock up for the rest of the week, figuring that an upcoming Fed meeting would make an excellent opportunity to take profits, based on his calculation that Fed Chairman Alan Greenspan would raise interest rates again (John happened to be right). And even when Qualcomm dropped like an anvil before the announcement, John was prepared to ride it out, at least to where he got in, figuring he was riding on free money.

At the close of the fourth day of the week's trading, John decided not to close out his position. The stock had made a move upward

Continued on next page

Continued from previous page

toward the day's close, and he knew that a strong close often leads to a strong open. The next day, the stock went up in the morning, just as he'd calculated, and he figured the mini-correction was over, so he bought another 100 shares. As soon as his order was filled, he watched the stock make a "two steps down for every one step up" digression for the rest of the day. When the stock had dropped about 18 points below his entry point, he finally implemented an exit strategy, based on how much it hurt to have just lost 5 percent of his trading capital—about $6,000. Ouch.

In other words, John didn't really have an exit strategy—and a "gut feeling" doesn't count as a viable system. Elsewhere in this book are helpful hints on exit strategies that incorporate cash management and trading strategies. Be sure you have an exit strategy that correlates upside potential and downside protection. Without an exit strategy and a clear exit price, you risk taking a thrashing.

It's important to stick with your trading strategy right up to the end, even if it's wrong. Some serendipitous and profitable turning point may be just over the horizon, but even if the stars are in alignment for you, it doesn't help you fine-tune your trading system. If you learn later that you have incorrectly set your downside exit point, the time to evaluate your error is after you've exited the trade, not during the trade.

While accepting a loss is hard, for some it's even harder to take a profit. People who are new to extreme investing often find themselves in a tizzy over taking a profit too early. They calculate profits in their head as a stock rises, or they remember a time when they exited a trade and watched the stock run another 10 points higher, or they stop to consider whether it might be wise to add to their position rather than stick to their exit plan. What do all these thoughts have in common? They show investors second-guessing their trading strategies. If you think it's wise to add to your position at some point, that needs to be part of your entry strategy, not something you do on the fly because something you bought shot up unexpectedly. Of equal importance is that each of these thoughts allows emotions to seep in, thus decreasing your ability to take a purely rational approach. Which brings us to the next of our common trading mistakes.

○ **Trading with euphoria, greed or fear:** Staying with losers and not taking winners is generally the result of euphoria, greed or fear. The only way to consistently succeed at extreme investing is to trade using reason alone, and never in response to gut feelings or emotions.

Let's start with euphoria. Never underestimate the negative power of giddiness. Not that there's anything wrong with a trade that makes you feel airborne, but trading when you're feeling high is counterproductive. Las Vegas depends on the "let it ride" mentality. Serving free drinks helps the process along. That's gambling as entertainment, folks—not extreme investing as a business. If you're high on the fumes of a recent trading experience, enjoy. Take the day off. Golf. Or just lumber around your office like King Kong for a while. Don't trade.

Greed is an unsettling force with strong emotional roots and a negative undertone. Greed can turn an otherwise brilliant trade into a flop. Extreme investors never kick themselves for taking a profit of any kind when it's part of their game plan—even when they sell something that keeps going up after they've moved on. But greed can never be in the plan. Use whatever Zenlike resources you have to resist it.

And fear. No one likes to admit to fear, but it's the single most powerful unseen force trying to nibble at the edges of every decision you make. Fear of loss, fear of missing out, fear of margin calls! Fear of getting up to go to the bathroom and coming back to find you've missed your moment and lost your money. Luckily, confidence trumps fear every single time. And confidence comes from doing your homework, believing in your plan and knowing your capacity to do the job as planned.

○ **Not writing down your plan, or failing to test and keep records that corroborate your success or failure:** As an extreme investor, your mental state is continuously updated as you think and act each day. To better control the design of your mental processes, it's absolutely critical to write down the things you want to learn, the concepts you want to apply and the system you eventually choose to follow. And then keep meticulous records of where the ride takes you, good and bad. The physical act of writing and the methodical act of record-keeping are powerful tools you can use to clarify your thoughts, influence your actions and maintain a proper perspective. Plus, what you commit to paper is the ultimate reality check, before or after the fact.

Using a written pre-flight checklist not only keeps you on task but is also a great way to not look back on a losing trade and kick yourself for having failed

> **Greed** can **turn** an **otherwise brilliant trade into** a **flop.**

to remember one key ingredient. Often a checklist will have several items on it that are all shouting at you to buy or sell something. As you prepare to invest, anticipation sets in and anxiousness follows. The urgency can become unbearable as you notice a winning situation rapidly escaping. You pull the trigger with confidence. Yet when things don't go as planned, you realize later that one of the elements on your mental checklist was waving a warning flag the whole time— a flag that you failed to see. Like a good pilot, use that pre-flight checklist. Don't head into an investment and then realize you forgot to check the landing gear before takeoff. Write down your trade parameters—and stick to 'em.

Keeping records is often viewed as, well, a pain in the bum. But committing your experiences as an extreme investor to paper and reviewing them is the only way to guarantee you're on the right track. Whether you made a good trading decision or a bad one, you can look back and learn what you did right or wrong. Don't let your daily experiences slip by without taking advantage of every single act. Write down what you did and review it often.

○ **Using inside information and tips:** Beginning traders never seem to learn this lesson the easy way. But they all learn it sooner or later. Insider information and tips almost always backfire. Period.

Insider information often finds its way into the heads of traders. Maybe a friend or relative at the top knows the upcoming quarter will end with a surprise earnings report to the upside. Or some company is rumored to be a takeover target, according to someone who works at the bank that's handling the financing.

If you insist on pursuing inside tips, do so with the tiniest amount of risk capital. Even if the information is correct, do you really suppose that you're the only one lucky enough to know about it? By the time you hear it, so have dozens of other people, all of whom learned it about a week after the pros have already traded on the news. And that's only if it's true. If it's not, you're headed in the wrong direction anyway. In either case, you're probably going to lose unless you develop some sense of using that information as a contrarian indicator.

Steve K. worked at a San Diego-based microchip manufacturing company in sales and worked closely with upper management. One day

personal playbook

he overheard his boss talking to the president of the company about his new stock options, and his boss assured him they would be adjusted for the upcoming stock split next month. Naturally, the rest of the company knew nothing about the stock split, and since insider information is highly protected, and knowing how wrong it was to act on what he heard, Steve waited until the next day and called his sister and told her to load up, which she did.

She bought 1,500 shares of the company's stock, and when it went up 11 points, she knew why, so she bought another 1,000 shares. The news hit and the stock went up for a nanosecond, but then it tanked. The news of the split had sent the stock higher in the days preceding the announcement, before she bought her shares, and when the news was finally made public, the stock was at its peak. Split announcements often cause a brief run up, but by the time she realized it wasn't going to bounce back, she had lost several thousand dollars. If inside information finds its way to your ears, don't trust that it hasn't already been factored into the current price of the stock.

By now you know there's a playbook—your own dog-eared, coffee-stained, personal playbook—that reflects the strategies you want to implement. But being aware of the X-factors—those "can't put a figure or a finger on it" factors like market mentality, trends and fear—can affect every game you play. These intangibles are as important as your playbook itself, but now you know that. So let's move on.

Tools
Of The
Trade

n the previous chapter, we briefly touched on the need to heed dependable common-sense tips, the catchy sayings and the tried-and-true axioms of the stock market and other forms of extreme investing. There is one more we'd like to add that is an appropriate introduction to the information that follows: "The market is always telling a story." Unfortunately, we often just don't listen.

However, unlike others, the extreme investor uses all the tools at his disposal to make surgically precise trading decisions (based on forces far greater than sheer gut instincts, the opinion of your brother or a lucky rabbit's foot).

As we mentioned in Chapter 1, the two main types of decision support tools are *fundamental analysis* and *technical analysis*. In simple terms, they are as follows:

Fundamental
Analysis

Fundamental analysis on a particular company, commodity, bond or other investment vehicle entails looking at the global picture and the investment you're pursuing as it fits into that global picture. For stocks, options and IPOs, this means investigating the corporate climate by looking at management talent, technology advantages, earnings and revenue growth and projections, and lots, lots more.

Fundamental analysis is generally used by investors rather than traders, since the information behind such analysis lends itself to a longer-term trading horizon. If you look at the overall market scene and note that a particular sector is doing poorly, like the pharmaceutical sector (which is made up of big companies like Warner Lambert, Pfizer and Eli Lilly), your analysis might begin with the external factors that are putting pressure on the sector. After all, if you look at the individual health of each of these companies, you will see mostly good news. Their stock prices should be up because of good earnings and high revenue numbers, but they *aren't* due to a given factor (or factors) suppressing the sector overall, like adverse governmental pressures or imminent regulations. (Bristol-Myers Squibb recently tanked based on bad news about one of its new drugs, but the sector didn't suffer much.) Often, a suppressed sector denotes and/or signals a wait-and-see game and is best suited to the longer-term investor.

> **Fundamental analysis** is generally **used** by **investors** rather than **traders**, since the **information behind** such analysis **lends itself** to a **longer-term** trading **horizon.**

Interest rates play an important role in fundamental analysis, as do other global economic factors you can read about in the news. One of these factors is inflationary trends, which might lead to higher interest rates, which can eventually make the entire stock market sag. You should also keep an eye on economic indicators, such as the GDP (gross domestic product) and employment rates. There are dozens of indicators out there.

If you're interested in trading stock options for a specific company, looking at an IPO or just want to day-trade a stock, it makes sense to have an understanding of what is happening to that particular company in terms of its outlook within the particular industry.

Lately, it seems the most important factor on the minds of most traders is revenue growth (sales growth). Internet companies can be making no money whatsoever (that is, be utterly unprofitable), but simply by virtue of the fact that their revenue is going through the roof, everybody jumps on the stock, option or IPO as if it's the last train leaving the station.

Amazon.com is a perfect example. A few years ago, the company went public, and people were buying books online in record numbers, every month driving sales figures up higher and higher. Still, even at the time of this writing, in spite of massive revenue, the company is not making any money, i.e., actual profit. It's an illogical scenario that can't continue indefinitely.

It's sort of like the car dealer who claims to sell automobiles below his cost. When asked how he does it, he proudly exclaims, "*Volume*. . . I sell *lots* of automobiles." Bottom line: At some point in time, either potential profits manifest themselves or the negative bubble bursts.

Thus, strong companies that have fantastic track records are often shunned because of their seemingly average—or average by comparison—revenue growth. No sizzle, if you will. Big companies like Procter & Gamble have annual revenue growth of 5 percent and bring in around $20 billion, but the slightest boo-boo on the earnings front slams the company's stock like it was in bankruptcy. Other stocks, like Cisco Systems and Sun Microsystems, may be very profitable, but what everybody has their eye on is the amount of business expansion they are experiencing. They suffer from the IPO syndrome noted above, which isn't to say the valuations for Cisco and Sun are wrong. Many fundamental analysts wisely argue that the companies that supply the picks and shovels for the Internet gold rush are a safe way to play the Internet sector.

What's important to remember is that there are myriad elements to look at in the fundamental analysis of companies, and it's an important tool. Yet fundamental analysis plays a slightly less significant role to the extreme investor than technical analysis, which is a better measuring tool for trading on momentum. Extreme investing goes hand in hand with shorter-term trading and catching the trend while it's hot, hot, hot.

Technical
Analysis

To many investors, technical analysis (TA) is just looking at a bunch of charts that reflect past market movement. People who read charts, however, seem to be able to plot out where a commodity or stock is headed next, usually better than those who do not read charts.

If you believe that history repeats itself, technical analysis makes a lot of sense. Even if you follow the theory that most things happen randomly, mass psychology is still influential in determining trends. Technical analysis is being used by the enemy (other traders), so you should be familiar with the tools they're using even if you lack total confidence in them.

Technical analysis involves a lot of that pays off in the end. So as you begin reading more and spending more time perusing Internet research sites (as we know you're going to, right?), don't let your eyes glaze over. You'll encounter all types of mind-boggling, cryptic jargon (stochastics, Bollinger Bands, oscillators and Elliott Wave Theory), so we can only encourage you to start learning what they are. There are many good books devoted solely to the language and mechanics of technical analysis—and it's a good idea to know what a technical analyst means when he or she refers to recognition and trend analysis.

Rather than attempt to explain in detail how TA works, we'll simply emphasize the importance of recognizing that trends are the most important thing the extreme investor needs to first identify and then start following up on—pronto. Simple, but critical to your success.

trend analysis

Technical analysis offers a visual means by which to put a finger on the pulse of the current mass market psychology. Whether you're interested in currency, major stock averages, industry groups, IBM or cattle futures, TA has tools you can readily find and successfully use to formulate a picture of the market and to get a handle on where it might be headed.

Interested extreme investors will still read *The Wall Street Journal*, pore over corporate earnings reports and subscribe to financial newsletters. But charts will tell them what the fundamentals are for a given stock or an entire market based on the direction in which its price is moving. If the fundamentals of a stock are weak, the price is generally reflected in the charts. The best thing about TA is that it provides clear-cut, fast answers that always reflect what's going on in the real world. Students of TA often recall a quote by financial expert Bernard Baruch, who said, "Show me the charts and I'll tell you the news."

When the market is telling a story, listen and learn.

S&P 500 Futures/Cash Market

Technical analysis is a method of evaluating securities (stocks, commodities, bonds, etc.) by looking at charts that show price changes over a given period of time (as little as a few minutes or as much as several years). The Dow Jones Industrial Average (DJIA) is a group of stocks used to track the overall market. Standard & Poor's 500 (S&P 500) is another group of stocks used as a benchmark for determining the health of the overall market, but because it is a market-value-weighted index (explained a little later), it is even more carefully watched and charted by traders than the DJIA.

The S&P 500 is a group of "big cap" stocks. Big cap means big capitalization, or stocks with huge market value. This is determined by multiplying the number of shares outstanding by the value of one share. Amazon.com has 337 million shares. Multiply that by the price of one share on any given day, and you have the market capitalization—many billions of dollars. Amazon may be considered medium cap compared to General Electric (GE), with almost $500 billion in market capitalization. And then there are the little guys, like Doggy Drawers,

Who Are These Guys, Anyway?

Start analyzing the stock market and you can't help encountering the Dow Jones Industrial Average (DJIA) and Standard & Poor's 500 (S&P). But why?

As for the DJIA, back in 1882 three young reporters—Charles Dow, Edward Jones and Charles Bergstresser—decided to begin producing handwritten newsletters (called *flimsies*) detailing stock market activity to be delivered by messenger to interested parties on Wall Street.

Two years later, the trio put together its first stock indicator—an index of railroad stocks that became known as the Dow Jones Transportation Average. In 1886, they introduced a second index, now known as the Dow Jones Industrial Average, which tracked 30 blue-chip U.S. stocks. Today, the DJIA is the world's most widely followed stock market indicator.

Theirs was an idea whose time had come, and in less than seven years they outgrew their tiny basement office. By 1889, they decided to turn their burgeoning *Customers' Afternoon Newsletter* into a formal newspaper they dubbed *The Wall Street Journal*.

> The **S&P 500 companies** are top **"market value"** picks **and** collectively **equal about 70** percent to **85** percent of **all publicly traded U.S. stocks.**

By comparison, the S&P 500 Composite Stock Price Index is a virtual newcomer, although its roots trace back even farther. In 1851, Henry Varnum Poor—editor of *American Railroad Journal*—wrote a book on transportation for the U.S. Treasury. This led him to form H.W. Poor Co. in 1867 (H.W. being the initials of his son, who was instrumental in the growth of the new publishing company) to publish railroad info. By 1886, the scope broadened to include *Poor's Handbook of Investment Securities*. Around 1900, newspaperman John Moody also published his *Moody's Manual of Industrials and Misc. Securities* (one of Moody's companies ultimately purchased Poor's in 1919).

In 1906, a third key player, Luther Blake, founded Standard Statistical Bureau to gather info on the top 100 U.S. corporations. Struggling through the '20s and the Depression of the '30s, Poor's fell into bankruptcy, and Standard Statistical Bureau merged with *Poor's Handbook*.

Introduced in 1997, Standard and Poor's 500 stock index now includes industrial, transportation and financial blue-chip companies, among others, which are primarily listed on the New York Stock Exchange (NYSE).

Continued on next page

Extreme Investor

Continued from previous page

> The S&P 500 companies are intended to cast a different snapshot of the market than the narrower DJIA, which only portrays 30 companies. The S&P 500 companies are top market value picks and collectively equal about 70 percent to 85 percent of all publicly traded U.S. stocks. Finally, the NYSE index debuted in 1966 to include all stocks listed on the "Big Board."

a blossoming canine clothing store, with 11 million shares, each worth around $5, representing a mere flea compared to behemoths GE and Amazon.

The S&P 500 index is made up of New York Stock Exchange (NYSE) stocks as well as National Association of Securities Dealers Automated Quotation System (NASDAQ) stocks. Big mutual fund managers and institutional traders (referred to here as volume traders) invest in this index. It's a way to put their money to work, sometimes as a permanent holding, sometimes just as a short-term holding pattern for idle funds. Mutual fund managers try to beat this benchmark index with their own stock picks. They all measure their relative success by how their fund did compared to the S&P 500 index.

The Answer, My Friend, Is Showin' In The Trend...

The S&P 500—cash, futures or both—offers a way to gauge what the overall market is doing. It's the most highly respected index, and it reflects both the moods and actions of buyers and sellers (as a whole) while serving as a trend indicator showing if the market is moving up or down at a given time.

As we mentioned, one form of the S&P 500 index is called the "cash" market (the cash market simply means that stocks are sold for cash and delivered immediately). Looking at a historical chart of the cash index, you see directional patterns, but it really tells you nothing more than what the market is doing today, or more accurately, what it finished doing just recently or maybe a long time ago. It's a running track record of the cumulative supply and demand for the entire basket of S&P 500 stocks selected by Standard and Poor's. It's comprised of 400 industrial companies, 40 utility companies, 40 financial companies and 20 transportation

Tools Of The Trade

companies, all chosen by Standard and Poor's to reflect the 500 largest companies by market capitalization.

But the S&P 500 is also traded as futures contracts, which means this group of stocks can be bought and sold just like any other commodities contracts (where buyer and seller agree that on a future date, a specified commodity, in this case a group of securities, will be delivered at a specific price).

Futures contracts are discussed in Chapter 9, but to understand this explanation, you need to know that futures contracts represent the "obligation to deliver" the value of the index on a certain date (the expiration date) at some time in the future. The S&P 500 futures contracts are bets on where that group of stocks will be in terms of price at some point in the future.

The S&P 500 futures contracts trade at the Chicago Mercantile Exchange, completely independent of where the actual S&P 500 stocks (cash index) are traded. The contracts expire quarterly. They are displayed on the exchange ticker as March (SPH), June (SPM), September (SPU) and December (SPZ). No matter what day of the year it is, one of these contracts is active for the current period and will expire in 90 days or less.

But there is a way to combine the cash index and the futures index to actually get some information on where the market is headed, at least for the short term. This is a very beneficial tool for day traders. Here's how it works:

The volume traders put gigantic amounts of money to work buying the cash index and selling the futures index, and vice versa. The term *arbitrage* is used to describe the process of weighing the two and moving money into the one that appears undervalued. Arbitrage is technically defined as the simultaneous purchase and sale of identical or equivalent financial instruments (in this case the stocks and the futures contracts that represent those stocks) to benefit from the discrepancy in their price relationship. This valuation discrepancy is based on a complex mathematical formula (that you don't

> **Arbitrage** is **the** simultaneous **purchase** and **sale** of **identical** or equivalent **financial instruments** to benefit from the **discrepancy** in **their** price relationship.

Futures Contract Symbols: What's The Deal?

Commodity futures contracts (one of the subjects of Chapter 9 in this book, but relevant to the S&P commodity futures discussed here) trade and come due at different times of the year, and each month they have their own symbols that appear on the exchange ticker tape. As such, S&P 500 futures contracts are cryptically indicated on the exchange, and there seems to be no logical explanation or apparent reason for these abbreviations. Or is there?

First of all, the SP in the symbol denotes—you guessed it—Standard & Poor's. Next, as in the military and international radio communications, letters are assigned words to avoid costly mistakes…B, C and D (which all sound basically alike) become Baker, Charlie and Delta to set them apart.

The months relating to S&P 500 commodities futures are assigned a third letter (in addition to the SP noted above) for no rhyme or reason other than they are basically not easily confused visually, so they use the following symbols to represent the months of the year: January—F, February—G, March—H, April—J, May—K, June—M, July—N, August—Q, September—U, October—V, November—X, and December—Z.

The S&P 500 futures contracts are quarterly instruments, so each contract expires at the end of a calendar quarter—March, June, September and December (H, M, U and Z).

---

really need to learn but that can be found on Internet Web sites like www.cnbc.com) that indicates whether or not the value between the two is fair.

The formula takes into account many different angles, like current interest rates, and what would happen to people's money if they just put it into a T-bill instead. It factors in how much money the stocks would pay in dividends over a period of time if people owned them outright instead of just the option to buy them later. It also assigns a value to the time remaining before the option expires (it's assumed that over the long haul, stocks will move up in value, a good bet unless some world calamity strikes). In other words, the formula is not a shot in the dark. It's a proven relationship that professional traders recognize and universally accept.

formula

With this formula, volume traders can quickly figure out if it's better to own the real thing now or to own the right to buy the real thing later. This process is employed when volume traders buy or sell based on information that indicates to them that one of the indices is currently undervalued compared to the other (this revolves around the concept of *fair value*, which is what the aforementioned mathematical formula is all about).

Remember, the benchmark of success for professional investors is often tied to the S&P 500 index, and these professional investors tend to put funds to work in association with this index in one form or another. So if the formula indicates that the futures contracts look a little too expensive at the moment compared to the value of the stocks themselves today, volume traders will sell the futures and buy the cash index. If the S&P 500 cash index looks overpriced, volume traders will sell the actual stock now and purchase the right to buy it later via futures contracts.

> The **important thing** is that **money flows** from **one** to the **other**, and when you know **which direction** it's going in, you can tell **in which** direction the **market** is **headed** when it **opens**.

The important thing is that money flows from one to the other, and when you know which direction it's going in, you can tell in which direction the market is headed when it opens. If money leaves the cash index, stocks go down (volume traders are selling stocks and buying futures). If money leaves the futures index, stocks go up (traders are selling futures and buying the actual stocks).

Fair value is what the people on the financial news refer to when they are reporting throughout the night, in the morning and especially right before the market opens. That's because any big discrepancy in fair value is going to send the market off in a certain direction, at least for a little while. Trading programs (see "Slow It Down, Please" on page 51) are used by volume traders to automatically do a lot of this buying and selling.

The NYSE is set up for program trading so that buy and sell orders for huge blocks of shares can be electronically sent to the exchange floor specialist—generally dedicated to dealing in only one specific stock—for

Slow It Down, Please

Program trading is when volume traders use computers to automatically execute big trades when certain conditions occur, such as when the fair value between the S&P 500 cash and futures markets has a valuation discrepancy. This automatic trading is a way big institutional investors get in or out quickly, with a simple touch of a button.

The New York Stock Exchange (NYSE) defines a program trade as either a group of 15 or more stocks from the S&P 500 index valued at any price, or a group of any size stocks from the S&P 500 index valued at $1 million or more. Program trading rarely lasts more than a half-hour and sometimes only lasts a minute or two until normal market order is restored. But sometimes program-ordered buying and selling is so intense that the market has trouble adjusting to these huge trades.

To maintain market stability, the NYSE established what traders commonly refer to as *trading curbs*. The NYSE applies program trading curbs whenever the Dow Jones Industrial Average (DJIA) moves 210 points higher than—or 210 points lower than—the previous day's closing price. This restriction on program trading remains in place until the DJIA returns to within 100 points of the previous day's closing price or until the end of the trading day. When trading curbs are in place, program selling can still take place, but there are certain rules in force that help prevent total "runaway" markets.

immediate order execution. In other words, volume traders compare the running price of the S&P 500 cash index in New York to the running price of the S&P futures contract in Chicago to determine if and when an index arbitrage opportunity exists.

Within seconds, volume traders who own the S&P 500 cash index might sell it and replace it with the cheaper S&P 500 futures index. Virtually all the volume traders make money this way—big corporate investors, brokerage firms and institutional investors.

In addition to program trading, if the market looks like it's about to move up quickly due to some wild market sentiment, volume traders who are anxious to establish or increase their long position in the market can do so with a single order (and do it really cheaply) by

volume traders

buying S&P 500 futures contracts, as opposed to buying an assortment of individual stocks.

Bearish traders who want to quickly grab some insurance against depreciation of their portfolios can sell a futures contract for protection. The futures contract allows an investor to leverage the full value of the entire 500 stocks, rather than the full value of all 500 stocks if bought individually.

Because of this, the stock market is quick to reflect both world events and local company news that might move the market in one direction or another. Program trading accounts for about one-fifth of a typical day's NYSE volume. Day traders can take advantage of these move scenarios by keeping an eye on what the volume traders are doing and going along with the trend by tagging along with similar buy and/or sell orders.

If there are more sellers than buyers of something, this generally means the price will move lower. If there are more buyers than sellers, this generally means the price will move higher. So the program trading that's triggered by either the cash index or the futures index being off the fair value is rather short-lived. As soon as the buying or selling takes place in response to arbitraging the spread, it doesn't take long for that action to drive the spread back to fair value.

14th Floor...Stocks, Futures And Fair Value

Despite the short life associated with bursts of program trading, any big move in the market is something to keep an eye on for investing opportunities. Naturally, extreme investors like day traders don't wait until program trading has run its full course; they enter and exit in anticipation of moves. It's important to get in just before the program trading starts and get out just before it ends (this is referred to as *front-running*).

Trading on this information offers big rewards. But as a cautionary note to traders, someone once said that front-running these program trades is like picking up dimes in front

Someone once said that **front-running program** trades is like **picking up dimes** in **front** of a **steamroller.**

Circuit Breakers

If the Dow Jones Industrial Average (DJIA) falls 10 percent, all trading on the New York Stock Exchange (NYSE) is halted for 60 minutes. If the DJIA falls 20 percent, trading is halted for two hours. If the DJIA falls 30 percent, trading is halted for the day. (If the DJIA falls any more than that, not only is trading halted, but the fire department knows to rush over to Wall Street and set up the nets and trampolines.) But there is no trading halt if the NYSE rallies to any degree, even 30 percent or more in a day, because exuberant rallies are considered a good thing, not something to be curbed.

of a steamroller or participating in the running of the bulls in Pamplona, Spain. Use S&P cash and futures program trading as one of your many trading decision resources, not as a single action criterion.

Film
At Eleven...

This section is not intended to give you a full, every-gory-detail explanation of fair value, but it will get you started. CNBC has an Internet Web site that explains this in more detail (go to www.cnbc.com, and at the home page click on the "Markets" tab, and then go to the left side of the screen and choose "Fair Value" from the list of options).

While we're on the subject of CNBC, each day at 6:30 p.m. and 2 a.m. Eastern Standard Time, someone will do the math for you, and they will tell you the difference between the spread and the next day's fair value. They will also tell you whether all this math and fair value stuff will have a positive or negative effect on the day's trading session if the futures and the cash indices hold their relative positions up until the opening bell. During the day, CNBC scrolls similar information at the bottom of the TV screen that will also help you figure out the current status of the S&P 500 cash index and futures contracts, if you know how to interpret it (again, go to the Web site).

Trader See,
Trader Do

In addition to fundamental analysis, technical analysis and understanding what the S&P 500 cash and futures markets are all about, there are many other events that can hypercharge investment movement, many of which are totally bogus but move stocks anyway. Much of the following only applies to day trading and options trading, but a better understanding of these events will help all your extreme investing endeavors.

Splitting Hairs

Stock splits are perceived as really cool things by average traders—but often for the wrong reasons. Stock splits are simply a means of making a company's stock appear to be more affordable. That's it. Most average investors, and a lot of traders, want to own more shares of a stock they like. More shares can be bought when they're cheaper. So companies split their stock, generally two for one. Unfortunately, this doesn't do a thing for the actual value of the stock, since doubling the number of shares only means that each share now represents a smaller portion of the company.

Jim D. is a trader who teaches an investment class in Los Angeles one night a week. When he gets to the part about stock splits, he tells a story about his young nephew, whose name is Benny. Benny likes to play "business," which the child does by pretending to fill out play invoices and memos (like he's seen big folks do). Benny was playing on the living room floor one day when he decided he needed more paper. Jim told him he had an entire pad of paper right in front of him. But he said he wanted two pads for two different things. So Jim took Benny's pad of paper and cut it in half with a paper cutter. Little Benny was extremely happy.

> Stock **splits** are **perceived** as really **cool things** by **average** traders—but **often** for the **wrong reasons.** Stock **splits** are **simply** a **means** of making a company's **stock appear** to be **more** affordable.

Thereafter, Jim used this scenario to explain to his students that, in reality, he performed a classic stock split with the paper. There were twice as many pieces of paper, but there wasn't any more paper than when he started. And that's what a stock split is all about—making the kids happy so they can have more shares.

warning period

In reality, stock splits are rarely offered by companies that cannot sustain growth: Companies never want their stock price to be too low since really low stock prices indicate weakness. Therefore, a split generally comes in conjunction with anticipated growth. The split itself, however, is a nonevent in terms of increased stock valuations. Corporate sales, revenue and earnings don't change just because you fiddle with the number of shares you have. Nonetheless, stocks generally go up right after a stock split is announced. And they often fall back down a few days later.

Coming Soon To A Theater Near You

Earnings season leaps out onto the scene to scare traders with news that can send a stock up like a bottle rocket or crashing to the pavement like an overripe cantaloupe. The month prior to an earnings report, stocks and options are traded in an attempt to second-guess what the actual report numbers will be—good, bad or indifferent—with whispered numbers being leaked or bandied about speculating on what the earnings (or loss) may actually be.

There are Web sites that do nothing but report on when companies' earnings are due out for release. Yahoo! Finance has a cool presentation, and there are many more out there. Some companies with weird fiscal calendars don't report during earnings season, but most do.

A big company that has a good earnings report can be reason enough to send the entire sector higher. If Intel's report is good, the computer chip sector goes up. If Cisco's report is good, the network sector goes up. And conversely, if a report stinks, the corresponding sectors tend to go down.

Just as important to the actual reporting is what's called the "warning period," when companies announce that they won't meet earnings expectations. If the warning period passes and a company you follow hasn't put out a warning, this implies that things are OK. Compaq made a goof at one point when it failed to put out an earnings warning. Investors made the assumption that the company had no reason to suspect that earnings would fall short. But earnings turned out to be under expectation, and the stock price tumbled. Soon thereafter came a class-action lawsuit claiming that the company essentially misguided investors. So there are exceptions—just because a company doesn't suspect a shortfall doesn't guarantee that it's not going to experience one.

The important thing to recognize is that if you're trading a stock, you need to know when the company reports earnings. If you have any doubts about what that report might reveal, it's best to pretend that it will be bad, since only *great* news is rewarded. Anything else is often punished. There's no reason to leave yourself exposed during these times.

> **Don't hope** for **good earnings reports** and **gamble** that one is coming up **unless** you're **really sure.** The **downside risk** is too **painful.**

Don't hope for good earnings reports and gamble that one is coming up unless you're really sure. The downside risk is too painful.

You're Going To Meet A Tall, Dark Stranger

Big, reputable banks and investment firms pay lots of money to seasoned analysts whose job is to rate companies and figure out what their stock prices should be 12 months from now. Many times the analysts who come out with rave reviews are the same underwriters who just took a stock public. But no matter how subjective and inaccurate, or how perfectly right-on they are, the important thing is that when they speak, it has an effect on that particular stock's price.

A company can be doing perfectly well, and an analyst might come out and say she thinks the stock is worth 10 points less than it's trading at, and she doesn't expect the same robust growth rate as before. The stock goes down the tubes.

Seasoned stock traders regard analysts with the same reverence as they might a circus sideshow hawker who tries to lure them into a tent to see the tattooed, bearded lady. Analysts are sometimes perceived as having a vested interest in channeling buyers in a certain direction. They can downgrade a stock on what seems to be trivial information or suspicious timing, and you wonder who's been buying up shares as soon as the downgrade is public. Is it the same company that issued the downgrade?

The point is that you need to stay clearly tuned into what's actually being said—and who's saying it. (Analysts can just as easily give a stock a really good boost just when you need it most, too.)

Cubes, Diamonds
And Spiders

So far, this chapter has provided information on decision support tools used by extreme investors. Some of you may think the research involved is overwhelming, especially if you have to perform it on every single stock you consider trading. That's where Cubes, Diamonds and Spiders come in.

These strange-sounding names represent *index unit trusts*, which are another form of specialty "baskets" or groupings of stocks that you can trade as a single unit. They trade like a stock with a unique trading symbol, but instead of representing a specific company, they represent a group of companies. You can trade an entire sector rather than a single stock. So listen up.

The NASDAQ 100 index (symbol QQQ), the Dow Jones Industrial's Diamonds (symbol DIA) and the Standard & Poor's Depositary Receipts (SPDR or "Spiders," symbol SPY) are baskets of stocks you can invest in as a group without buying each stock individually.

The QQQ (Cubes) represents the top 100 NASDAQ companies. The Dow Jones DIA represents the entire 30 stocks that make up the DJIA. The S&P SPY represents the entire portfolio of the 500 stocks that make up the S&P 500 cash index.

In one transaction, you can buy or sell shares of all these stocks just like you would buy or sell shares of any single common stock. That means you buy or sell shares that represent the collective performance of that particular index using a single transaction. They all day-trade (as a group) just like a regular individual stock.

When you buy Cubes, Diamonds or Spiders, you're investing in the shares of the selected companies that are represented by that particular index, so the index trust as a whole will go up or down in value in accordance with the larger overall index. The price of each of these unit trusts varies in accordance with a percentage of the value of the underlying index. In other words:

○ the QQQ group of shares represents about 5 percent of the value of the actual NASDAQ 100 index,

○ DIA shares cost about 1 percent of the Dow Jones Industrial's index value, and

○ SPY shares trade at about 10 percent of the value of the S&P 500 index.

The bottom line is that when you invest in these unit trusts, you get the advantage of diversification without the hassle of buying an unwieldy number of individual stocks. And the entire group conveniently trades just like it was one stock, with its own share price.

All three of these unit trusts are not actively managed like mutual funds are, which means the trust does not try to outperform the index on which it's based. The unit trust simply tracks along with the index, which means there's a lot less overhead in the form of fees that are traditionally associated with mutual fund management.

New investment vehicles are appearing on the horizon all the time that expand on the concept of buying *groups* of stocks that trade with a single ticker symbol, like one individual stock would trade. For example, Merrill Lynch has "HOLDRs" (for Holding Company Depositary Receipts), which are like little baskets that hold handfuls of similar stocks.

The Internet Infrastructure HOLDR (symbol HHH) contains just a few stocks of the biggest and most influential companies that provide the nuts and bolts that hold together most e-commerce Web sites. The Internet Infrastructure HOLDR includes such stocks as Inktomi (INKT), which develops software that enhances the performance and intelligence of large-scale networks; Exodus Communications (EXDS), a provider of Internet system and network management solutions; and VeriSign (VRSN), which provides Internet-based secure communications and e-commerce online. Merrill Lynch also has HOLDRs that represent the pharmaceutical industry (symbol PPH) and telecommunications companies (symbol TTH).

Just Cube It

Gail C. in Simi Valley, California, fancies herself a mini-extreme investor. She trades the QQQ index, which she swears is the greatest trad-

"I grew up on a farm in Arkansas and left home to study art history at the University of Virginia," Alexis Zanone says. Upon graduation, Zanone moved to New York City to work for a photography agency. Struggling on a meager $25,000 salary, she still managed to eke out a social life that included a circle of friends who worked in the investment banking industry. She couldn't help but notice they were taking home three times as much as she was. This fact got her attention.

As luck would have it, her cousins' family were the founders of Quick & Reilly (Q&R), one of the original discount brokerage firms (which today has about 120 branches nationwide) and a parent company for many Wall Street services, including Suretrade, a deep-discount Internet brokerage company.

In the spring of 1997, Zanone approached Quick & Reilly for a job and was hired as an assistant in the Client Services Division of the Clearing Unit, providing back-office services to brokerage firms such as Suretrade.

"Quick & Reilly was really a pioneer in getting brokerage firms on the Internet, and I was exposed to all kinds of financial data and capabilities," Zanone notes. "I bought some Q&R stock ($350 worth), and it doubled in three months." (Q&R was bought by Fleet Bank.)

"I was immediately intrigued by the stock market," she says, "and started to buy all the Internet stocks (like AOL, Yahoo! and Lycos), and this was when they were going up 10 to 15 points a day. As I got more interested, I spent hours after work looking at the charts and times sales for my picks and others, and it kind of became my hobby.

"Then, in the spring of 1998, I made $17,000 on strong reaction to stock splits and stuff." She lost $14,000 of it a few months later, due to not taking profits, which she shamelessly admits.

> **"I** was a **trader** at **heart. I** was **hooked."**

Granted, she had some built-in advantages—due to her family affiliation—but she didn't squander the opportunity, as others might have. Soon she became a sponge, soaking up information and pumping everyone around her for market insights and trading techniques. "I was a trader at heart," she beams. "I was hooked."

At age 26, she started keeping a detailed journal of profits and losses—noting why each happened—and its resulting dictates became her investing bible. She became an info junkie. She watched CNBC while getting ready for work. If she heard a tip of sorts, she checked it out at work, and if it looked

Continued on next page

Tools Of The Trade

Continued from previous page

promising, she made some buys. Often, they were right on, and 20-point jumps were not uncommon.

She sought volatile movers and rode them up and down daily. With tight scrutiny and constant analysis, she found herself researching the Internet for stock insights almost continually (see the list of her favorite research sites on page 61). She read *The New York Times* every Sunday for any news she could use, wrote down weekly highs and lows of owned stocks, and discovered that her hobby now represented 20 or more extracurricular hours per week. "Just mining for nuggets" is how she describes her after-hours activities.

> **By** the **summer and fall** of **1999**, **she** was **profiting** an **average** of **$250** per **day part-time, with lots** of **$1,000**-or-more **days** as well.

By the summer and fall of 1999, she was profiting an average of $250 per day part time, with lots of $1,000-or-more days as well. Many trades and profits were realized by limit orders that were executed while she worked at her day job. And she kept upping her purchases, diversifying and steadfastly following the rules and messages of her journal and constant market research.

"I was also desperately trying to find myself, to determine my style, what I was going to do and how I was going to do it," she says. "I studied all kinds of traders—retail, institutional, proprietary and day traders—looking for ways to go.

"Through friends I met due to my interest in stocks, I was also introduced to lots of high-level traders, and studying them helped, too."

At age 29 with an investment war chest now well in the tens of thousands of dollars, Zanone drops the bombshell. "I quit my job three months ago, and I'm now in my second week of being a full-time, professional, direct access day trader. There's no question [about it]…I'm extreme."

See Chapter 5 for the further extreme adventures of Alexis Zanone.

ing vehicle ever invented. She is really interested in, and invests heavily in, high-tech computer companies, software and hardware, and biotech companies. As such, she does virtually all her shopping on the NASDAQ. But when the NASDAQ 100 index came along, she did some rethinking. She determined that this one investment portfolio mirrored what she liked anyway, and she loved the convenience of trading one symbol to trade all 100 NASDAQ stocks (she was trading between 30 and 40 of them already).

Since she likes virtually every stock represented, she feels as if her homework has been done for her. That's because unit trusts, and the QQQ in particular, represent stock leaders in their respective industries, all of which are widely held by the biggest and best institutional investors.

Gail still has all her favorite tech stocks in play (and then some) but now spends far less time analyzing her group, thanks to the QQQ Cube. She uses the time she saves to analyze and trade other stocks—in other categories she was previously too busy to deal with—and now benefits accordingly. The indices can be a wonderful addition to the fleet-footed extreme investor's portfolio.

part two

Day
Trading

If extreme investing were a NASCAR race, day trading would certainly be the pace car.

Day trading has set the standard for individuals who seek to maximize their investment experience. It has kicked open the doors of high-risk, high-return activity for anyone who wants to enter.

The following chapters paint a picture of the world of day trading—the sorts of people who are doing it, how they're doing it and where they fit into the bigger stock trading picture.

The Ultimate Video Game

Most stock traders understand the nature of real-time quotes and the importance of immediate trade executions to success. But many traders don't know how to use this electronic information and capability the way market makers, professional traders and institutional investors do.

It's an edge that, once learned, no trader will ever choose to work without. Day trading, incidentally, contrary to what many think, does not require an up market. Success depends instead on volatility in *either* direction. And as exemplified by recent market moves, both up and down, today's marketplace is an extremely lucrative arena.

With the aid of a computer and high-speed Internet access, extreme investing—and day trading in particular—is the ultimate video game. And like any other game, you get better with practice—and as your knowledge builds.

Trading Styles
And The Old Tick-Tock

Day traders, by definition, make lots of trades during the day, and they generally don't "take home" positions (meaning they liquidate all their positions by the market close each day). But there are other forms of day trading for the extreme investor that extend the trading window a bit further. Understanding basic trading techniques will help you figure out which avenue might work best for you.

Day trading can be broken down into subgroups determined by the rapidity with which a trader gets in and out of a stock.

○ **Seconds and minutes—spread trading, grinding and scalping:** This category of day trading is characterized by limited exposure, rapid-fire trading and lots of tiny profits accumulated on a continuous basis, shaving 1/16ths or 1/8ths from the spread or riding market momentum. Decisions are usually made based on the ticker (what the last sales price was for a given stock, and if it's higher or lower than the previous price). There is very low tolerance for loss (often 1/4 point). Within this category, 20 minutes is considered a long time to hold a stock.

○ **Minutes and hours—traditional day trading and specialist trading:** This category features a slightly longer-term focus and typically liquidates at the end of the trading session. Like scalpers, traders within this category seek entry and exit points based on perceived buying and selling peaks and valleys, retracements and trendline pullbacks (these are technical analysis terms that refer to predicting future stock movement). This manner of trading relies heavily on the ticker and daily graphs, and there is medium tolerance for loss. Within this category, three hours is a long time to hold a stock.

○ **Hours and days—position trading and swing trading:** This category encompasses a longer trading horizon than day trading, sometimes extending over days. Buy and sell indicators factor in more fundamental data, as opposed to the technical indicators used by scalpers and day traders. This category of trader uses daily and monthly graphs with moving averages, among other tools, and there is a higher tolerance for loss. Within this category, two weeks is a long time to hold a stock.

liquidate

The Birth Of Day Trading

How did this form of fast-paced online investing get started? It happened in 1984 with the creation of the Small Order Execution System (SOES; rhymes with "toes"). The SOES is an electronic mechanism by which small orders (not huge blocks of stock) can be bought and sold. Direct access to NASDAQ stocks via the SOES was established by the National Association of Securities Dealers (NASD) to ensure that individual investors had better access to NASDAQ and the ability to trade NASDAQ stocks without being subject to the control of professional market makers.

The SOES was dormant until the crash of '87. During the crash, small investors simply couldn't get their orders placed because of the overwhelming volume. Some brokers weren't even answering their phones because they were overloaded with calls. Since the job of market makers is to provide a "fair and orderly" market, which they didn't do too well in 1987, a furor resulted that uncovered the benefits of trading on the SOES, which many saw as the first glimpse into the future of global stock trading. Since then, the concept of SOES trading has expanded into what we have today—a move toward fully electronic trading platforms.

The true day trader's strategy is to liquidate at the end of the day to limit exposure to a negative overnight surprise (though this prevents benefiting from any positive overnight surprises as well). The swing trader, or position trader, buys (or shorts) stocks for more than just a momentary move and isn't necessarily worried about closing out his trades at day's end. He's no buy-and-holder, but he will hang onto a stock long enough to ride more than a moment or a day's momentum. There are advantages to the slower pace, the most important being that it is less torturous on your nerves. Swing trading may not be as heart-stopping as, say, scalping or bona fide day trading, but it still requires mastery of the game.

Fast
And Furious

Now let's have a look at the opposite end of the day trading spectrum—scalping, which is the fastest and most furious of all day trading

Terry G. in Northern California grew up playing video games. Once, he got a black eye from a game called Asteroids. Actually, his wife gave him the black eye, but the video game was indirectly responsible. The La Quinta Inn in Palm Springs was packed the night in question, and Terry and his wife were in the hotel ballroom having dinner with friends. During a lull in the friendly (but boring) conversation, Terry excused himself to go to the men's room and on the way found a four-machine mini-arcade, and one game in particular called Asteroids.

> **The black** eye **ensued** after **Terry** compared **her** friends **back at** the **dinner** table **to** a **game of Pong.**

It's an older game, and you don't see them around much any more, but it was his favorite game at the time, and there was a young kid playing who had just cleared 60,000 points. (Terry had never made it past 46,000.) He watched the kid with his mouth agape, wanting to congratulate him, but staying quiet so as not to ruin his concentration.

The kid's score kept heading up—70,000, 80,000, 90,000 points, then over 100,000. Finally, his spaceship got hit. Game over. Such is life.

For Terry and the kid, it all happened so quickly. But Terry's wife didn't think so. What seemed like minutes to Terry was actually almost half an hour, and Terry's wife had to go in search of him. The black eye ensued after Terry compared her friends back at the dinner table to a game of Pong, an old, once-state-of-the-art video game featuring nothing more than a dark screen, two white paddles and a ball. Whack! She packed a solid right hook.

What Terry's wife didn't understand was that this obsession with video games was soon to become the foundation of their family's livelihood. That's because day trading is a video game—and Terry eventually became a successful day trader.

In this game, you play against thousands of others who represent many different skill levels. You have a joystick of sorts (your mouse and keyboard) that controls your character (the cursor). You also have access to an unlimited number of what could be called armor plates, warp shields, protection zones and extra lives that you can add to your character before each game. You can add these protective devices by setting up internal warning signals based on your running profit and loss figure—plus, you can set flags that indicate when your preset downside limits are reached.

Continued on next page

You can buy the best weapons, add speed to your vehicle and dive into mountains of strategy (you choose the screens, graphs, indicators, values and settings you want). Still, your video screen doesn't look like a dungeon or a space station, and there aren't any fire-breathing dragons.

Instead, your screen is more like a sleek flight simulator—with gauges and graphs and buttons and data flashing before you, all of it valuable information indicating when it's time to take evasive measure or pull the trigger (to stay out of the market or hit the buy/sell button).

And just like any other game, you get better by combining your accumulated knowledge and your mastery of the rules—which, in turn, equals your skill at day trading.

These days, Terry sits at his computer and analyzes stock patterns (using charting, the basis of technical analysis), which he uses to pick his entry and exit points for the stocks he intends to trade the following day. He spends approximately three hours after the market closes each day going over recent price movements, looking for stocks with chart patterns he's learned indicate that a stock is undervalued and poised to move higher or overvalued and poised to move lower over the course of a few days.

He knows how to play the game—and he's driving his score higher and higher with each passing day. He is an extreme investor. . .playing the ultimate video game.

techniques. Many traders find scalping to be totally unappealing, too grueling and wrenching, no matter what the upsides. Scalping (sometimes also called "grinding") is for the caffeine-through-an-IV crowd.

Day trader Simone Q. in New York City is amazingly equipped to keep up with this rapid pace. She was 23 years old when she started scalping, and it came naturally to her. She grew up with a computer in front of her (first her father's, then her own) and feels just as at home with a mouse in her hand as a telephone.

Here's a summary of how she works her trading technique: Simone keeps her eye on a select group of high-volume, very active, fast-trading stocks. She gets in quickly when she sees a trend developing and gets out when she's "scalped" three-quarters of a point on the trade (as little as one-eighth of a

grinding

point sometimes, one-quarter or more other times). She tolerates only slight moves against her. That is, if her calculations prove incorrect, she exits her position at a small loss and moves on to another setup.

This strategy is so fast-paced that she never feels remorse about bailing out on a trade, since she knows there will be other opportunities jumping out at her any moment. The important thing is that she rarely takes more than a one-quarter-point loss. On 1,000 shares, one-quarter point represents $250. On good days, she is successful at three trades for every one that flops, and she trades in and out maybe four times in an hour. If you do the math, she makes about $500 an hour. Sometimes the market isn't moving, so an hour or so may pass without her doing any trading. She says she makes about $2,000 on a good day.

> It's **basically** like **playing** a **video game** running at **warp speed** with **monsters** that will **eat** you and **bombs** that will **end** the **game** in a **second** unless you've put in the **required** hours to **learn** how to **survive.**

Naturally, Simone has bad days, too. One Monday she lost just over $7,000 (she admits she was trading with a hangover) and not only made poor risk management decisions but was "slow on the draw" regarding the good trades she identified. Scalping requires lightning-fast dexterity, a good memory, a mastery of the rules and access to the fastest technology on the planet. It's basically like playing a video game running at warp speed with monsters that will eat you and bombs that will end the game in a second unless you've put in the required hours to learn how to survive.

Scalping is the most active form of trading, involving many "round trips," an expression used to describe the act of buying and selling the same stock. Extreme investors can trade hundreds of times in a day, and the commissions are significant. Traders who scalp may not even know that INTC, the stock they've traded all day, is Intel Corp. They don't care if Intel makes computer chips or kitty litter. They only care about short-term movements in price. They trade on market momentum, a science all its own.

Degrees
Of Extreme

Have you ever created a spreadsheet? Creating a spreadsheet is pretty easy. But if there were a spreadsheet-building contest that pitted you against someone who spends all day, every day, taking a spreadsheet software product to its limit, would you win? Before you would consider jumping into the contest, you'd want to have months of experience using the software. So it goes for the day trader.

Becoming a day trader means knowing the rules of the game and all the tricks and tools of the trade—especially when the game is so fast-paced and the rules so complex, as is the case with scalping.

A lot of brokers recommend scalping as the best way to day-trade, maybe because it generates the most "tickets" (commissioned trades). But in reality, scalping represents a one-dimensional strategy and is too frenetic for many traders. However, scalping is an extreme form of trading that can make small profits add up.

To summarize, day trading can be altered to fit your pace, and the slower the activity level (i.e., swing and position trading), the more forgiving the experience. But no matter which form of trading you choose, you have to know the basics about the playing field. All day trading is accomplished using the same rules. These rules begin with understanding what goes into a stock trade—how you buy and sell.

Going Long Vs. Going Short

Going long means you have bought a stock in expectation that it will go higher in price. You intend to buy it at one price and sell it at a higher price. Going short is the opposite. You borrow the stock from your broker so that you can sell it at the current price, with the expectation that the stock is going down. That way you can buy the shares back again

playing field

 from somebody at a lower price and repay your broker and make a profit. It's like selling your roommate's tennis racquet for $100, knowing that later you will be able to buy another one for $75 as a replacement.

The ability to go short means day traders can make money as the market's going down just as easily as when it's going up. Naturally, you can make money as the market rises by going long on a stock. That's what most investors do. But the extreme investor takes advantage of market volatility in *both* directions.

Market Orders Vs. Limit Orders

Many investors buy and sell stocks for years without ever grasping how stock exchanges work and how buy and sell orders are transacted. It's important to understand what the bid and ask prices represent, and what the "spread" is.

The first thing you need to understand is that a stock market is a place where buyers and sellers trade with each other, and only once in a while do both buyer and seller simultaneously blurt out an identical price at which they're willing to make an exchange. Usually it's a tug of war between what one side wants to pay and the other side wants to sell for. That price is registered electronically via computers for the NASDAQ, but the NYSE still does it the old-fashioned way, with people actually talking to one another and flailing about. Both use the same basic pricing system of one-sixteenth of a dollar being the norm, though soon the decimal system will be introduced.

The "bid" is the highest price a buyer is willing to pay for a stock at the moment. The "ask" is the lowest price a seller is willing to sell that stock for at the moment.

Some traders buy stocks by placing a "market" order. This means that they are willing to pay the current asking price. It's like someone who sells a used Porsche. He or she has an asking price. The seller might be asking $36,000 for his or her 1989 Porsche, and you as the buyer agree without haggling. If you do not make a counteroffer and just end up paying the guy the $36,000, that's like buying a car using a market order.

Used cars vary in features and wear, but in the case of stocks, a share of eBay is a share of eBay—all shares are the same color, quality and condition. So that makes it easier to pay whatever the market price happens to be at any given *bid*

If you're **knowledgeable**, the **reason** you **placed** a **market order** was because **you didn't** mind **paying** a premium for **owning** those **shares** right **away**, **whatever** the **market price** was.

moment because, in theory, you've checked the merchandise thoroughly by reading up on eBay. An anxious trader might be extremely confident about the current momentum and be sure eBay is going to move upward in price, and as such they might be willing to buy eBay at whatever the asking price is.

When you sell, you can also place a market order, which means that you are willing to sell at the current bid price. In other words, somebody out there is looking to pay more than anyone else at this moment for your shares of eBay. You place a market order to sell, and that guy who has his hand up in the air gets your stock. He's actually not waving his hand in the air, but the point is he's made the best offer, and you filled his request by selling at his price.

Stock prices, however, usually don't work in such slow motion. In fact, they can be quite fast-moving and volatile. One minute a guy could be offering 100 shares of a company at $75 a share, and by the time you place your computerized order, the guy already sold his 100 shares, and the next guy in line wants $76 a share for the same 100 shares. With your market order, you just bought them at $76, or $100 more (for 100 shares) than you anticipated. But if you're knowledgeable, the reason you placed a market order was because you didn't mind paying a premium for owning those shares right away, whatever the market price was. This is an extreme way to buy stocks, but not extremely prudent most of the time.

The alternative is called a "limit" order. If you want to buy a stock, and you know what the current price range is at the moment, you send an order through your computer that limits what you're willing to pay. If you don't want to pay more than $75 a share, you place a limit order for that amount, and if no one is willing to sell at that price, your order doesn't get filled (it sits there until someone wants to sell at your $75 price). If the

market order

The Ultimate Video Game

In Chapter 4, we learned how Alexis Zanone fell into stocks and trading through happenstance, and how it quickly led her down a path of discovery and intrigue to a bold career decision.

By late 1999, while her near-obsession with stocks was resulting in a steady flow of profits into her personal investment account, it also stimulated a desire to seek out others with like interests and experiences. "I was using the Internet heavily as a tool for stock research and started using it to look for new trading ideas and opportunities, too," Zanone says.

Socially, she hung out with those with similar interests—which included some who were employed as full-time RJ (real job) institutional traders, so she was trolling for insights while she worked and while she played. One instrumental contact was a young man she met in a night-school class who introduced her to technical analysis, small cap stocks and professional day trading.

> **"I set a goal of making a thousand dollars a day and started reaching it consistently using my limit order technique."**

"While using the Internet to learn more about day trading, I had also reached a personal trading level where—by setting limit orders for my positions before work—I was earning about half my annual salary in a month," Zanone casually adds. Was this a fluke?

"I set a goal of making a thousand dollars a day and started reaching it consistently using my limit order technique," she says. "This gave me enough confidence to leave the corporate world and trade on my own from my laptop computer." Scary—but exciting.

The young man she met in class was Landon Ray, a legendary day trader of dramatic proportions (you'll meet up with him again later in this chapter) who is wildly successful and a pied piper of sorts. Through Ray and his friends, she was invited to visit the Broadway Trading office in New York City—a mecca of sorts where elite day traders elect to ply their craft. One glimpse into the inner sanctum where nimble fingers and intense research win or lose thousands, hundreds of thousands, in minutes—seconds—revealed to Zanone her own future. There and then, Zanone decided to become a full-time professional day trader.

Today, Zanone has opened her own trading account at Broadway (requir-

Continued on next page

ing a substantial investment in the tens of thousands) and is in her second week on the direct access system that allows her to make real-time stock trades—just like having a seat on the exchange. Her goal: "I'm going to make a million dollars in my first 12 to 18 months." There's no "I want to," "I hope to" or "I'll try to." She says, "I'm going to."

Alexis has every reason to be confident. A million reasons.

ask price of a stock is $76 (somebody wants to sell at $76) and the bid price is $75 (some other guy wants to buy at $75), you can place a limit order somewhere in-between, thus becoming the new person with the best offer to buy or sell. You move to the front of the line and become the new best bid or ask price leader.

Merry
Market Makers

Who are these people who represent the bid and ask prices? The bid or ask price might be on behalf of a brokerage firm that has a client who just phoned in an order to buy or sell. It might represent a Charles Schwab customer who wants to trade over the Internet. Or it might be a market maker.

A market maker is a brokerage firm or bank (sometimes both) that maintains a firm bid and ask price in a certain security. Market makers faithfully stand by, willing and able to buy or sell at publicly quoted prices, thus providing individual traders with a chance to buy or sell even if other traders aren't willing to do so. In other words, market makers keep the market alive by constantly maintaining a bid and an ask (they're constantly ready to buy or sell), and as compensation for providing this service, they are allowed to make money in the process. That's because they can act as either brokers or dealers.

As brokers, market makers execute other people's orders. As dealers, market makers execute orders for their own accounts, taking small profits accomplished using a market maker spread—the difference between the price at which a market maker is willing to buy a security and the price at which he or she is willing to sell it. Rules regulate how and when market makers can wear the dealer or broker hat.

NYSE market makers operate differently than NASDAQ market makers. There is only one NYSE market maker for each stock that trades on the NYSE. But on the NASDAQ, a multiple market maker system is used, mainly because NASDAQ is an electronically based system that can allow multiple orders to be compiled and transacted from all over the country, instead of being done by one single guy on the floor of the NYSE.

So What's The Spread?

The "spread" is the difference between the bid and the ask price. Using an example where the bid price is $75 and the ask price is $76, the spread is $1. So since stocks trade in fractions as small as 16ths (day traders actually deal in much weirder numbers, like 64ths and even up to 256ths), imagine how someone might squeeze in between the two and buy from the one guy for $75.25 and then sell to the other guy for $75.75, making a 50-cent profit on the deal, satisfying both the buyer's and the seller's best offers. The problem is that the spread is usually tiny, and even when it's not, the video game virtuoso with the lightning-fast fingers has already completed the trade while the rest of us are just thinking about keying it in.

Keep this in mind as you read the following deeper explanation of how market makers do what they do.

It's vital to understand the basic principles of how markets are made as the means of providing a platform for trading. You need to understand how market makers provide liquidity, execute orders for customers and trade for their own accounts. It's equally important to understand how market makers maintain a "fair and orderly" market, and what market makers do to fake the market in one direction so they can buy or sell at a better price.

Market makers are extreme investors by profession, and they play every single day. Extreme investors need to know how market makers work because they will be trading with them and because market makers are in the business of making money at your expense, which is easy for them to do if you don't know how they operate or why they are providing a liquid market in the first place.

Let's start with the terms "market" and "liquidity." You probably know what both are and can intuitively figure out what they mean in the context of the stock market. But in case the concept is hazy, a market is simply a common ground where people buy and sell things. Buying and selling opportunities are limited, however, if there is just one person buying and one person selling. Either you want what he has and he is willing to accept what you want to pay, or the trading day is over. If there are a thousand people gathered to trade a particular item, establishing the true fair value of that item is accomplished with greater ease than if you have just a few interested traders. When you have lots of interested traders, hundreds or thousands, all ready to buy or sell, it's called a liquid market.

Now visualize one person in charge of coordinating the sale of a particular corporation's stock for the day, say the micro cap (tiny) stock of a company called Doggy Drawers, that cute little company we talked about in Chapter 4 that got its start making little doggy sweaters. If only a few people are standing around waiting to see if the price goes down enough for them to be mildly interested, there won't be much liquidity. One trade might take place every 20 minutes. That's not a liquid market. Now picture the guy in charge of Hewlett-Packard's stock. He's got so many people who want to buy and sell that he has to limit the number of people he takes orders from. Not just anybody can walk up and attempt to buy stock from him—only a few licensed folks on the NYSE floor can. These licensed people represent people-on-the-street traders.

If thousands of people want to buy or sell Hewlett-Packard stock that day, then the odds are good that as soon as one person bids a price, somebody else will be standing by to accept that bid and sell to them. That's a liquid market. Lots of buyers and sellers actively participating means there's always someone to sell your stock to at some price, and you can always buy stock because somebody out there has it for sale. Extremely liquid stocks can trade many times per second. Hundreds of transactions, and thousands of shares, in five seconds.

In the world of day trading, the greater the liquidity, the greater protection you have from being stuck with an unfortunate trade. That's because if you identify your error quickly, you can reverse your purchase immediately by liquidating your position to anyone in line to buy back shares. If you make a bad move with an illiquid stock, it may be hard to sell your shares.

The Man Behind The Curtain

The person who coordinates the buying and selling of a particular company's stock is called a market maker. This guy is a member of the stock exchange. He's licensed and governed by laws and rules. He can actually create a market for stocks by buying and selling for his own account when the public is not buying or selling. He sells from his own account if there are more buyers than sellers, and he makes money trading that stock in exchange for allowing buyers and sellers to enter and exit their own positions in an efficient manner. And all this generates an astoundingly accurate representation of fair value, as determined by the free market. In a nutshell, that's how the NYSE works. There is one market maker per NYSE company, and that person's sole job is to keep his own company's stock liquid—and make money in the process, of course.

NASDAQ market makers work differently. At the NASDAQ, several market makers can represent one company's stock, not just one guy coordinating all the trades. And the NASDAQ is electronic. There are other differences, but for now all that's important is that you understand the basics of how each works so you know who you're up against. The most influential market makers in the NASDAQ indicate where big money is headed, establishing short-term trends day traders can act upon. We'll talk about who they are later, but first, here's a primer on the NYSE vs. the NASDAQ, and why you need to know the difference.

The NASDAQ And The
Next Generation Of Trading

The NASDAQ is viewed as the stock exchange for the next century, partly because it was born as an electronically based hybrid. The NYSE was born a long time ago and still operates by way of waving arms, pencil and paper, and a lot of howling (the NYSE is sometimes referred to as the "museum"). The NASDAQ, on the other hand, is wired, meaning all NASDAQ trades are executed by computers. As a result, the NASDAQ market has leaked into cyberspace, which has made it easily accessible to

If you want to meet a legendary day trader, you want to meet Landon Ray. He is a true celebrity within a small, tight, sub rosa community, and he is not easy to reach. He is always busy. He makes what, for an average person, would be a lifetime of profit over and over again—and he is only 28 years old.

Ray grew up in Half Moon Bay, California. He went to college, earned average grades (with little effort), dropped out, bummed around the world with friends for a while—through India, Israel, etc.—returned to a host of odd jobs, from being a waiter to selling flowers at open-air markets. Then, at 22, he had a revelation: "I felt the world was passing me by, like I was living in Renaissance Italy and ignoring painting. My generation was really up to something—the Internet start-ups, big advancements in technology, a wild stock market—and I was missing the whole thing," he recalls. "I wanted to get involved."

He began reading newspapers and the business section, looking for insights and ideas. Then one day, his father spotted a cover story in *Inc.* magazine on the success of a new day trading firm. He was fascinated at first; intrigue turned to amazement and then to challenge when the story told how even the company's 20-year-old receptionist was making a killing ($80,000 a month) in the stock market. " 'If she can do it, so can I,' " he thought. His father thought so, too, and agreed to bankroll Ray if he wanted to give it a try.

> **Dogged determination** led to **progress**, and soon **Ray** was **making $4,000** in **one** day; **the following** month, **he** made **$25,000** in **one** day.

In 1997, Ray ended up at Broadway Trading in New York City, and his very trusting father pulled $50,000 out of his IRA, crossed his fingers and handed it over to a 25-year-old with a dream. The rest—as they say—is day trading history.

At Broadway, Ray saw guys making $4,000 or $5,000 a day—or more. "It was incredible," he relates excitedly. Moving to New York, he opened a $50,000 trading account and went to work. He lost about $15,000 over a two-month period (which is actually a success story, as most new day traders lose more at first). It didn't get better for a while…breaking even, losing a little. But then, as time and money were running out, things turned around with a vengeance.

Continued on next page

Continued from previous page

After nine months, pressure and looming failure became the mother of invention. Ray refocused, buckled up and dug in. Failure was not an option.

Dogged determination led to progress, and soon Ray was making $4,000 in one day; the following month, he made $25,000 in one day. Focus and discipline were the order of the day. "Waiting until a course of action is obvious is the key to trading," he says. "It's like being a cat in the grass holding off 'til just the right moment." Soon, $50,000 and $100,000 weeks were regular events. Virtually anything became possible.

Today, Ray has thousands upon thousands of trades under his belt, winning more often than not, and so far netting him six figure months and seven figures annually many times over. He caps things off with, "If I've learned anything at all, it's patience. The more I wait, look and listen, the clearer my course of action becomes."

Ray is an all-star example of an extreme investor, but he generously allows that he's not alone. "I guess I've been responsible for a number of people getting started, but, hey, there are guys out there doing a lot better than me."

the public. Fueled by a rapidly expanding interest in faster, cheaper, better ways to invest, a new breed of stock trader has emerged.

The NASDAQ recently merged with the American Stock Exchange. The NASDAQ also plans to make other changes that will improve the ease with which extreme investors can make trades. But the NYSE isn't far behind. It has seen the NASDAQ expand based on its electronic trading architecture, and the NYSE plans to join the revolution. And as world markets join in, cybertrading will expand even more dramatically. The German Deutsche Boerse, for instance, is in the process of setting up electronic trading of its own, so the number of extreme investors will soon expand—all across the globe.

Since it's all computerized, access to NASDAQ stock quotes can be refreshed with up-to-the-millisecond updates, and executions can be completed without the help of a middleman. In other words, individual investors can see what the big institutional investors and market makers are doing as they do it, and they can trade right alongside them.

What this means is that every individual trader who sets up

with the proper hardware and software can now get pricing information at the source. With that information, day traders can take full advantage of the action in the market.

When you become a day trader, you essentially become a micro-market maker.

The Day Trading Playing Field

Recent changes directly impact how day traders operate and how day trading itself is done. Execution speed and market access are at the heart of the matter.

When day trading first hit the scene, it was impossible to succeed at home using your own remote trading equipment unless you had a direct connection to a trading execution system via a high-speed ISDN (integrated digital services network) or T1 (high-speed access) line. Dial-up modems were grueling. Now we have DSL (digital subscriber line) and cable modems, which are faster and more reliable than dial-up analog phone line modems, and they are the minimum requirement for serious day trading.

However, the longer your trading horizon, the slower your connection speed can be. Hard-core day traders need the fastest on earth. Position traders, who may hold a stock for a week or more, can enter and exit with casual aplomb, requiring only a sleepy 56K modem.

Online And Direct Access Trading—All Aboard!

Lots of companies provide access to the markets through the Internet. Among them are Charles Schwab, Ameritrade, E*TRADE and Quick & Reilly. Some companies, such as Datek Online, offer both Internet access and direct access connections, which bypass the Internet and tie directly to where trades are executed. But the Internet seems to be able to handle most day trading requirements.

Internet-based and direct access firms are springing up all over the place. Little firms are being bought by bigger firms. CyBerTrader, for example, one of the industry's highly regarded trading outfits, was recently swallowed by Charles Schwab. Some of the first brokers to offer services designed for day traders were Block Trading, All-Tech Investments Group, and Broadway Trading.

Companies like Broadway Trading account for about 8 million shares a day, or nearly 1 percent of NASDAQ trading volume. Broadway, in New York City, does not offer Web-based services to the general public but instead aims specifically at full-time day traders. Some of these day traders commute to Broadway Trading and use its in-house computers, software and network connections, although many more dial up into the company's servers from remote locations (such as at home).

This is an industry that's evolving at lightning speed, so we can expect an eventual trend toward lower fees and greater access. The bottom line is that trading is getting cheaper and much more pervasive. The price per trade among most companies has gotten very competitive, and most discount brokers charge online investors roughly the same amount, between $9.99 and $19.99 per trade.

Charges for Level II Direct Access are sure to undergo some competitive price shifts as well. Level II Direct Access (discussed later in this chapter) is used by virtually all day traders and can cost up to $100 per month, or it can be provided free to active traders (each provider of this service has its own pricing policy).

How Big Is Big?

How many people—full-time professionals and part-time amateurs—now trade stocks online? Merrick Okamoto, president of TradePortal.com, a leading Level II Direct Access execution firm in Irvine, California, says, "The explosion of growth of the Internet has launched a huge new market and category of individuals trading online. According to Jupiter Research Group, today's overall online trading market is estimated to be about 7 million investors, and it projects [that number] will grow to 20 million in four to five years."

On the other hand, Pacific Day Trading Services in San Jose, California, which monitors trends in the day trading industry, presents a different story: It expects the number of customers trading securities online to reach 23 million by 2003. "These estimates are for the overall online trading market," Okamoto says, "and not specifically the day trading portion, which is harder to pinpoint because most firms specializing in this segment are privately held."

> Just **five** or **six** firms **now** control **as much** as **80 percent** of the **existing day trading market.**

Still, a recent estimate by the *Los Angeles Times* put the number of full-time professional day traders at only about 4,000, in contrast to Jupiter Research Group's estimated 7 million part-time amateur investors. However, industry experts like James Lee, president of the Electronic Traders Association, expect the number of professional day traders to grow as investors learn and master market nuances.

What they lack in numbers, day traders more than make up for in volume. Lee says 14 to 16 percent of the approximately 600 million shares traded daily on the NASDAQ exchange comes from day traders, up from about 7 or 8 percent just last year.

Today, there are approximately 40 firms in the United States that offer day trading to investors. Most are small and undercapitalized, but they are trying to catch and ride the wave of this new and rapidly growing segment of the marketplace. Lee estimates that just five or six firms now control as much as 80 percent of the existing day trading market.

What does all this tell us? Although no one knows definitely how big is big, we do know one thing: "Day trading is a very young, dynamic industry," TradePortal.com's Okamoto concludes. "Watch for explosive growth and exciting change in the days, months and years ahead. It's an exciting wave to ride."

"I was born in 1972 in St. Petersburg, which at the time was Leningrad, Russia," he begins. Vladamir Efros is 27—and only 10 months into his new career as a full-time professional day trader. "When I was 6, my family immigrated here, and I grew up in upstate New York."

Always fascinated by business, Efros took his first opportunity—the $2,000 he received for his bar mitzvah (at age 13)—and invested in silver through a brokerage account. A year later, he sold it for $3,000. In 1986, he discovered baseball cards, so he invested his silver windfall and started setting up at local shows and flea markets, and selling and trading via mail order as a vest pocket dealer. An entrepreneur in the making.

> "In **my** first **two weeks**, I **lost $3,300**. The next **few weeks** were flat. **After** that, I **lost another** $3,300 in **14 days**. Then, **six weeks** in, **it began** turning **around."**

At 15, he teamed up with an older friend and partnered to start a baseball card store called Bases Loaded. At 16, Efros became sole owner of the store, and upon graduating high school he sold the store but kept some choice baseball cards for his own private collection. He went to off to study economics at the University of Rochester.

After two years, his college career swerved off course when he dropped out to manage a rock band called Yolk, which did OK for about three years but then disbanded. His earlier interest in things financial resurfaced.

"In 1997, I went back to school and studied finance and management information systems at Binghamton University in upstate New York," Efros says, "but I wasn't sure what I was going to do careerwise. I'd only narrowed it down to business. I didn't have a clue."

Then, in 1998, the stock market experienced a major correction. Having done nothing in this arena since he was 14 (the silver deal), now—having just turned 26—it again caught his attention. Thinking it might be a good time to take advantage of some bargain-basement prices, he liquidated about $10,000 worth of his prized baseball card collection (for a quick $3,000), which he slammed into stocks without hesitation.

"I opened an online account at T.D. Waterhouse, $12 a trade, etc.," he says. "I tried various strategies used by friends, winning here and there, but eventually I lost most or all my profits." Limited funds allowed Efros to only buy one

Continued on next page

Continued from previous page

or two stocks at a time, not enough of a sampling to give him a chance to really break loose.

After he convinced his brother to lend him $10,000, he began to diversify into many of the hot tech stocks, like AOL. His first big score was Data Broadcasting Corp., which he bought at $17 per share due to a subtle tip in a *Business Week* article. He sold the stock a few days later at $36 per share. He developed a formula and looked for large companies that were about to spin off an Internet division as a new IPO offering (see Chapter 7). "I began mining business news for little nuggets on IPO spin-offs," he says—and his $10,000 online investment account grew to $28,000 by the spring of 1999.

Not long before graduation from college, Efros got a glimpse into the inside of a day trading operation. It was then that he knew he had found his future in the day trading room. Bundling his online account money with other funds (remaining baseball cards, loans, etc.), he amassed an investment war chest. He took a week-long training class in professional day trading and started trading mini-blocks of stock 100 shares at a time (the limit new day traders usually buy and sell until they are up to speed). Efros' progress then became the classic scenario of serious, eventually successful, professional day traders.

"In my first two weeks, I lost $3,300," he notes. "The next few weeks were flat. After that, I lost another $3,300 in 14 days. Then, six weeks in, it began turning around." He found the secret was not in making money, but rather in controlling risk. "I started concentrating on not losing money instead," Efros says, "and I started getting it." Over the next month, he recovered most of his earlier losses, and a month later he went positive in his account for the first time—with $18,000 in profits that month alone. His advice to those wanting to day-trade? "Find someone who's experienced to train you."

Just two months short of completing his first full year as a professional day trader, Efros notes, "My initial goal was to make a million dollars in my first year. And I'm on track. After 10 months, I'm 80 percent there. I'm rockin'."

Who's Driving This Train, Anyway?

Dedicated day traders want to know everything there is to know about what's going on behind the scenes and how stock orders are processed. That's because some methods are more efficient than others. But these days knowing all the details is becoming less and less important. That's because with each passing month, the Securities and Exchange

Commission (SEC), the NYSE and the NASDAQ all seem to be moving toward simplifying and streamlining what used to be a rather complicated process.

This book cannot possibly cover every aspect of order handling; it's a complicated, ever-evolving subject. Fortunately, most reputable brokerage firms execute orders at the best price they can without burdening you with the decision as to which channel you want your order routed through. With that in mind, let's dig a little deeper.

Day trading, an electronic endeavor, involves four possible routing systems for buying and selling stocks. The NYSE has one routing system—called SuperDot—for posting bids and offers for the purpose of executing trades. The NASDAQ uses three routing systems for posting bids and offers: Electronic Communications Networks (ECNs), the Small Order Execution System (SOES), and SelectNet.

Swing traders may trade NYSE stocks, but day traders generally do not because the fast, in-and-out trading can't be done as effectively there. That's a function of how the NYSE operates, using one market maker for one stock, with everything housed in one physical place (on Wall Street). It's still more of a manual process.

Remember that the NYSE has been around a long time, and electronic trading was retrofitted to work with the older ways of the NYSE. The NASDAQ, on the other hand, was born of the electronic age and involves many market makers situated all over the place, so the order routing system is much more complex, but it's also much more efficient and potentially more volatile. This is good for day traders.

"Now Leaving On Track Three..."

ECNs, SOES and SelectNet are used by traders to make their orders visible to other buyers and sellers, and in some cases they can be used directly to execute orders with the click of a mouse or tap of a key on a keyboard.

Specifically, these three systems allow individuals to bid and offer shares. They also allow any individual trader with the proper computer setup to have a front-row seat to the best pricing and immediate access previously enjoyed only by the market makers.

routing system

ECNs are independent computer networks established by broker-dealers to handle order processing. They attempt to match your buy or sell orders with what's already in their own computer system, and if they can't, your order is posted on something like a bid board, which is called a Level II Direct Access screen. That screen (discussed later) is just a list of who's offering to buy or sell which stock, how many shares, and at what price. There are six ECNs out there now, and market makers can use any or all of them to post their stocks for purchase or sale.

The National Association of Securities Dealers (NASD) provides the remaining two routing systems—SOES and SelectNet. SOES was created in 1985, but it didn't become popular until the crash of 1987, when a whole bunch of small investors couldn't sell their stock because the huge trading volume overwhelmed the limited phone access to brokers and thus trade executions were difficult or impossible to make. SOES was not well known until then, but after the crash, word spread that there was this thing called the Small Order Execution System that let small traders buy and sell stock without necessitating the assistance of a broker. Average investors could deal directly with a market maker through SOES.

Last is SelectNet, another electronic order routing system, which was established as a way for market makers to communicate with each other. Day traders can buy and sell through SelectNet, but only the market makers have access to these electronic transmissions, so your offer to buy or sell isn't really out there for the whole world to see.

The point is, there are differences between the three routing systems that serious day traders may want to learn more about if, for instance, they intend to become scalpers, or if they really want the advantages offered by each and the awesome informational/execution power traders can have at their fingertips.

Regular online trading accounts, such as those through E*TRADE and Charles Schwab, cater to day traders and do not allow you to specify a routing system. They figure out the best way available through their particular resources and execute the trade for you. The truly gory details on these three NASDAQ routing systems, while interesting, are outside the scope of this

On The Edge

Here's a unique story of an extremely young professional day trader. Michael Ray (does his last name sound familiar?) is only 20. When he started trading at age 19, he had absolutely no experience as an investor or in buying and selling stocks.

Michael was coursing his way through his second year at Santa Barbara City College in California while his older brother Landon was in New York scoring big as a professional day trader. Watching from the sidelines, he questioned whether he should get involved while the market was hot or finish college first. At the beginning of 1999, he put school on hold and—with the intention of giving it a year—decided to try to capitalize on the opportunity at hand.

Without any experience, but based on his older brother's success, he was able to borrow a start-up fund from relatives and open an account at his brother's firm of choice (Broadway Trading in New York). He then began learning and operating at his brother's elbow.

> "I've **probably traded** about 10 **million** shares in the last **year**, just following the **rules.** I can **buy 100,000** shares and **make** or **lose** $30,000 in a **day.**"

Michael's a quick study, and he's definitely making his mark, but if you ask him specific questions about the stock market—if it's something outside the realm of his high-tech Level II Direct Access screen information—he's at a total loss. Yet he is as intense and focused—and has become just as successful—as some of those around him who have many years of stock market and trading experience under their belts.

Michael reflects, "I've probably traded about 10 million shares in the last year, just following the rules. I can buy 100,000 shares and make or lose $30,000 in a day. At the end of each day, I go through my journal of what was bought and sold, and whether I lost or made money. Then I look at why. What rule did I break or use correctly? It's a ritual everyone should use."

By listening up and following every day trading rule to the letter, Michael Ray is succeeding—by any standards.

book, but you can learn more about them from any number of books on day trading—go to any of the online booksellers and search with the phrase "day trade." Dozens will come up.

Stepping Up—Level II Screens

While there are plenty of day traders who don't choose their order routing systems, very few go without Level II screens. There are three levels of information about the markets, each one displayed on a computer terminal—Level I, Level II and Level III. The first level shows who's out there with the high bid (the person or broker-dealer willing to pay the most) and the low ask (the one willing to sell for the least). The Level I screen tells you what quantity is attached to the bid and ask. You might see that 100 shares are on the bid side and 1,000 shares are on the ask side, meaning that there are a lot of shares for sale at the moment, at least in proportion to what you know about the willing buyer out there who just wants 100 shares. But this is often misleading information. That's where the Level II screen comes in.

real-time information

The Level II screen is used by extreme investors to monitor what the market makers are doing. Not only do you get the real-time information associated with the Level I screen, but you also get to see who is in line right after the guy with the highest bid and the lowest offer. It's like going to an automobile supermall with every car dealer imaginable there, from Ford to Ferrari, showing all their cars, each one with a price tag on the windshield. A Level I automobile showroom would have all the cars for sale out of sight and only a few out front, and only one would have a price tag on it. OK, this analogy is very Detroit, but the point is that Level II screens show a lot more detail (see the sample screen on page 93). Let's look at a realistic example.

On the Level I screen, if someone wants to buy 100 shares at $50 per share, and somebody else wants to sell 1,000 shares at $50 1/8, you might assume the stock is headed lower because there are so many shares for sale compared to the number of shares somebody is willing to buy, at least at the best bid and ask prices.

The Level II screen might show you that right beneath the guy who wants to buy 100 shares are 10 more people, market makers or broker-dealers who want to buy thousands of shares, also at the $50 price. (Generally, the first in line with the highest bid or lowest offer gets his order filled first.) You might also see that once the 1,000 shares are sold and out of the way, nobody else is in the queue to sell except a few isolated individuals or dealers who only have 100 shares at $50 ½. In other words, with a Level II screen, you can see how many buyers and sellers there are and at what price.

On top of all this information is another important clue regarding who exactly is behind the bid and the ask. Each Level II entry not only displays the bid and ask list but also identifies who is attached to each bid and ask by means of a four-letter abbreviation. If you see MASH, which is Mayer & Schweitzer, you can probably guess that it's a Charles Schwab trader, as MASH handles Schwab's trading. If you see MSCO, you know it's Morgan Stanley Dean Witter; MLCO is Merrill Lynch, and GSCO is Goldman Sachs. If you see one of these guys selling at a frantic pace, you had better not buy because these big guys may have orders to sell millions of shares, and they're just selling what they can. That selling pressure is likely to drive the stock price down.

This isn't everything there is to know about broker-dealers and which symbols mean what to whom, but it's enough to know that Level II screens give day traders a lot of information necessary to win at this wild video game.

Oh yes, Virginia, there is such a thing as a Level III screen. But to get Level III access, you must be a registered professional market maker. Level III screens have the same quotation attributes as Level II but are used only by market makers to enter (or update) their orders.

> **Each** Level II **entry not** only **displays** the **bid** and **ask** list **but** also **identifies who** is **attached** to each **bid.**

What's Next?

There you have it—the rudimentary layout of the day trading environment. If our examination of day trading basics has piqued your inter-

Level II Screen

| AMAT | + | 87 1/16 | b 87 | | a 87 1/16 23 x 5 | | 8.71M | 11:13 |

MMID	C	Bid	BSi...	Ti...	MMID	C	Ask	AS...	Ti...
INCA	+	87	23	11:13	INCA	-	87 1/16	5	11:13
REDI	+	87	20	11:13	MLCO		87 1/8	10	11:11
MASH	+	87	10	11:13	MASH	-	87 1/8	5	11:13
ARCA	+	87	8	11:13	ISLD	-	87 1/8	1	11:13
SLKC	+	87	1	11:13	NITE	-	87 1/8	1	11:13
ISLD	-	86 15/16	1	11:13	GSCO		87 1/4	10	11:08
NITE		86 7/8	10	11:12	MSCO		87 1/4	10	11:06
FBCO	+	86 7/8	1	11:12	SHWD		87 1/4	1	11:11
MONT		86 7/8	1	11:02	RSSF		87 1/4	1	11:09
LEHM		86 13/16	1	11:09	FBCO	+	87 3/8	1	11:12
FLTT		86 3/4	1	11:09	CIBC		87 7/16	1	11:06
PERT		86 3/4	1	11:05	SBSH		87 1/2	5	11:12
SELZ		86 3/4	1	10:59	PERT		87 1/2	4	11:05
JPMS		86 3/4	1	10:58	HRZG		87 1/2	3	11:11
MLCO		86 11/16	10	11:11	ARCA		87 1/2	1	11:12
AGIS	-	86 5/8	5	11:12	DEAN		87 1/2	1	11:02
BEST		86 5/8	1	11:01	SELZ		87 1/2	1	10:59
MSCO		86 9/16	10	11:06	REDI	+	87 9/16	1	11:13
MADF		86 9/16	1	11:11	BTRD		87 5/8	5	11:11
WARR		86 9/16	1	09:19	GBIC		87 3/4	7	11:10
HRZG		86 1/2	20	11:11	MWSE	-	87 3/4	5	11:12
GSCO		86 1/2	10	11:08	BRUT		87 3/4	3	11:02
NTRD		86 1/2	7	11:03	JPMS		87 3/4	1	10:58
BRUT		86 1/2	5	11:02	LEHM		87 13/16	1	11:09
PRUS		86 1/2	1	11:02	NFSC		87 7/8	20	11:11

Key:

MMID: Market Maker I.D.

C: Change

Bid: Bid Price

BSi: Bid Size (how many shares are desired)

Ti: Time of Bid

Ask: Ask Price

AS: Ask Size (how many shares are for sale)

Sample Courtesy: eSignal, www.esignal.com

est or made you want to look for the next logical steps that will lead you into this arena, then we've accomplished our goal. Here's a glimpse of what is available to assist those who seek more extreme investing—and where the experts in the field suggest you turn first.

Let's start with a story. Matthew Ostrowski of On Line Trading Expo, a trade show for day traders, once worked for a large retail paint store. Inevitably, a certain percentage of customers would come in, buy paint and be back a few months later complaining that it was an inferior product or a bad batch because it peeled and cracked off. And the store would have to agonizingly explain that "it ain't the paint"—it's all in the prep work. Successful painting is 80 percent preparation and 20 percent application. Says Ostrowski, "The same is true for successful day trading."

It is interesting to note how differently day trading firms and traditional brokerages view the importance of preparing their new customers for day trading. Many Level II Direct Access companies, such as TradePortal.com, CyBerCorp.com, eSignal and Tradescape.com, have aligned themselves with top-quality day trading educational organizations—such as the Online Trading Academy in Irvine, California—that provide in-depth programs to train potential customers long before they ever sit down to make a high-speed Level II Direct Access trade.

What's even more interesting is that a student's cost for the Online Trading Academy course is currently fully recoverable in the form of discounted trades and services offered by these companies, which remain in effect until the full tuition is recovered. Thus, the cost for training is nothing. Mainstream day trading brokerage firms, on the other hand, generally don't offer training but instead may recommend training resources.

> ## Successful **painting** is **80 percent** preparation and 20 percent application. "The **same** is **true** for **successful** day trading."

Getting back to your day-trading homework: There are lots of ways to learn. Besides classes, there are all sorts of online tutorials and mentoring programs (where instructors work with you in real time). And there are many good books and video tutorials on the subject.

The Internet alone offers hundreds of ways to get to the bottom of extreme investing.

Says Merrick Okamoto of TradePortal.com, "In addition to seminars, online training and education, reading books and personal disciplines—like technical analysis and keeping a journal—we encourage comparison shopping before deciding on any Level II Direct Access software or broker.

"Companies offering this type of service generally have *demo* buttons on their Web sites, and we suggest downloading each one and test-driving it to see how it performs and how you like it. You can execute actual real-time trades without committing to a purchase, sort of like shooting blanks. How can you argue with that?"

The Extreme Investor Challenge

You now have an insight into the incredible world of day traders, a special breed of extreme investors. You've learned there are several styles of trading that vary according to the time you hold a stock. You've also learned that you will need specialized computer access to trade successfully, and you understand that the pros recommend treating any extreme investing regime like a true business.

Today's stock market isn't your dad's tired old Buick anymore. If you're considering stepping into a new, flashier high-speed vehicle of any type,

---

The Extreme Investor's Bookshelf

Here's what day trading professionals are reading:

❍ *The Electronic Day Trader* (McGraw-Hill), by Marc Friedfertig and George West

❍ *The Disciplined Trader: Developing Winning Attitudes* (McGraw-Hill), by Mark Douglas

❍ *How to Get Started in Electronic Day Trading* (McGraw-Hill), by David S. Nassar

❍ *Reminiscences of a Stock Operator* (John Wiley & Sons), by Edwin Lefevre

❍ *The Strategic Electronic Day Trader* (John Wiley & Sons), by Robert Deel

❍ *Trading for a Living: Psychology, Trading Tactics, Money Management* (John Wiley & Sons), by Dr. Alexander Elder

❍ *Trading to Win: The Psychology of Mastering the Markets* (John Wiley & Sons), by Ari Kiev

we strongly suggest some form of driving school before you take it out on the track. Otherwise, it could lead to another type of "crash course" in trading.

For the stock market in general, and with day trading specifically, there's a great deal to master before you put any money into an account and begin trading. For those who still decide to shoot first and ask questions later, remember: "It ain't the paint."

part three

Other Extreme Investments

In the following chapters, we will look at some forms of speculating that investors should thoroughly investigate when seeking greater risk/reward benefits, which is the hallmark of the extreme investor.

As you will see, while these aren't the speed-of-light endeavors that, say, scalping is, there are plenty of heart-pounding moments to be found on slower-paced but equally extreme financial paths such as initial public offerings (IPOs), options, futures trading and junk bonds.

For those looking to broaden the scope of an existing portfolio with an eye toward more extreme performance, these pages are intended to present an introduction to these extreme investment vehicles and a starting point for further investigation.

Finally, we will take a look at some of the outer quarters of today's dynamic investment world in search of cutting-edge trends, new directions and practical insights for the prospective extreme investor.

Make Me An Offer: Initial Public Offerings

nitial public offerings are among the most extreme ways to speculate. Investing in the stock market is risky enough as it is, but investing in a company that has no stock trading history makes it even more speculative. The initial offering of a stock for sale to the public is actually the first time the open market is allowed to cast its vote for a company in the form of buying its stock.

If a company has proven management, wildly sought-after products and awesome earnings potential, it's considered a hot IPO, and its stock price will reflect that perception when the stock is finally offered for sale on the open market. In other words, if a company's future looks promising, investors will buy its stock more readily than if it's a completely unknown company.

There's a lot of volatility involved in the IPO market. This favors the extreme investor; we'll discuss how in a moment. But first, it's important to understand what's fueling today's IPO trend.

A Flash In The Pan
Or A Sky Full Of Fireworks?

Trying to determine whether you're looking at a momentary glimmer of promise or something closer to a genuine explosion is certainly the trick of working an IPO.

When a company "goes public," it is essentially allowing investors to buy a piece of the company as a way to raise money to expand the business. A company that shows early profitability or potential for significant revenue growth has a much better chance of introducing a successful IPO than a company that has a track record of weak or fluctuating revenues and nebulous growth potential. Growth potential, not current profitability, has been the hallmark of the latest big IPOs.

That's because everybody wants a piece of the next Microsoft or AOL, and they want it while it's still relatively cheap. If the company has demonstrated wondrous financial results prior to going public, this is a marvelous indicator of future growth and success. But since the Internet itself is new, Internet stocks typically have little or no actual earnings.

Still, these Internet hotdogs usually have business plans that make investors drool over the prospect of owning a piece of the next new twist in high-tech. Internet IPOs have everyone's attention these days, and this trend will continue because the Internet represents today's electronic version of the industrial revolution.

But Internet IPOs are not the only hot issues available to the extreme investor. New IPOs are issued almost every day for companies ranging from Spanish broadcasting networks to new pet supply stores to Martha Stewart. Yet today, some of the best and most explosive tend to be in biotech and pharmaceuticals, computers and the Internet, telecommunications

The **Internet** **represents** today's electronic **version** of the **industrial** **revolution.**

and fiber optics, and all the companies that interact, to some extent, with these sectors.

But there's still money to be made on even the least extravagant, lowest-profile companies. A new auto parts company might issue an IPO that proves successful, for instance, though it may not rocket up or down quite as drastically as some of its higher-profile counterparts.

Shhhh...

Once a decision to go public is made by a company, its board of directors finds a lead underwriter (an investment company that handles selling the stock). Then the company creates a prospectus (also called an S-1 document), which details financial data and information on the management team, the target market, competitors, growth strategy, and more. The company registers this document with the Securities and Exchange Commission (SEC), which imposes a "quiet period" that usually lasts from the time the company hires an underwriter until after the stock for that company has traded publicly for about a month (i.e., 25 days after the official IPO date).

The quiet period is when the corporate officers have to be, well, *quiet*. What this really means is that the corporate officers—and all the banking and underwriting people involved in taking the company public—can't be blabbing about things that would unduly hype the stock.

If some new or meaningful piece of news occurs, it's all supposed to be in the legal documentation monitored by the SEC. If anything happens that materially changes the prospects or actual day-to-day business of a company, it has to go into the S-1 as an official addendum. So if a company is about to go public, and three weeks before the IPO the company signs a contract with a huge new customer, the quiet period legally prevents anyone from within the company (or the underwriters) from leaking the good news to the press (or anyone else, for that matter).

The venue for such news remains in the official S-1 filing only. Rumors outside this document are dealt with harshly if they can be traced to company insiders. The SEC uses every tool at its disposal to make sure that only officially documented facts move the stock price.

Bridge Over Troubled Waters

Underwriting is simply the act of assuming risk, as when bringing a corporation's new securities issue to the public. If the underwriter blows it and prices the stock wrong, or makes any number of potential mistakes, the IPO can actually cost the underwriter money. That's because underwriters keep shares of the companies they take public in their inventories. If the underwriter prices the stock at 10, and it trades at 8—and the underwriter has 20 million shares in its inventory—that hurts.

Underwriters are usually investment banks, and they're the intermediaries between an issuer of a security (the company) and the investing public. Investment banks frequently maintain broker-dealer operations, and they offer investor services, but they don't accept deposits or make loans, leaving that to the regular banks.

Once the preliminary prospectus is filed with the SEC, the company has to wait for reviews, approvals and amendments, and the lead underwriter begins the process of lining up other investment banks that will help sell the stock to their clients. In other words, the primary underwriter (an investment bank like Morgan Stanley Dean Witter or Merrill Lynch) acts as an agent in the sale of the company's shares when it goes public. As an agent, the underwriter sells shares to its own customers, which may include big insurance companies, or other big investors, or even extreme investors (like you) who have an account with Morgan Stanley or Merrill Lynch. But the underwriter usually pre-sells blocks of shares (hundreds of thousands) to other investment banks who want to buy shares for their own portfolios or for their own corporate clients and individual customers.

Unfortunately, most small investors don't get in on the deal until the stock goes up for sale publicly on a stock exchange (typically the NASDAQ or the NYSE). Here's why:

The investment banks gauge their big customers' interest in buying into the IPO and try to suggest an appropriate price based on expected demand and other market conditions. The ultimate pricing of an IPO can change, and usually does, depending on the investment climate, buying interest and other factors.

Some Internet companies have such a wildly anticipated public offering that the price is raised before the stock is actually offered for sale to investors on the open market (the stock market). Underwriters might calculate that $14 per share is an appropriate price, but they might learn that they can get even more, so the next day they increase the price to $16, and—whoa!—that's too low, too, so the pricing is finalized at $17 per share when the stock finally hits the market.

It's all a juggling act right up until the last minute on the day of the offering. The price is fixed, the shares are put up for sale, and the public takes over from there, either trading the stock higher or lower, depending on whether there are more buyers than sellers or more sellers than buyers.

Small investors are often frustrated by the fact that they miss out on all the cool IPOs—or if they do get involved, their involvement is too late. The price small investors get after the preferred investors are done buying is usually much higher than that appealing-sounding $17 per share they heard about on the news.

> **"Small investors** are often **frustrated** by the **fact** that they **miss out** on all the cool **IPOs."**

Here's the typical small-investor scenario: The frustrated investor enters a market order, which instructs the broker to buy stock at the best price currently available, but when the stock finally becomes available, it's at a price near the high for the day. The little investor is stuck holding a stock that is about to start its descent. The big move up in the stock price is over.

IPOs can shoot way up during the first few minutes or hours of trading and then decline to less exuberant levels, leaving the last buyers stuck in the unlovely position of buying high and selling low, or buying high and waiting for the price to rebound in the future.

The lead underwriter is supposed to make sure the company's stock trades smoothly when it's offered for sale to the public. That's the lead underwriter's job as agent. As soon as the stock can be traded publicly, it may rocket up from its initial offering price, tempting IPO participants who got in first to sell and take a quick profit. But that profitability is based solely on the fact that they had an inside advantage, which is decidedly unfair to the rest of the public, who didn't have that special opportunity.

Therefore, selling shares obtained prior to their being available on the open market is frowned upon by the lead underwriter. To prevent this practice, which is called *flipping*, the lead underwriter can impose penalties on brokers, thus discouraging the practice. But all this only applies to you if you got in early. So how do you do that?

Getting In On
The Fun Is Not Easy

The traditional way to get in on an IPO is to buy shares directly from one of the investment banks carrying the deal, which can be done through your existing broker. Big underwriters like Lehman Brothers, Merrill Lynch, Morgan Stanley Dean Witter, and Salomon Smith Barney accept individual accounts, but you generally need a pile of money to get in on the ground floor before the shares are offered through normal market channels.

In other words, your chances of getting a crack at a new IPO improve if your broker is large because it will have distribution alliances with traditional investment banks, and you can participate if you ask. It helps if your account is large, or you do a lot of trading, because even if you have an account with a big broker, IPO shares are saved to reward a firm's biggest, most active and longest-standing customers.

Investors with accounts of less than $50,000, who make only a few trades per month, or who have opened an account within the past 90 days have only a slight chance of getting in on the fun, excitement and extreme aspects of hot, new IPOs.

Once you hook up with a broker that's big enough to have access to IPOs, there's no guarantee the broker will have access to all IPOs. They will only be able to get you in on the ones for which they have negotiated shares for themselves, which they in turn pass along to their customers. More brokers are allowing their customers access to IPOs because it's good PR and attracts new customers. These brokers now include such names as E*TRADE, Charles Schwab, Fidelity, DLJ*direct*, and

> More **brokers** are **allowing** their **customers access** to **IPOs** because it's **good PR** and **attracts** new **customers**.

Upping The Ante

"If your relative or close pal isn't a top executive at a company going public and you're not an institutional investor, your chances of getting in on a hot IPO drop drastically," notes IPO columnist Jed Graham in *Investor's Business Daily*, a newspaper all extreme investors should read.

"Industry estimates of the share of initial public offerings going to individual investors [including the rich clients brokers cater to] range from 4 to 20 percent. There remains incredible demand, and underwriters always give preference to their best customers," Graham explains.

However, while traditional brokerages still handle most initial public offerings, online brokers are making inroads for a greater share. "But a surge in demand has overwhelmed the modest increase in the number of shares available to individual investors," Graham notes.

His advice? "Some investors complain that they can't sit in front of their computers all day, so they miss what can be a narrow window for applying to buy IPO shares," says Graham. "Others say they've improved their chances of getting IPO shares by using services that alert them when online brokers begin accepting orders. These services include eWebWatch.com, IPOpatrol.com and NetWatchdog.com."

That's the FYI on IPOs.

> While **traditional brokerages** still **handle** most initial **public offerings**, online **brokers** are **making** inroads for a **greater share**.

Wit Capital. Each has its own parameters for allowing investors to get involved in its IPO programs. These discount brokers are more likely to let extreme investors in on IPOs, compared to the full-service brokers (Merrill Lynch, Morgan Stanley Dean Witter and Salomon Smith Barney). That's because the full-service brokers tend to cater to bigger clients, and the smaller investors get lost in the priority list.

E*TRADE allows qualified customers to place conditional offers to buy shares of an IPO. You tell them how many shares you're interested in buying and the maximum you're willing to pay for them, and E*TRADE puts you in an allocation pool with the other potential buyers. While shares are generally allocated to customers randomly, they wisely review all applicants' past IPO trading patterns, and investors with a history of short holding periods (flipping, which we discussed earlier) receive a lower allocation priority for future offerings.

According to E*TRADE, the rationale for allocating shares to customers who tend to hold for longer periods is that it helps E*TRADE get access to more offerings and more shares, because issuers of new stock seek to build price stability in the aftermarket. (The *aftermarket* or *secondary market* is the actual stock market, as opposed to the primary market, which is where sales of an issue take place before the company's stock is traded publicly, as described earlier.)

What E*TRADE is trying to say is that the underwriter is keeping track of which brokers have the highest flipping ratios, and it may limit future IPO opportunities accordingly. So in turn, the subbrokers monitor which of their individual customers are guilty of flipping, and they respond accordingly, too.

"Danger, Will Robinson!"

In the 1960s TV series "Lost in Space," the lost Robinson family wandered galaxies trying to find their way back home to Earth. In numerous planetary adventures along the way, young Will Robinson and his robot sidekick encountered many tricky situations in which the friendly machine would flail its arms and blurt out the warning, "Danger, Will Robinson. . .danger!"

Today, small investors could use just such a friend when weighing IPO ventures (or *adventures*). In lieu of a protective droid, a good rule of thumb is to ask yourself these two logical questions instead:

1. Why didn't the large investment banks and big investors—both institutional and private—gobble up all existing shares and make them available to their own clients and customers? Why are there some left? Do they know something you don't? When an IPO is readily available to even the smallest of investors, your radar should be warning you.

2. When a retail stockbroker is heavily promoting an IPO as a hot opportunity, it again begs the question: "Why?" It has already gone through many hands (and much scrutiny) and apparently was not only generally passed over by the big boys, but for some reason it now requires a sensational buildup to sell to small investors. Hmmmmm. Carefully weigh the offer and ask: "What's up here?" before blindly jumping aboard the IPO Express.

DLJ*direct* only gives shares to customers with a certain account size ($100,000 or more). DLJ uses a Dutch auction bidding process, which is too complicated to describe in detail here but basically involves secret bidding, and the price of the stock is lowered until it hits its first bid (the highest price any buyer is willing to pay), and it's sold at that price.

Wit Capital, like E*TRADE, uses a prioritization method that allocates randomly to all investors who respond to its solicitation e-mails within a certain time frame. Wit Capital puts those who sell their IPO shares in the first 60 days of trading at the bottom of the priority list for upcoming IPOs. Wit doesn't have account size prerequisites.

'Tis The Season...
Or Is It?

Timing is everything when it comes to IPOs. Sometimes an entire season is just not good for IPOs, and none of them do very well. This can be one of the best times to get in if you're a patient investor. A company that has the misfortune of going public during one of these unfavorable cycles can often lead to your realizing the proverbial windfall somewhere down the road.

That's because, during one of these cycles, stock prices stay artificially low based on the selling pressure of the overall market. Under normal market conditions, the IPO would have risen because of a healthier market sentiment. Until recently, however, IPOs have been perennially in season.

If you wait for the IPO to settle into a *trading range* (where the highs and the lows of a stock price stay the same over a period of time, usually days or a few weeks), opportunities often reveal themselves. After stabilizing into a sound trading range, the IPO may break out and the price may rise. Some IPOs fizzle out into a *flat trading pattern* (they don't seem to go up or down in price) and then slowly drift lower, which allows you to be thankful to have avoided the early feeding frenzy that left many buyers paying too much for a stock that settled down to reality. There are many such near misses.

News You
You Can Use

The IPOs with solid financials and/or serious long-term potential soon become subject matter for analysts. Professional analysts issue research reports that are made available through investment periodicals like *Investor's Business Daily*, TV news channels that cover financial events (like CNBC and CNN's "Moneyline"), specialized radio financial program broadcasts and almost all discount and full-service broker Web sites.

The research reports come out about a month after the IPO and include revenue and earnings estimates, plus information on why a particular company might have an advantage over the competition.

This information can help you decide if you want to buy the shares or not. But remember that analysts can have underlying motives that allow them to get fuzzy with positive thinking in the direction they'd like to see a stock move. And sometimes analysts flat-out disagree with one another. It's very subjective stuff, but all the opinions and data can be weighed and used to make decisions on which post-IPO stocks to buy.

Buy The Parent, Own The Prodigal Son

Jim A. from Burbank, California, got involved in an Internet IPO for Net2Phone (NTOP) in a unique way. First, his homework revealed that the company had an edge on the technology that allows people to use the Internet to make overseas, long-distance calls for a lot less than normal telephone rates. He liked what he read in the prospectus, but instead of buying Net2Phone stock, he bought stock in IDT Corp. (IDTC), a company that has a large interest in Net2Phone as a subsidiary. IDT Corp. is a telecommunications company that offers a broad range of integrated long-distance telephone and Internet access services. He considered buying IDTC safer than buying stock in the Internet company itself, a strategy worth considering.

Playing Extreme
In The IPO Aftermarket

Just because you can't get in on an IPO at the initial offering price doesn't mean you can't get in at all. Getting in early is good, but jumping on the coattails of a rising star is also an extreme way to take advantage of a new IPO.

Hot IPOs almost always leap to artificially high levels. The feeding frenzy takes hold, and the upward momentum can last for several days or sometimes weeks. But there's always a cooling-off period, and for some IPOs, the heat never comes back. But for the extreme investor, the speed with which these stocks rise and fall creates an opportunity to take advantage of the momentum in either direction. (See the "Working With A Net: Risk Management" section in Chapter 2, and consider these same rules, as they also apply to investing in an IPO.)

Various Web sites can keep you informed about upcoming IPO activity. You can get free weekly e-mail updates on the IPO market. It's not difficult to learn about the previous week's filings and recent pricings (IPOs that got the final go-ahead and that are being traded), and you can even find out which companies are soon scheduled to go public.

Most companies, however, only release a tentative date on which they plan to go public. These dates change frequently according to market conditions. Buy.com, for example, was scheduled to price in late January 2000. Then it was put off until the first week of February, and it finally priced on February 8. Rarely does a company actually go public on the exact date the company was expected to.

Developing IPO Radar
And Intelligence

Here are some Web sites where you can find virtually every shred of information you'll need to get involved in an IPO.

○ **www.IPOCentral.com:** Hoover's IPO Central provides a list of companies going public for the current week. It features a very well-written section for beginners, including a clearly explained bit on what to look for and how to read a prospectus. This site is good for a quick reference on which companies are being traded this week (click on "Trading") versus the companies that are about to be traded (called "priced," which means the IPO price is finally determined so it can be traded the next day). Hoover's offers detailed information to members and basic information on the underwriters and anticipated pricing dates to nonmembers.

○ **www.edgar-online.com:** Click on the "IPO Express" button, and you can get a list of upcoming IPOs organized by date, with underwriter, pricing, and even a column that indicates whether or not the issue is Internet-related. The site also shows ticker symbols, which others sometimes do not. EDGAR (Electronic Data Gathering Analysis and Retrieval) is a Web-based provider of real-time SEC filings. The SEC's EDGAR system is government-run and supplies filings to EDGAR Online Inc. for distribution over the Internet. (For more information, see "Meet EDGAR" on page 111.)

○ **www.redherring.com:** *Red Herring* is a magazine (and an online Web site) all about new companies. This site has some of the best news articles on what's hot and why. It has an IPO calendar that includes an interesting column of information for each IPO. This Web site has a directory of underwriters that allows you to locate companies the underwriters have recently taken public.

○ **www.ipo.com:** This Web site offers its opinion on hot IPOs, plus recent IPO pricings and IPO filings. It also has an IPO FAQ section.

○ **www.ipohome.com:** This site has a section called "IPO of the Week" and an appealing and clearly presented compilation of IPO information.

○ **www.ipomaven.com:** This site has its own spin on IPO data and news. It has a little section labeled "Best of IPOs" that indicates which IPOs have gone up most by price and percentage increase. It also has an earnings section for recent IPOs so you can see which IPOs are associated with companies making money and which are hooked up with losers. This site allows you to look at groups of IPOs, such as "Best of IPOs," for a particular date, or you can click on an IPO for further information on the company's financials, officers, etc., and a description of what the company does.

Meet EDGAR

The Securities and Exchange Commission (SEC) was founded in 1933 to protect investors from the kinds of practices that resulted in the crash of 1929. Since its inception, the SEC has developed regulations for publicly held corporations based on the premise that full disclosure regarding the business and financial status of a public company produces an open and fair market. The reports the SEC requires companies to file are available to the public as soon as they are written.

Public companies must file many types of reports with the SEC, including an extensive annual report that contains year-end audited financial statements (10-K Report), a quarterly report (10-Q Report), a time-sensitive document reporting significant corporate events (8-K Report), and proxy statements, which are reports to shareholders prior to a proxy vote (a proxy vote is when shareholders allow someone else to vote for them at a shareholders' meeting).

> **Since** its **inception**, the **SEC** has **developed regulations** for publicly held **corporations based** on the **premise** that **full disclosure** regarding the **business** and **financial status** of a **public company produces** an **open** and **fair market**.

Originally, SEC filings were submitted and available to investors via hard copy. In the 1970s, the SEC contracted with an outside company to create and distribute microfiche film copies to designated SEC public reference rooms.

In 1984, the SEC started the EDGAR (Electronic Data Gathering Analysis and Retrieval) pilot program to create an electronically accessible database providing a more efficient and less costly way for the investing public to get the information. A gradual phase-in schedule was established, which mandated that public corporations file SEC documents electronically.

Today, full disclosure and accurate information are readily available to all investors in SEC public reference rooms for prompt scrutiny and accurate investment planning.

○ **www.ipofrontline.com:** This site has a summary of the day's IPOs as well as the ones scheduled for the very next day (though you can never be certain when the actual pricing and aftermarket sales will take place). Subscribers to the site get access to every NASDAQ IPO from the moment the market makers show their orders through the beginning of trading, minute by minute.

○ **www.ipolockup.com:** This Web site tracks lockup periods so you can be forewarned. Lockup periods typically last six months (but sometimes as few as four months); the lockup period is a time during which company insiders (employees, management, major shareholders and venture capital investors) can't sell their stock in a company that has recently gone public. When that period ends, there is the potential for many new shares to be sold on the market, temporarily creating an oversupply, and thus a fall in price.

○ **www.SEC.gov:** Many general investment guidelines and a great deal of specific information, some directly related to IPOs, are available on the SEC Web site. There is also a toll-free information line: (800) 732-0330.

Prospectus
Pointers

As we stated earlier, there are ways to take advantage of IPOs even if you get in late. Since the majority of IPOs do poorly (as measured against the broader market), your late arrival to the game can often protect you as you watch for the overall trend of a particular IPO to mature and stabilize. Read the company's prospectus before investing, and you can surmise which company's stock might rise and fall, and which ones might be more apt to rise and then rise further.

To do this, you need to know how to read a prospectus. Unfortunately half the darn thing is written by lawyers and accountants, so you skip that half and go directly to the sections that describe the products and services, only to find that even these sections leave you scratching your head.

Even though the SEC prevents blatant misrepresentation, it's still hard to tell if the company's products and/or services represent the next Palm Pilot or some bogus magic act that leaves the elephant standing on the stage after the curtain is removed. The solution is to get an education on the market you're investigating and learn how to read a prospectus to glean the important stuff.

Prospectuses are available without charge from FreeEdgar.com, an SEC Web site. Many companies put their prospectuses on their own Web sites; if they don't, they are available upon request through the underwriting broker (the underwriting broker is always printed on the cover of the prospectus).

> **You** will **be most interested** in **reading** certain **sections** that **call** for some **useful interpretation.**

There are lots of sections in a prospectus—far too many to list here—and most of them are self-explanatory, such as the financial sections that make up much of the report, and the list of officers and details on the competition.

As an extreme investor, you will be most interested in reading certain sections that call for some useful interpretation. Once you get a prospectus in front of you, here are some pointers to make those sections more understandable, starting with the cover, which has vital information.

The Cover Page—Your First Clue

The underwriter is indicated on the bottom of the front page of every prospectus. Sometimes there are several participants, and you'll be able to figure out who they are right here. In a nutshell, you want to see names on this cover page that are reputable firms with a lot of experience as underwriters of viable companies that go public.

Goldman Sachs, Merrill Lynch, and Morgan Stanley Dean Witter are some of the best-known companies of them all. When they bring an issue to market, it's got clout. They do their due diligence and rarely introduce a total flop, although every now and again, it happens.

The smaller investment banks often take the smaller companies public. Not that small companies or small underwriters

Bigger Is Better

Here's a list of the bigger firms that take companies public. These under-writers have good reputations within the industry, and they have track records backing winning companies and their IPOs.

- ○ Goldman Sachs
- ○ J.P. Morgan
- ○ Morgan Stanley Dean Witter
- ○ Merrill Lynch
- ○ Robertson Stephens
- ○ Credit Suisse First Boston
- ○ Donaldson, Lufkin & Jenrette
- ○ Pincus Warburg

are bad, but their offerings tend to be built upon relatively less substantive foundations. To be considered big, a company has to have a market capitalization (the share price multiplied by the number of shares issued) of at least a few hundred million dollars. A lot of small regional banks have a good track record taking companies public, but exercise caution when you see a peewee company going public via a peewee underwriter. If you haven't heard of the underwriter, at least verify its history and reputation.

Prospectus Summary—The Overview

Start with the "Prospectus Summary" and the section on "Recent Developments," and glance at the financial stuff. The summary offers a pretty good overall picture of what's going on within the company in terms of products, sales, customers, past history, and financial track record, and what you read here may be enough to send you deeper into the prospectus or to throw it out altogether.

The "Recent Developments" section identifies any notable recent events, including how the company has performed in the previous quarter. It's also where you'll find *amended filings*, which is the information that comes up after the

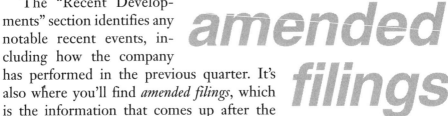

amended filings

initial prospectus is issued. Consider it a big warning flag if this section doesn't feature mostly good news. The rest of the "Prospectus Summary" is a condensed version of what comes later under the "Business" section, which is the blow-by-blow account of what the company does.

Risk Factors—The Nitty-Gritty

Most companies believe they can overcome most obstacles and that they will rise to the top if only they get the money they need to expand. But when you read a company's prospectus, you might think the opposite when you get to the section titled "Risk Factors."

Most of these sections read like the business is up against big competition, the company's products need help, the product life cycle is in question, and the business may go down if XYZ company decides to move to a new technology standard. This doom and gloom is normal for a prospectus because both the company officers and the underwriters have to be totally upfront about potential speed bumps to avoid lawsuits.

Don't be shocked at such dismal prospects and dire warnings. Don't ignore them, either, because this is where you'll find the mud puddles.

What's Underneath Those Underwriters?

To learn more about the history of a securities firm or broker, you can call the National Association of Securities Dealers at (800) 289-9999, but it's easier to use the association's Web site. Go to www.nasdr.com and click on "About Your Broker." Then click on the "Perform an Online Search" link, and then use the pull-down menu to select either "Bank" (most underwriters that take a company public are investment banks) or "NASD member firm" (you may have to try both), click on "Firm" (under the pull-down menu), and then it's easiest to click on the "Firm Index" over in the left column and locate the underwriter in question from there. You'll be able to review any previously registered customer complaints, legal or regulatory actions against them, and financial disclosures. This Web site will tell you about any substantial or alleged problems with an underwriter.

To get information regarding an underwriter's reputation, read the financial press (e.g., *The Wall Street Journal*) and check the underwriter's ads (called "tombstones" in the trade). These ads show public offerings carried out by an underwriter, which give you a clue about previous success taking a company public in a particular industry.

> # If **most** of a **company's business** is coming **from** one **customer**, that's a big **negative** no **matter** how **profitable** the **company** is and no **matter** how much **revenues grow.**

For example, if most of a company's business is coming from one customer, that's a big negative no matter how profitable the company is and no matter how much revenues grow. This dependence makes a company's prospects, and its stock price, vulnerable. The same thing goes for a company that depends on a particular supplier to make its products. If Intel is the only chip your widget uses, and Intel can't supply what you need for some reason, business will look bleak unless you find a second source for that chip.

This is just one example. There are many more red flags to look for, and recognizing them requires specific knowledge about the industry in which the company is involved.

What We Really Meant To Say...

In a prospectus, disclaimers follow every positive statement, because if something can go wrong, the company is duty-bound to mention it. A recent Internet company's prospectus offers a good example of the disclaimer syndrome. The "Risk Factors" section contained the following subsections, each followed by a detailed explanation.

○ We have incurred substantial losses and expect to continue to incur losses for the foreseeable future.

○ Our future operating results may fluctuate and cause the price of our common stock to decline.

○ Our business model is new and unproven, and we may not be able to achieve profitability.

○ Our recent growth has strained our resources, and if we are unable to manage and sustain growth, our operating results will be impaired.

○ If we are not able to generate significant advertising revenue, we may not be able to achieve profitability.

○ If we do not respond to technological change, our stores could become obsolete and we could lose customers.

○ If we are unable to successfully defend against pending legal actions against us, we could face substantial liabilities.

The Business Of The Company—
Is Everyone's Business

Learning about the business of the company should be your first priority in finding out if the company has a shot at success. Your analysis of what the company does for a living requires that you know something about that company's particular business climate and landscape. The more you know, the better. If you know nothing about the industry, you are taking a gamble, since you'll have no real reason to believe the company offers something unique.

the more you know, the better

Almost 10 years ago, Roger V., a programmer in Seattle, was asked to develop a blob of code that would connect a little handheld device to a server without wires. This was way before Palm Pilots—and even before everyone had a cellular phone. The wireless concept was not yet hot. In fact, it was so cold in terms of practical application that only a visionary could extrapolate a winning future for such devices. But Roger saw the potential for wireless devices. And he was interested in the whole telecommunications industry, so he read up on recent developments and industry plans.

While doing his research, he ran across a company called Globalstar, an outfit that designs, constructs, and planned to operate a worldwide, low-Earth-orbit, satellite-based digital telecommunications system (say *that* three times fast!). Roger followed Globalstar and eventually invested in the company soon after it went public in 1995.

Remember that his background was in programming, so he was comfortable with high-tech matters already, and because he was interested and knowledgeable to some extent about the whole industry, he was able to read the company's prospectus and determine that it had an innovative and bright future.

The point is, he was prepared to read about the business of the company in the prospectus because he already knew the industry. His knowledge of this particular technology equipped him to read a prospectus on any given wireless company and at least understand what they were talking about in terms of product offerings and potential.

You should understand what the company does and all about the industry in which it competes. Read. Talk to experts in the field. Don't assume that a company has leading-edge stuff just because it's in a business everyone thinks will go up, up, up. You need to know *why* this company has a better chance of succeeding than the rest—before climbing aboard, buckling up and lighting the fuse.

Within this section of the prospectus, you should find information on the company's growth strategy. To know if a company's growth strategy makes sense, again, you need to know the business. Assuming you do, you have a chance of figuring out if a company has a clue in terms of growth strategy.

Use Of Proceeds—Where The Dough Goes

A prospectus must outline what a company intends to do with the money it receives as the result of selling shares in the company. This section of the prospectus is called "Use of Proceeds," and it pretty much spells out where the dough's gonna go. Specifically, the company must describe how much it's going to spend and on what. Capital expenditures associated with technology and systems upgrades, sales and marketing activities, acquisitions, and research and development are all normal and good.

If a company plans to use most of the money from its IPO to pay off debt or shift gobs of it to pre-IPO investors in the form of dividends, this is ghastly. You don't want to pay for a company's past debts and obligations; you want to pay for future expansion. Some portion may be allocated to repay debt under an existing credit facility, but hopefully this is a small amount.

The Officers Of The Company—The Lineup

This section of the prospectus paints a portrait of who's running the company. Look for a group of leaders with a good track record. Know who's doing what and if they've done things in the past that lead you to believe they can do it again with this business endeavor. This element of a prospectus is extremely important, and it's frequently the part that's most overlooked. That's because it takes some digging beyond what's in the prospectus.

The prospectus will mention

> **Don't assume** that a **company** has **leading-edge stuff** just because it's in a **business everyone** thinks will go **up, up, up.**

the primary players and their backgrounds. A mini-resume accompanies the names of each executive officer and director. But these mini-resumes don't tell you how these people did at their previous companies, or if they were replaced because they did a rotten job for their last employer.

One way to dig deeper is to research how a person's company did while he or she was an employee. Standard & Poor's corporate profiles (at your library) lists public companies and how they've done financially over the years. Or just go to your discount broker's Web site to get past performance for the company (this only applies to public companies, of course, as private companies don't have to show anyone their financial information).

Financial data is readily available for past years, so you can see revenue growth (or lack thereof), earnings performance and lots more. E*TRADE, Charles Schwab and most discount brokers have this data, and they make it available to all their customers for free.

Another way to find out more about executives involved in an upcoming IPO is to call the company's investor relations department to see if you can get information. Investor relations departments are prepared to talk to potential investors and may fill you in on what kind of experience the top executives bring to the game.

Selected Consolidated Financial Data— Dollars In A Nutshell

Sometimes this section is titled "Summary of Consolidated Financial Data" instead of "Selected Consolidated Financial Data." This is where the accountants give you numbers on revenue, profits, losses, cash, debt, etc. If you aren't familiar with reading financial reports, here are a few things to look for.

First, always look for year-over-year increases in revenue. If revenue for a company's most recent fiscal year is equal to or down from the previous year, it may mean things aren't so good. That's what makes the technology sector and Internet companies look so attractive—even if they're not even close to being profitable yet, their revenue growth is exploding, sometimes 50 percent or more per year. If growth is not stellar, look for a reason why in the following section of the prospectus titled "Management's Discussion and Analysis of Financial Condition and Results of Operations."

Look at the company's operating margins. If operating margins are shrinking, profits are shrinking. The reason this is less important than revenue growth is that there are more good excuses for having a descending operating margin than falling revenue—like the company is in transition, acquiring companies, adjusting to competition, tooling up for a next generation of product, or other such reasons. Maybe the company has lower operating margins because it just ran a series of winning ads on Super Bowl Sunday, and it's in the process of pulling in market share and building brand recognition, all of which may have an effect on short-term profits.

If operating margins are suffering, you should again flip to the "Management Discussion" section for an explanation. Company execu-

Who's Planting The Seed Money?

Big companies that provide venture capital to start-ups are big because they've picked the right businesses to back. There will always be losers—and all venture capital firms know this—but to stay in business, you have to pick more winners than losers. It's not a guarantee, but something to factor into your decision on whether or not this IPO is the one worth following. Here's a list of some of the bigger venture capital firms:

○ Credit Suisse First Boston

○ Kleiner Perkins Caufield & Byers

○ Sequoia Capital

○ Softbank

○ Benchmark Capital

○ CMGI

○ idealab!

○ Comdisco Ventures

○ 3i Group

○ Chase H&Q

○ Goldman Sachs

○ Morgan Stanley Dean Witter

tives are anxious to explain their strategy if it's good, and if operating margins are not good, they are obligated to tell you why.

Another element worth noting has to do with debts and liabilities. You don't want a company's debts and liabilities to be more than its assets. In addition, look for anomalies such as abnormally high interest expenses, and look for an explanation if accounts receivable are rising faster than revenue. All this will be discussed in the "Selected Consolidated Financial Data" section.

One last note on finances: Look for companies going public that have an association with big venture capital firms like Kleiner Perkins Caufield & Byers or Sequoia Capital. An IPO's performance is directly related to its venture capital foundation. Companies with financial backing tend to do a lot better in terms of stock appreciation than those without such backing.

A Risk Disclaimer
Of Our Own

Read the prospectus on a given company carefully, and use it as a tool to decide whether it's worth investing in. If this book had a section called "Extreme Investor Risk" as it might appear in a prospectus, it would probably read something like this:

"You should consider carefully the inherent risks involved before you act upon what's contained herein, and do not assume that this is a complete compendium of all necessary information on IPOs, as there are uncertainties not presently known to us which could result in investments that could materially affect the value of your portfolio in a negative manner."

Say what? Stated in clear and concise extreme investor street talk: "This chapter is only a brief overview and is certainly not intended to provide you with everything you need to know to successfully invest in an IPO." But if you're seeking more extreme investment opportunities, take the time to give IPOs a look-see—and do your homework.

The Stock Options Option

ven at its most basic level, the intricacies of stock options may make your head spin, so we've tried to keep the information in this chapter as clear and concise as possible. This chapter is meant to give you a basic working definition of stock options as an investment vehicle and to provide insights into the extreme techniques and strategies savvy investors are using.

So before you read another word, know this: Stock options are tricky, and you'll need a full-blown tutorial not found in these pages before you can begin to take advantage of this complex opportunity. That said, let's take a look.

Stock Options—
Worth The Trouble?

Before we get started, let us add that stock options are gaining popularity as an investment vehicle for the extreme trader. Why? Although they are inherently complex, they offer a unique trading proposition. And on the pages that follow, you will find out how stock options increase investment horsepower for the extreme investor.

In essence, when you *buy* a stock for $50 and it goes up $10 (to $60), you've made a 20 percent profit. When you buy an *option* (which we'll explain) on a $50 stock for only $5, and the stock goes up $10 (to $60) and you sell your option, it might have increased in value to $7.50. When the adding and subtracting is done, you've spent only $5 to make a tidy $2.50 profit. A whopping 50 percent return! Big difference.

The bottom line: Stock options, handled correctly, give the extreme investor a lot more bang for the buck.

That's the end of the easy read. So settle in, buckle up and brace yourself for a mental journey into this ultrachallenging investment proposition.

What's It All About
Stage One

In life, as Martha Stewart would say, "Options are a good thing." (In reality, options in Martha Stewart's *company* are even better.)

Let's say your neighbor comes over one day and you have a chat about your front yard. You tell him you're going to plant grass this spring, and you'll need to either hire a gardening service to trim your lawn or buy a lawnmower and do it yourself.

Your neighbor tells you he has a brand-new lawnmower he won in a contest, and his yard is all rocks, so he offers to sell it to you for $100. You've seen the same lawnmower at Sears, brand new, for $200, but you haven't decided for sure whether you want to hire a gardener or mow the lawn yourself.

You think a minute. Your neighbor wants to sell his lawnmower and will probably soon do so by putting an ad in the paper. He'll easily get his $100. So you tell him you'll give him $10 for the option to buy his lawnmower for $100 sometime between now and spring if he'll just hold off selling for a bit.

Your neighbor now stands to make $110 if you buy the lawnmower (the $10 he got for the option and $100 for the mower). And if spring comes and you choose not to buy the lawnmower, your neighbor can still put an ad in the paper,

> **Stock options** are a **bit trickier executionwise.**

and he gets to keep the $10 you paid him for the first right to buy. That's what an option is all about. And while stock options are a bit trickier executionwise, they are basically the same thing in concept.

The Right,
But Not The Obligation

Stock options are a way to lock in the price of a stock, which you are willing to buy or sell, at some point in the future. The definition of a stock option is "the right, but not the obligation, to buy or sell a stock at a stated price within a specified time."

Let's say a stock is worth $50 today (as in our earlier example). Hold that figure in mind. Now let's say you decide to pay $5 for the option to buy it at $50 six months from now. That means that if the stock goes up $5 (to $55), you'll break even. You paid $5 for the option, and you'll pay $50 for the stock, so that equals $55. But if the stock goes up to $60, you make $5, because you can still buy it for $50, and if you add in the price you paid for the option, which makes your total investment $55, you make $5.

If the stock goes to $40 (which could happen just as easily as it going to $60), you won't want to follow up on that particular option to buy it at $50 because you can now buy it on the open market (stock market) for $40. You'll simply forget about the whole mess and lose the $5 you paid for the option.

lock in price

To Be Or Not To Be
That Is The Option...

Virtually all options are sold sometime prior to the expiration date. Only rarely are they converted into actual stock shares; when that happens, it's called *exercising* the option. (When an option holder wants to own the shares, it usually makes sense to sell the option and just buy the shares on the open market, but in some rare cases the math may prove that exercising the option makes more sense—usually not, though.) Because options are just place holders, they carry no intrinsic value, unlike stocks, which entitle the shareholder to voting privileges, dividends and other benefits, in addition to actual partial ownership of that company. Stocks represent tangible assets. Options are only worth something within the context of a transaction and can expire worthless, like your $5 option (noted above) might.

Options, however, are a much more efficient way to leverage your money than owning stock. If you choose a winning stock and get the timing right, an amount of money invested in options will yield a much higher return than if you bought the stock with the same amount of money.

Unfortunately, trading options is part of a zero-sum game, meaning somebody is going to lose. In fact, more people lose money trading options than they do trading stocks. Investors can be fatally attracted to the lure of the leverage, but it's that very leverage that eventually costs them a proportionately greater loss.

Consider the example above (where you paid $5 for an option to buy the stock later for $50). If the stock goes to $100, you make $45 (in theory, the value of the option should go up about $45). That means you turned a $5 investment into $45, a really great return. If you had bought the stock for $50 outright and it went to $100, at which point you sold it, well, $50 is also a great return. Doubling your money is always lovely. But buying the stock tied up $50 of your investment capital for however long you held the stock vs. just $5 per share you paid to reserve the right to buy the stock.

Stock
Option Lingo

Options are either *calls* or *puts*. A call option gives the holder (the guy who paid the five bucks) the right, but not the obligation, to buy a certain quantity of stock from the "writer" (the person who sells the option) at a certain price up to a specified date (we used six months in our example). A put option gives the holder the right, but not the obligation, to sell a stock at a fixed price for a predetermined period of time. Our example above is a call option.

Remember that when you buy an option, it gives you the right, but not the obligation, to either buy (in the case of a call) or sell (in the case of a put) shares of that stock at a fixed price for a fixed period of time. And while we're defining terms, in our $5 option example above, the price at which you were allowed to buy the stock ($50) is called the *strike price*.

"Options are **traded** in **100-share** lots **known** as **contracts."**

Options are traded in 100-share lots known as *contracts*. If you buy one contract, you control (i.e., have the option to buy or sell later) 100 shares. If you buy 10 contracts, you control 1,000 shares. Options are assigned a date after which the option expires.

So if you have one contract for AOL (America Online) and it's good until January, and your strike price is $70 per share, that means between now and January you can buy 100 shares of AOL at $70 apiece. That option would be abbreviated as follows: AOL JAN 70 CALL (a call option for AOL, expiring in January, with a strike price of $70).

Since one contract represents 100 shares, if that option trades at 2 1/2, that automatically means one contract costs $250 (100 x $2.50 = $250). It'd be nice if they'd just do the math for you, but they don't.

Every time you see a price attached to an option contract, you must calculate yourself and multiply by 100 to arrive at what your actual price will be, knowing that the price they've given is for one share, and that the contract you're buying is for 100 shares. So 10 contracts for options that trade at 2 1/2 would cost $2,500 (1,000 x $2.50 = $2,500). If you bought those 1,000 shares of AOL stock at $70 per share, that would cost $7,000, which means you can control those same 1,000 shares for a lot less by owning the option. Here's how trader Ron W. from Santa Monica, California, worked a few option trades on AOL recently.

Betting On AOL
You've Got Foresight

Ron W. really likes America Online. In 1999, while other people grumped about AOL, complaining about the banner ads and monthly costs, Ron felt that buying AOL options was the best bargain this side of the Mississippi. Ron met his wife on AOL, too, so perhaps he's a tad biased, but he has always considered AOL a solid company with a bright future.

While investors warned that AOL's earnings did not justify the stock price, Ron knew AOL was not only the biggest Internet service provider, but that it was likely to stay the biggest, judging by its growth record in the industry.

So later that year, he bought 10 AOL November 80 calls. That means he purchased the right to buy 1,000 shares of AOL up until the following

at the money

November, for a price of $80 per share (the strike price). Incidentally, options expire the third Friday of the designated month. That means the seller of the option (the person Ron bought it from) was betting that the stock price would go down, or at least not go up much. The seller gets the advantage of receiving the premium for offering the option.

Here's one of your first real ventures into the concept of stock options:

The November 80 calls Ron bought in July were what's called *at the money*. That means the price of AOL at the time he bought the calls was $80. In our $5 option example earlier, where you bought the option to buy at $50, and the stock was currently trading at $50 the day you bought the option, it was also at the money.

So with Ron's example, if AOL had been trading at $85 when he bought the November 80 calls, those would have been called *in-the-money* calls. His option allowed him to pay $80 between now and November, and the stock was already at $85.

in the money

If AOL had been trading at $75, Ron's option buy at $80 would have been called *out of the money*, which, in this case, would be for any AOL call options at a strike price under $80. Buying out-of-the-money options is a lot cheaper than buying in-the-money options, but you stand to make less money with out-of-the money options when the stock moves in your favor.

Call It What You Will

To summarize, if AOL is trading at $80, any option with a strike price of less than $80 is called out of the money, any option with a strike price of more than $80 is called in the money, and if the strike price is $80, that's called at the money. Not too difficult, eh?

The more a stock option is in the money, the more expensive it is. That should be pretty clear because there's money—potential profit— already built into it. Using our $5 call example from the beginning of this

out of the money

volatile chapter, let's say that a stock is trading at $50 today, and you want to buy an option that's good for six months, like last time, but you want your strike price (the price you can buy the stock for between now and then) to be at $25 instead of $50. Do you think the price of that option is still going to be just $5?

That would be an insanely great deal for you—and these miracles don't happen. Because if you could pay $5 for the option to buy a stock at $25 ($5 for the option, $25 for the stock, that's $30) and it's worth $50 today, you'd make $20 immediately.

So don't count on that crazy scenario. By the way, the difference between the option strike price in this example ($25) and the actual value of the stock ($50) is $25, which is called the *intrinsic value*.

How'd He Do That?

Back to Ron. If the price of AOL was at $85 when Ron bought the November 80 calls, then there would have been an intrinsic value associated with the option totaling $5 because he could exercise the option now, buy the shares at $80, and turn right around and sell them for $85 on the open market.

But Ron actually paid $18 per share for the option, more than just the $5. So if Ron paid $18 per share for his 10 contracts, and each contract represents 100 shares, his grand total would come to $18,000 ($18 per share, or $1,800 per contract of 100 shares, or $18,000 for Ron's 10 contracts). By the way, the price you pay for an option is called the *premium*.

Note again that the difference between the strike price ($80) and stock price that day ($85) was $5. So $5 of the $18 was intrinsic value, right? Pay attention—there'll be a pop quiz on this tomorrow!

If you're still following, you'll note that there is $13 left over in Ron's AOL maneuver, and that equates to what's called the *time value*. Time value is the amount you pay for an option, minus the intrinsic value. That means for the privilege of being able to lock in the purchase price of AOL at $80 in November, four months away, Ron had to

intrinsic value

rate of erosion

pay $13,000 of time value, plus $5,000 for the intrinsic value.

Which means that AOL would have to go up $13 per share just for him to recoup the time value that was built into the price of the stock alone. AOL would have to go up $18 past the $80 strike price, to $98, for Ron to break even.

The time value of an option erodes over time. In other words, the closer the expiration date gets, the less the time value is, and the rate of erosion gets faster and faster as that day approaches. So imagine that you buy an option on November 18 and it expires on the 19th (the third Friday in November), so the value of the time associated with one day is almost nil. Pennies. But there's big money attached to the time value of an option that's six months from expiring, because good stocks (the kind you'd expect to buy a call option for) are expected to rise over time.

Then there's the fact that the more volatile a stock is, the more expensive its options are. So Ron was paying a lot of money for his options. If he had just bought $18,000 worth of AOL stock at $80, he would have owned 225 shares. And if AOL were still at $80, he'd still have all his money. Not so with the option. If November rolled by and AOL was still at $80, Ron would have lost all $18,000 of his capital in a puff of theoretical smoke.

Fortunately, AOL climbed to almost 90, and Ron sold his options a few weeks after he purchased them for $27, netting him $9 per share ($27 minus the $18 he paid), or $900 per option contract—$9,000 total profit on 10 contracts. Notice that he didn't wait until November. He never exercised the option—that is, bought the actual stock—but he traded the option, buying at one price and selling when it appreciated later, but before expiration.

Had he owned the shares outright, his profit would have been a little over $2,000. He leveraged himself into a much better position by trading the options, at the risk of losing it all. Now *that's* extreme investing.

There's **big money attached to** the **time** value of an **option** that's **six months** from **expiring**, because good **stocks** are **expected** to **rise** over **time.**

Betting Against
A Stock Using Put Options

A lot of companies make bombs and rockets—literally. The Patriot missile is one such product. And in the United States' attempts to protect the world from tyranny, we shot lots of them off not too long ago in the the Middle East.

As the news got out that we were quickly depleting our supplies and fast running out of bombs, people started to investigate who was making these things so they could invest in the companies before the rush of new orders came in. A company called Raytheon makes the Patriot missile. So "Buy Raytheon" was on the minds of astute investors.

A lot of people bought Raytheon stock, not knowing that Raytheon was about to take a dive from $70 per share to less than $20. Raytheon operates three businesses, including commercial and defense electronics, engineering and construction, and aircraft. It's not just a bomb maker, and it has occasional cross-company business problems like many other corporations.

Meanwhile, Ron (the same Ron who was into AOL) investigated Raytheon and found that its net income was going to be offset by the absence of a $100 million pretax gain from divestitures and an increased effective tax rate, all of which he claims to understand, and which indicated to him that the stock was going down.

Ron expected the price to decline from its highs in the 70s to somewhere in the 50s range, so he bought a put. Remember, that's the right, but not the obligation, to sell a stock at a fixed price for a predetermined period of time.

In this case, he bought 5 October 68 put contracts, meaning that he owned the right to sell 500 shares (5 contracts x 100 shares each) for $68 a share any time between now and the third Friday in October. With Raytheon trading in the low 70s, this meant that Ron bought an out-of-the-money put option. He paid about $5 each, or $2,500 altogether.

Ron watched Raytheon drift around the same price, in the 70s, for weeks, and began to wonder if he'd chased a losing position when suddenly the stock started to drift lower. He had several weeks left until his options expired. Time was running out.

Ron had several alternatives. He could sell the put option and take the profit, or he could hang on for a while in hopes of the stock going even lower.

Instead, he decided to sell and then buy another put with the profits he made, letting him bet with "house money," so to speak. Ron sold his 5 October 68 puts for $5,000, took his $2,500 profit and bought 5 October 63 puts (his new put options cost $2,500), which left him with a risk-free way to ride any further downside move in Raytheon. The worst that could happen is that the stock would go up and Ron would break even, still having his original $2,500 profit.

As it turned out, he sold his October 63 puts for a profit, too, and then moved on to greener pastures, although Raytheon eventually plummeted down to less than $20 per share. (He didn't kick himself for missing out on such a huge move because, like all good extreme investors, he never regrets making a profit, no matter how small.)

Alternative
Option Strategies

Here's where we step it up again, as we now start delving into more strategic thinking that goes into the mind of the more knowledgeable extreme investor.

Remember that the value of an option is determined by its intrinsic value and its time value. The intrinsic value is the amount, if any, that an option is in the money. The time value is a little trickier, but it's a price that reflects the time remaining and the volatility of the stock, all of which come together in what's called the *premium*, which is what you pay for the option (not including commissions). There are formulas used to determine time value and formulas used to determine

> The **time value** is a little **trickier**, but **it's** a **price** that **reflects** the **time remaining** and the **volatility** of the **stock.**

On The Edge

Linda Tors is a homemaker in a suburban community north of New York City. She is in her mid-40s, married and the mother of two young daughters. On weekdays, while her husband works and the kids are in school, Linda trades stock options from her home on a quiet, tree-lined street.

She learned stock options by working as a metals trader in commodity futures (see Chapter 9), which led to her becoming an options broker on the floor of the American Stock Exchange for a company called Timber Hill Group. Then it came time to settle down and begin raising a family, and that meant leaving the fast-paced, demanding life of a full-time professional floor trader behind. Or did it?

In the fall of 1999, Linda opened an online trading account with Interactive Brokers (www.interactivebrokers.com), a subsidiary of her old employer, Timber Hill Group. Her primary interest was in this company's unique ability to give her direct trading access to all four options markets at the same time—American Stock Exchange (AMEX); Chicago Board of Options Exchange (CBOE); Philadelphia Exchange (PHLX); and Pacific Exchange (PCX). "I have the bid and offer information from each exchange in front of me at all times," she says. This gives her an edge even pros working on the floor don't have because they cannot trade the other exchanges. Having all four at her disposal allows her to find the absolute best price in any market at any given moment.

For the past seven months (as of this writing), Linda's day has begun with dropping the girls off at school and returning home at 9:15 a.m. While firing up the computer and going online, she listens to CNBC on television, deciphering what the spin doctors are saying. She gleans news about the market, gathers insights on particular stocks with a high profile that day, and pays attention to how big brokerages are rating certain companies and their stocks. From an options standpoint, she looks for trends that will help keep her a step ahead of what the pack is currently trading.

When the market opens at 9:30 a.m., she looks for activity of interest. Once she gets a feel for that day's market, if there's something she wants to take a position in or something that looks like it's going to be moving, "I jump on the bandwagon," she says, and starts actively trading.

In a quiet house, in the glare of her computer screen, this day she looks at Microsoft, which is now trading at 71. She chooses to buy a May 60 call. She clicks her mouse to buy 5 contracts (each contract is an option on 100 shares) at 11 5/8, so she has just spent a little more than $5,800 ($11.625 x 5

Continued on next page

Continued from previous page

contracts x 100 shares per contract). Her desired exit point is 11 7/8. It could happen in seconds…or tomorrow…or never. When it does rise the quarter-point she's looking for, with another click of her mouse, she'll sell her option and pocket a tidy $125 profit (5 contracts x 100 shares per contract x $0.25 profit = $125). "And I'm a happy trader," she chuckles. And so it goes week-day mornings in the Tors household.

She does this for two hours each morning. "I have to leave the house at 11:30 a.m. to pick up one child from school," she adds, "but if it's an active day, I'll come back and trade for another [few hours], until 3:15 p.m., when I leave to pick up my other child from school."

So how is she doing? "I opened my account with a small amount of money—only $3,000 in the fall of 1999," she says. "I try to average about $2,000 a week. Obviously, some days are better than others." Her best day ever? "I made about $7,000 in one day," she smiles. Her average? "My target is $500 a day."

Is Linda Tors an extreme investor? If she can take a $3,000 account and build it up to $35,000 in just seven months—trading stock options from home, just a few hours a day—on her block, Linda Tors is extreme. Knowing what we know about options trading, heck, she's extreme on any block.

Her suggestion to anyone interested in options trading? "I happened to have stock option trading experience, so I started with a leg up, but if I didn't, I'd read books, visit online brokerages, gather information and then just do it," she says. "Open an account with a small amount of risk capital, start trading just one con-tract at a time in inexpensive options, and you'll quickly get a feel for it. Then, if stock options are for you, you can ramp it up from there."

> "I **have** to **leave** the **house** at **11:30** a.m. to **pick up** one **child** from **school, but** if **it's** an **active** day, I'll come **back** and **trade** for **another few** hours."

what the estimated cost of an option should be. Suffice it to say, by way of explanation, that the price you pay for any option is ultimately deter-mined by the bid and ask—i.e., what a willing buyer decides he would like to pay for an option, and what a willing seller decides he would accept for the option. Formulas do not create the market price; buyers and sellers do.

The Stock Options Option

complex strategy

Once again, back to Ron. And for what it's worth, know that Ron doesn't always make winning trades. He was recently beaten up on two airline options, for example, when he bought calls just before some clown decided to cut oil production, so fuel prices went up, thus making it more expensive for planes to fly, making the whole transportation sector tank. The moral? Some of the best-laid plans go haywire for reasons you can't possibly anticipate.

Anyway, another key to trading options lies in understanding some of the trickier maneuvers that are available to options traders. So let's look at what Ron might have done with his Raytheon put option had he decided to pursue a more complex strategy.

When To Hold? When To Fold?

Let's assume that Ron's October 65 put had increased in value because Raytheon had dropped to $60. Remember that one put option gives him the right to sell 100 shares at $65. If Raytheon is trading at $60 and Ron can sell at $65, that's $5 per share better than the market price. So in this case, Ron's option is in the money, and he'd likely be thinking about selling his put. Does he have alternatives?

In this example, Ron is thinking about selling his put, which means he's obviously concluded that Raytheon isn't going to drop much further. In fact, let's say he thinks it may even go up again. Instead of selling his put and keeping the profit, he buys an October 60 call to protect his profit while opening up a new opportunity for making money. Here's how that works:

If he holds both call and put options until expiration and the stock ends up at $60, his call is worthless. (The calls had a $60 strike price, so it wouldn't be prudent to exercise an option to buy a stock at $60 if it's worth $60.) But his put is still worth $5 because his $65 put allows him to sell at $65, even though the stock price is at $60 (see the $5 profit?).

If the stock goes back up to $65, his put is now worthless, but his call is worth $5. His call option allows him to buy shares at

Some of the **best-laid plans** go **haywire** for **reasons** you can't **possibly anticipate.**

$60, when they're trading at $65, which gives him $5 profit. But his put option, which allows him to sell at $65, has no value at all because the stock is already trading at $65 on the open market.

Anything in between will net out to $5 worth of profit, too, as the put and call are both then valuable. As one goes up, the other goes down, right up until the stock reaches a maximum of $65 or a minimum of $60.

If the stock goes lower than $60 or higher than $65, Ron makes money in proportion to how far the stock goes in either direction, and it's virtually risk-free. One option will expire worthless, but the other one will be profitable according to how far the stock climbs or drops above 65 or below 60. (We've not factored in the costs of the options, which means that if the stock remains in this $60 to $65 range, Ron may lose more on the cost of the worthless option than he makes on the profit of the valuable option, but for understanding this example, you can forget this detail—the point is that the risk is very small.)

"I'm Sure" Vs. "I Think"

Ron could have taken another route that's called a bear spread, which options traders can do when they think a stock is headed down but are not entirely confident. In this case, the options trader would buy one put and sell another put with a lower strike price.

For example, let's say Raytheon is trading at $69 per share. Let's also say that the October 70 puts are trading at $6, and the October 65 puts are trading at $4.

Ron would buy the October 70 put and sell the October 65 put. That means he would spend $6 multiplied by 100 ($600) to buy one October 70 put contract, but he would receive $4 multiplied by 100 ($400) as payment (the premium) for selling the put and thus the rights associated with fulfilling his end of the put options contract (i.e., for the put he sells, Ron will have to buy 100 shares at $65 from the holder of that option no matter what the current stock price is).

Now say October rolls around. The worst-case scenario is that Raytheon closes above $70. If it does, Ron only loses $200—the difference between what he paid for the put and what he received for the put he sold ($600 - $400 = $200).

If Raytheon ends up at $65, however, the put he bought is in the

The Stock Options Option

money by $500, and the put he sold will die worthless. If the stock goes to $60, the put he bought is in the money by $1,000, but he has to honor his obligation on the contract he sold, so he will lose $500, but remember he made $400 just by selling the contract in the first place, so he ends up making $900.

Delta Dawns For The Extreme Investor

If you're considering options, it's because you want to take a little larger risk and leverage your money on a stock you think is about to move. In your decision-making process as to which month to buy (remember that typical options are available for periods of up to nine months out), and at what strike price to buy (strike price being the price at which you are contractually allowed to buy or sell at), it's best to make sure that the option value has the potential to move significantly when the underlying stock price moves.

> As a **general rule** of thumb, if your **time horizon** is only a **few days**, **forget** options **entirely** and just **trade** the **stock.**

However, option values and stock prices don't correlate on a one-to-one basis. Sometimes a stock can go up or down several dollars, but the value of your option only goes up 50 cents. What's the deal here?

The relationship between the price movement of an option compared to its underlying stock is called the *delta*, which is a measure of how much an option premium (the price of an option) changes when the underlying stock price changes. A delta of 1 means the change in the option's premium moves in direct correlation to the change in price of the stock itself.

A delta of 0.5 means that if the price of a call option is 5, and the underlying stock goes up one point, the price would be 5 1/2 (it moved 0.5 x the underlying stock movement, which was 1 point).

Delta is also an approximation of the probability that the option will finish in the money, and the delta increases as an option gets deeper in the money. The shorter your time horizon, the more you need to maximize your return by trading options with higher deltas.

As a general rule of thumb, if your time horizon is only a few days, forget options entirely and just trade the stock. If you plan to hold for a week or several weeks, trade options with high deltas. Only when your time horizon is way out there is it a good idea to trade options with a low delta.

S&P Index Options Vs.
S&P Index Futures

Options on the S&P 500 index (SPX) and the S&P 100 index (OEX) represent ways to invest in these indices using options, instead of buying all 500 stocks in the S&P 500 or all 100 stocks in the S&P 100. Such a busy transaction would be really cumbersome and feature lots of commission costs, too.

So if you want to own all 500 or 100 stocks (i.e., participate in their value without actually owning all of them), you can trade options on the indices instead. These options give the holder the right to receive a cash payment for the amount the option is in the money times the index multiplier, which is $100 for the SPX and the OEX.

If you have an SPX June 900 call and the SPX closes at 930 on the option's closing date (the end of the third week in June), you would receive $3,000 ($30 x $100). With index options, you don't get the right to buy the actual underlying stocks like you do with regular stock options. You get the cash they represent. Index options are settled in cash, and you never take delivery of the actual stocks.

Index futures contracts are a little different from index option contracts. With SPX futures contracts, each point is worth $250. If the SPX is at 1,900, one SPX futures contract would be worth $475,000 ($250 x 1,900 = $475,000). Big bananas. These futures contracts are generally traded by professionals, and each day their accounts are adjusted (credited or debited if there is a gain or loss) to reflect changes in the price of the contracts they own. The most heavily traded index futures contracts are on the S&P 500 index, which trades on the Chicago Mercantile Exchange.

Selling Calls And Puts—
Extra Extreme

If grasping the concepts presented so far haven't been challenging enough, get a load of what's next: We're going to switch from the standard practice of buying calls and puts to selling them.

When you sell a call option to someone, you are giving him or her the right to buy stock from you at a fixed price (and before a certain date). This is just the opposite of when you sell a put. When you sell a put, you give someone else the right to sell stock to you at a fixed price (if you give someone the right to sell to you, that means you will have to buy it). When you sell a put, the person you sell it to has the option to "put it to you" (sell it to you).

When you buy an option, you make money if the stock goes in the direction you anticipated. Your profit depends on your ability to analyze your situation and ride the trend for as long as there is one. Option buyers have to constantly watch and analyze the market.

Option buyers also determine if they want to exercise the option or not, but more often figure out when to sell the option prior to its expiration date (remember, options are rarely exercised). Option traders must figure out how much profit they want to hold out for—or how much loss they are willing to bear.

Option sellers, on the other hand, profit by selling an obligation to perform, and they must wait to see if the option they sold will be exercised. That's all an option seller can do—unless he changes his mind and neutralizes his position (done by purchasing the underlying stock associated with the option, for example). The seller of an option has limited profit potential. In fact, his profit is predetermined, based on the amount he received for issuing the option. But his downside risk is not necessarily limited.

Option buyers don't have to exercise their options if they don't want to. They can't be forced to complete the trade. Not so for option sellers. They are obligated to perform according to the option contract.

As in the example at the beginning of this chapter, if you bought an option to buy your neighbor's lawn mower for $10, he has to sell it to you according to the contract. The option buyer pays a premium to the option seller, usually just a small fraction of the total stock's value. And the option seller must perform.

When you **sell** a **put**, the **person** you **sell** it to **has** the **option** to "**put** it to **you**" (**sell** it to **you**).

Zowie! Recall for a moment what a put is—when you buy a put option, you obtain the right to sell the underlying stock for the strike price by a certain date in the future.

So if the stock is trading lower than the strike price, you make money because you can sell it for a higher price. As the stock goes lower, you make even more money.

The opposite is true when you sell a put option. When you sell a put, you receive money in exchange for agreeing to buy a stock at the strike price on or before some date in the future, if the purchaser of the put decides to exercise. This may sound like a call, but it's far from it: The seller of an option responds to the buyer's decision to exercise or not; when you buy an option, you get the right to exercise.

Close Only Counts In Horseshoes

Ashton L., 49, lives in a cabin in the ski town of Mammoth Lakes, California. Ashton only skis when conditions are perfect. And on days he's not skiing, he sits at his computer and trades options. He can't really day-trade because he has to use a regular modem and phone line, so options are his game.

Any money he makes in his option account goes directly to his Schwab account, which he uses to trade stocks for the long haul—his Schwab account is his buy-and-hold account. But sometimes he has his eye on a stock he wants to own, and his technical analysis has indicated the entry point he's looking for, but the stock is being stubborn and won't come down to a price he's comfortable paying.

This happened to Ashton with Xircom, a company that offers connectivity tools for people who want to connect their portable PCs to servers remotely.

Ashton watched the market and drooled over Xircom's growth rate. He finally decided he wanted to pay $45 for the stock, but it kept hovering around the $50 range. Ashton was unable to buy his stock at the price he wanted because the stock wasn't cooperating, so he decided on the following strategy.

When you sell a put, you're selling someone your obligation to perform—in this case, to buy something at a fixed price and in a fixed time period. So Ashton decided to sell a Xircom put, and that way he would win no matter what. By selling 5 November 45 puts on Xircom, Ashton got to keep the premium for selling the contracts (5 contracts for around $2 each—the price at that time for the puts—x 100 shares per contract, so he received just under $1,000), which meant that he was potentially obligating himself to buy Xircom for $45 at some point in the future no matter how low the stock went.

That was perfect for Ashton, since he intended to buy the stock at $45 when it got to that point anyway. The only way Ashton could get hurt is if the stock went much lower than $45. If it went to $43, he'd have to buy the stock at $45, but he'd still break even because of the $2 per share he made by selling the put in the first place. He was protected down to the $43 level. Anything lower than that and he'd lose money.

Ashton didn't lose. But he chortled a bit over the fact that Xircom went directly into the 70s, meaning that he never did buy or own Xircom, but he did make money by guaranteeing that he'd buy 500 shares for $45, which the option buyer never exercised for obvious reasons (only a dimwit would make Ashton buy 500 shares at $45 when the market price is $70). Ashton was happy with the money he made, although he was right about Xircom going up. Perhaps he should have just bought Xircom stock at $50.

Selling Naked Puts—Without A Net

The process Ashton went through with his Xircom adventure is called *selling naked puts*, naked meaning that you have little or no protection from a move against you.

If Xircom had fallen down to its previous lows of the year, at around $21, Ashton would have been vulnerable to say the least. He would have had to buy 500 shares at $45 when they were only worth $21. Selling naked puts is quite risky, and it's a practice for only the most experienced and extreme investors.

There are ways to protect yourself when you sell options. When you sell a call option, for example, you are giving the buyer the right to buy a particular stock from you, which you are obligated to sell to him at a fixed price up until the option's expiration date. You can protect yourself from a move against you by purchasing the underlying stock so you already own the shares that you might have to sell to the option holder if he decides to exercise.

Move Over, Floor Traders!

Earlier, we mentioned that stock options have only recently come into vogue as an investment vehicle for savvy extreme traders. One big reason, as with the day trading of actual stocks themselves, is the ease of access individuals find trading online via the Internet.

Broad access to multiple markets has come about directly at the expense of old-line professional traders who work the floor of the four main options exchanges: the American Stock Exchange (AMEX, remember?); Chicago Board of Options Exchange (CBOE); Philadelphia Exchange (PHLX); and Pacific Exchange (PCX).

Once considered too intricate, volatile and risky for the average investor, a long bull run in the market—coupled with direct access (via the Internet) and much smarter traders calling their shots—has caused a dramatic increase in the number of direct trades placed electronically. And it is taking a toll on all traditional option exchange floor traders.

In 1999, nearly 450 million options were traded, up more than one-third from the previous year. And while the number of brokerages offering online trading, with increasingly complex order execution capabilities, is dramatically increasing, the value of once highly prized, desirable membership seats on the various options exchanges is decreasing.

> While **today's mix** of **traders** is **perhaps only 10 percent** electronic **traders** and **90 percent human floor traders**, all that is **rapidly** changing.

At the CBOE, the cost of a seat is less than half its $700,000 price of only a year ago. The same at AMEX—a near 50 percent decline. PHLX has fared even worse, with a current seat price of only about 20 percent of where it was only a year ago.

And while no one knows exactly how things will shake out, only one thing is sure: Thanks to online trading and the Internet, the times they are a changin'.

While today's mix of traders is perhaps only 10 percent electronic traders and 90 percent human floor traders, all that is rapidly changing. If current trends continue, these numbers may become exactly reversed.

Technology is forcing this long-established investment arena to reinvent itself. Stay tuned.

Understanding options trading is conceptually challenging at first. Just understanding the terminology is like learning some kind of doublespeak. But in time, with effort and due diligence, the pieces will start coming together, and—as with any extreme endeavor (whether sports or investing)—one finds that mastery lies only in practice, over and over, again and again.

Are Commodity Futures In Your Future?

n the eyes of respected economists, the perfect market-place is one where lots of buyers and sellers meet—with no specific person or group controlling the market—and where everyone has access to information about supply and demand. The commodity futures market provides just this sort of ideal environment.

First, let's start by clearly defining what *commodities* and *futures* contracts are. Then we'll take a look at the global marketplace in which they trade.

By definition, commodities are "physical substances such as metal, grain or even foreign currencies." Commodity futures are "standardized, transferable contracts built around the delivery of a commodity at a specified price, on a specified future date." People buy and sell these contracts, and this fits all the prerequisites for being a form of extreme investing.

At some point, you might hear someone refer to commodities as *derivatives*. Derivatives are "any financial instrument [not just commodity futures contracts—stock options, too, among others] that is linked to, and whose value depends upon, an underlying instrument or asset." The value of derivatives is *derived* from the underlying instrument or asset. Easy enough.

Cash Vs.
Futures Markets

There are two types of markets. One is called the cash market, and the other is called the futures market. Cash markets are no more complicated than they sound. You pay cash, and you take delivery now. You might go to the magazine kiosk while you're at the mall and buy the latest copy of *Entrepreneur*, paying cash for it.

Later, while you're flipping through the magazine's pages, you come across a postcard urging you to become a regular subscriber. You fill out the card, drop it in the mail and become a prepaid customer. By doing so, you leave the cash market and enter the futures market.

You have agreed to pay a predetermined price for future delivery of a magazine you want, based upon a simple contract you enter into, which establishes what you get, when you get it and what you'll pay. That's basically what the futures market is about.

The futures market involves commodities of all kinds, from beans to gold, and contractual arrangements to deliver (or take delivery of) a specific quantity and quality of those commodities at some point in the future.

When delivery as such occurs, it is in the form of an ominous negotiable instrument that indicates that you own, say, 112,000 pounds of sugar, which is waiting for you in a warehouse somewhere in Hawaii. (Just

> The **futures market** involves **contractual arrangements** to **deliver** (or take delivery of) a **specific quantity** and **quality** of **commodities** at some **point** in the **future.**

kidding; you won't be doing this. The vast majority of people who trade commodities contracts never take actual delivery, unless they are end users and want or need the product.)

Supply And Demand
And Price

Predetermining what a futures contract is worth gets a little sticky when the cost of producing whatever you're buying fluctuates. Just the fact that there are competitive influences out in the marketplace that may affect the price is enough to make most valuations a moving target.

But at any given moment, buyers and sellers actually set the market price as they trade back and forth on a daily basis. And since nobody

The Good, The Bad And
The Ugly Possibility

The rise in price of a futures contract can be huge when compared to the rise in price of the underlying commodity. Futures contracts can easily rocket up over 100 percent within a week, and in some cases just moments, while the price of the underlying commodity itself has only risen by 15 percent.

It works in much the same way as the mortgage on your house. If you bought your house for $200,000, you probably made a 10 percent down payment upfront. That means you paid $20,000 in cash and borrowed the remaining $180,000 from a mortgage company or bank.

Three years later, you sell your house for $300,000, and you pay back the $180,000 you borrowed (give or take, after factoring in interest payments, taxes, insurance, etc.).

That means you invested your $20,000 in cash and made a cool $100,000. That's good. Similarly, futures contracts allow you to leverage a small amount of money into a large profit. But remember, futures contracts can leverage your losses, too. And that's bad.

If your house goes down in value to $100,000, you still owe what you borrowed on it—and in this case, it would be a whopping negative $80,000. Investment-wise, that's downright ugly.

knows for sure what the future total output of a particular commodity will be, and people sometimes can't predict the ultimate quality, either, price determination is always undergoing modification.

And so is demand. When the price of a commodity is too high, people use less of it, and they may even switch to something else, like jewelry made of silver rather than gold. Or taking the bus instead of driving a car when the price of gasoline goes too high.

Here's a hypothetical case: Let's say every dog owner wants to dress old Spike and little Fifi *only* in genuine gold-studded collars. This sudden surge in popularity may cause a scarcity of gold, which in turn drives the price for this precious metal up—way up—which in turn causes the demand for gold to go down (fast) and in tandem, so goes its price. The point is that producers keep a watchful eye on market demand and steer prices and production accordingly.

But in reality, the actual price of commodities is determined to a large extent by futures contracts, which are considered to be a far superior indicator than the prices set by businesses out in the current marketplace.

The futures contracts used to trade these commodities are standardized. Every contract comes with preset measurements that include quality descriptions, quantities and even where the goods are to be picked up or delivered, so that futures traders only have to worry about price. And if the price comes down enough, the supply should meet the demand, and production should match what people buy and use.

Hedging And
Risk Management

Everybody who makes, mines, grows or otherwise generates a commodity runs the risk of losing money. Nobody can tell what's coming tomorrow, so companies that own actual commodities often decide to transfer some of that price risk to extreme investors (like you) who might willingly take on that risk in hopes of making money.

In The Beginning

Futures trading started with grains and other farm commodities back in 1859. In fact, before the early 1970s, the only commodities traded on an exchange were things like wheat and corn—basically just simple agricultural products. Futures trading was adapted for coffee in 1955. But let's go back to the beginning and see how it all got started.

Back in the mid-1800s, wheat production was at an all-time high. Farmers took their wheat to Chicago to sell because the city served as a hub between the Midwest and the East, and Chicago offered railroad access and had all the modern stuff, like telegraph lines.

> They **no longer** had to **point** to a **big silo** and say, "Hey, **there's** my **8 tons** of **wheat.**"

So the farmers would arrive in Chicago with their wheat, or other grain, and sell it to dealers, who distributed it all over the country. Chicago turned into "the place" where farmers and dealers met to buy and sell grain, which they called "spot" grain, meaning that the grain was exchanged for cash for immediate delivery on the spot.

This marketplace grew, but despite Chicago's modern technology, it didn't support the massive storage facilities for storing everybody's grain. Soon it became clear that farmers could sell their crop to buyers prior to its actual delivery, so they didn't have to ship it all the way to Chicago, and in fact they learned they could sell their crop before it was even harvested. They no longer had to point to a big silo and say, "Hey, there's my 8 tons of wheat." So buyers and sellers began to commit to future exchanges of grains for cash prior to delivery and forgot about the physical meeting in Chicago, which, incidentally, still hosts the largest commodities exchange in the United States.

A farmer would agree to sell 5,000 bushels of wheat to a dealer, for example, at a fixed price and a predetermined delivery date that made both parties happy. The agreement they entered into represented a futures contract. These contracts gained popularity because they were so convenient, and they were valued as tradable commodities, even used as collateral for bank loans. The contracts were being traded themselves, so if a dealer suddenly decided he didn't want his wheat any more, or he needed less, he could sell his contract(s) to some other dealer. Farmers, on the other hand, might transfer their obligation to deliver wheat to another farmer.

The grain price fluctuated depending on what these contracts were trading for. If a crop was weak due to bugs or lack of rain, people who had contracted

Continued on next page

Are Commodity Futures In Your Future?

Continued from previous page

to take delivery held more valuable contracts, since the production would be lower and the price higher. If the harvest was bigger than expected, the seller's contracts became less valuable. And eventually these contractual obligations were being traded by people who had no intentions of delivering or taking delivery of anything. These people were extreme investors who made a business out of speculating.

What they're doing is called *hedging*, and what you're doing is called *speculating*. Here's how it works. Let's use oranges as an example. An orange grower knows that some years are great for orange crops, and others don't fare as well. A freeze can wipe out half his lovely orange grove; conversely, beautiful weather can leave trees with so many oranges that the neighbors are throwing them at each other.

If oranges are abundant, the price of oranges drops dramatically because the supply exceeds the demand. To make sure this year is pretty much like other years (and to make sure he can still send his kids to college), the orange grower can *hedge* his unpicked oranges by opting to sell them today for delivery at a point in the future using futures contracts.

In unprotected, nonhedged situations—without a futures contract—if prices drop, the orange grower will have to take a smaller amount of money for his oranges, maybe even losing money because it cost more to grow them than he made selling them.

But if he sells a futures contract that locks in a delivery date and a price that guarantees some profit, the loss on his oranges will be partially offset by a gain on the futures contracts he sold. It's not always the growers who speculate on orange crops. Often, it's the person who depends on the oranges.

The people who make orange marmalade can trade orange futures contracts, too. The marmalade maker can lock in a price now for the oranges he requires later, so if the orange crop turns out bad for the year, he isn't totally at the mercy of the harvest. In other words, hedging allows the marmalade maker and the orange grower to buy or sell oranges that *don't exist yet* as a means of protecting *both* parties in the event of abnormal market conditions later.

Keep in mind that futures trading is generally not used as a means by which to literally transfer commodity ownership, and very few traders deliver or take delivery on futures contracts. You won't, either. But as a speculative trader in commodity futures, you play an important role in the entire economic process.

Traders buy commodities when they think market prices are lower than they should be (or will be in the future). And they sell commodities when they think market prices are higher than they should be (or will be in the future). The problem is, very few speculators agree on what's too low or too high.

Thar's Gold
In Them Thar Futures

Some investors buy stock in companies that mine gold, like Homestake Mining Co. Because it has intrinsic value, gold is viewed as a commodity that makes sense to own (either outright or through the stock of gold mining companies) when inflation fears are high or when world political events (read: wars) or other calamities strike that may endanger financial markets.

Consider George T. in Los Angeles, who has made good money trading gold futures. When he sees a short-term potential for gold to rise or fall in price, he buys or sells a futures contract for gold. The leverage he is able to employ has made him a lot of money by catching the gold market as it rose in late 1990 when the Gulf War was looming, for example, and during other times when the world appeared a bit fragile. Small moves have made him big money.

George has a checklist of things he investigates before trading gold futures, information he gets from the Internet (sometimes he just uses *The Wall Street Journal*). He checks for the following bits of information:

❍ The "open interest," which refers to the number of outstanding contracts for each maturity month, which gives him insight into the liquidity of that contract (highly liquid futures contracts are easier to buy and sell because there are more interested buyers and sellers out there)

leverage

Loop The Loop

Despite the fact that you're an extreme investor, you're never going to want to get so extreme as to close a futures position by taking delivery of a herd of cattle, a towering silo of corn or a gleaming pile of gold, as tempting as it may sound. (Nor will you want to deliver any of these commodities per your contract.)

All commodities traders exit a futures contract by offsetting it—which means you place an order (online or through your broker) that is exactly equal and opposite to your initial futures position.

If you bought a futures contract, you exit the position by selling the same quantity and delivery month contract. So if you bought a soybean futures contract, you close that position by selling a soybean contract with the same quantity, same month. If you sold a futures contract, you exit your position by buying the same quantity and delivery month. For example, if you bought 5 CBOT September soybean futures contracts, to offset that position you would sell 5 CBOT September soybean futures contracts.

❍ The "open," which is the opening price, indicating the range of prices for the day's first trades

❍ The "high," which refers to the highest price at which gold futures contracts traded for the day, and the "low," which is the lowest price at which gold futures contracts traded during the day

❍ The "change," which refers to the change in settlement price from the previous day's close to the current day's close

❍ The "lifetime high and low," which are the highest and lowest prices recorded for each contract maturity from the first day it traded to today

George uses technical analysis to determine entry and exit points, and he then buys or sells the particular gold futures contract he's been watching.

George also trades options on commodity futures. These are not futures contracts, but options on those contracts (see Chapter 8). That means the buyer of an option has the right, but not the obligation, to exercise his option and thus to either deliver, or take delivery of, whatever has been optioned—in this case, gold.

Remember that stock options trade in lots of 100, so that one option contract represents

100 shares of the underlying stock. Corn and other grains are traded in lots of 5,000 bushels per contract (so you can get an idea how much grain we're talking about here, one bushel equals four pecks—pray for the metric system—which is equal to about 35 liters of grain). So if corn is priced at $2.50 per bushel, the value of each contract is $12,500—and you might be able to control that $12,500 contract with a margin of only $500 (which is like putting a security deposit on a contract).

Each type of commodity contract has a fixed trading quantity and minimum margin attached to it—like 5,000 bushels. If it's one contract of cattle, it's 40,000 pounds of cattle—generally one railroad car full.

Gold trades in lots of 100 troy ounces. So at $283 per troy ounce (today's market price), a gold contract is worth $28,300 ($283 x 100 = $28,300), so George can control that contract for a margin of $2,000. Every commodity's minimum margin is a variable based on the market and is set by the exchanges based on its volatility.

Risk Disbursement, Quick!

Here's how and why a gold mining company would want to hedge its future production using futures contracts.

Suppose a mining company has to pay about $300 per ounce to pull the gold out of the ground and then turn it into saleable units. Perhaps it sells its gold to circuit-board companies or jewelry suppliers. Pretend it's January, and the gold mining company knows that in April its next load of gold will be ready to ship, and it also knows that the April contract is currently trading at $340 per ounce.

The gold mining company management suddenly reads a big news article in *The Wall Street Journal* and now has fears that the Russians are about to dump lots of gold on the open market, which would lower the price so drastically that the gold mining company would lose money.

The gold mining company can hedge its future production by pre-selling its upcoming gold. That way, it can lock in a profit. The buyer of the gold futures contract does not have to be a company like Intel or Tiffany's and, in fact, is probably not someone who wants to take delivery of gold at all.

The trader is an extreme investor who makes money trading gold futures contracts. Only one in 20 commodity futures contracts is between an actual producer and an end user of that commodity, because there are so many traders who get involved, which provides liquidity and a healthy marketplace.

Trading International
Currency Futures

Cathy F. in Denver has a degree in economics and some banking experience. She lived in Val d'Isere for more than a year (in the Alps) working as a waitress, but aside from that, she's been in the world of finance all her life. She trades currency futures because she likes following international events and dealing with money. She trades from home, by phone, for herself.

Trading currency futures requires knowledge of current economic and political conditions throughout the world and an appreciation of market psychology, all of which influence currency prices. Cathy follows economic policy as it is disseminated through central banks and government agencies and tracks economic reports, which she thinks are fun to read.

Governments and central banks influence the cost of money by making it cheaper or more expensive to borrow (i.e., interest rates). And our Alan Greenspan is the most influential decision-maker in the world with regard to interest rates.

Because there are Greenspans sprinkled around the world doing their best to allegedly create economic stability, Cathy has to determine who's doing a good job and who is not and factor this into her investment decisions. Inflation levels and inflationary trends are constantly on her radar screen.

Who's Doing What, Where, And Why?

Currency tends to lose value during inflationary times or when inflationary pressures are perceived. Inflation causes purchasing power to decrease as more money chases the same goods and services, so the currency has less demand in the currency markets.

Cathy considers the Euro (the recently introduced standard European currency) to be a good move in the direction of stability but with some negative consequences that involve short-term valuation, as the currency tends to jumble together a weird mix of economic indicators.

You turn on the evening news and hear: "Today, the U.S. dollar gained a penny in value against the German deutsche mark." You might think "So what?"

But you wouldn't think that if you were an online day trader in world currency futures—or if you're someone like Willy Hauptmann of Worldwide Currency Trading in Angwin, California. This little news item *could* mean that, with an investment as small as $560 (at today's exchange rate), you just made $1,250—and did it from home, using your own personal computer! And people like Hauptmann, with his trading school, can show you how it's done.

Using the deutsche mark example above, here's what happened: The generous margins in currency futures provide extreme leverage for small investors, allowing you to control a contract worth many times the value of the actual money you initially deposit (your margin). Thus, even a small move in the value of the currency will have a proportionately large effect on the value of your margin deposit.

"In a typical currency futures contract, which generally averages about $100,000," Hauptmann says, "a rise or fall in value of just one-onehundreth of a cent equals a $12.50 profit. And if it moves a full cent, it's 100 times that—or a $1,250 profit—and on a $560 margin deposit, it represents more than 200 percent profit to the holder of that currency futures contract. Even small shifts in international politics can cause movement like this to take place in a matter of hours, minutes or even seconds in world currency futures trading."

> **Even** a **small move** in the **value** of the **currency** will **have** a **proportionately** large **effect** on the **value** of your **margin deposit.**

In 1972, the Chicago Mercantile Exchange (CME) created the International Money Market (IMM) to begin trading in seven foreign currencies. This allowed small investors to trade in world currency futures, too. Before that time, only big international banks and huge investment funds traded in these markets.

"Today," Hauptmann adds, "anyone can control hundreds of thousands of dollars worth of international currency and, with the click of a mouse, can trade and profit from his or her home or office in markets all around the world and many thousands of miles away." It's like having a $500,000 seat on the floor of the CME. "Today, you can open an account and send buy and sell orders directly to the trading floor in a matter of seconds—just like they do."

Continued on next page

Are Commodity Futures In Your Future?

Continued from previous page

Worldwide Currency Trading, Hauptmann's company, teaches newcomers the terminology, philosophies and strategies of successful trading in world currency futures. Hauptmann provides custom software; hands-on, in-person seminar training ($2,500 for a one-day session); and a follow-up program of paper trading leading to actual trading with a month's worth of e-mail and telephone support.

"Think of a commodity brokerage as being a large auto mall, where many types of vehicles are brought together under one roof for you to choose from [in this case, financial vehicles]. When you choose world currency futures as the vehicle you want, I become the driving instructor." After a moment, he adds, "Now, how you drive it, once you leave my school, well, that's up to you. I cross my fingers and hope you remember everything I taught you, but in the end, it's up to you. You're the driver.

"Today's high-powered online world currency day trader can be anybody. . .from your butcher or insurance man to the student or housewife next door," he notes. "With the click of mouse, from their businesses or houses, they turn small shifts in value into buy and sell commands that are executed in seconds halfway around the world. Isn't that exciting?" he asks. Indeed.

You can contact Hauptmann at Worldwide Currency Trading, 600 Whispering Pine Lane, Angwin, CA 94508, (707) 965-3261.

Many European countries' economic climates parallel each other, unlike in Latin America, where some economies can be doing very well while others flounder. Trade levels fluctuate greatly in Latin America, which is another factor Cathy works into her currency trading analysis.

If a country has a trade deficit, Cathy can generalize that there will be a tendency in currency markets to devaluate that country's currency. Government budget deficits also move a currency lower. It is the everyday yin and yang of international currency that Cathy carefully weighs. It's a continual ebb and flow—sometimes gentle, other times volatile and violent.

Armed with a running knowledge of current events, Cathy makes buy and sell decisions based on short-term indicators. She looks at bar charts (technical analysis) that show each day's opening and closing prices, and the day's trading range, some covering a few weeks of historical data and some showing years of data.

Since currency contracts are subject to actual delivery at the end of each calendar quarter, and Cathy does not want to physically take delivery of a pile of Swiss francs, French francs or any francs whatsoever, she closes out her position or rolls it over into the next month.

international currency

In other words, when a contract comes close to the delivery date, and nothing about the market has changed to indicate a new valuation of the currency Cathy's trading, she sells the contract coming due and rolls that money into a new contract, but for a month a little further into the future. Sometimes she just cashes out, which means if she bought a contract, she sells an equal but opposite contract to close her position.

From Wall Street
To Main Street

Today, there are a number of ways for the individual investor to trade commodity futures. One is over the Internet, where you can set up an account with any number of brokerages (see the list on page 161) and trade online directly or with a broker's assistance.

Cathy F. uses the advice of a broker through whom she trades. All her currency trading is done through the CME and her broker. She's adamant

Go Ahead—Sweat The Small Stuff

If you choose to use a commodities broker to make your trading decisions, be sure to discuss management fees and commission rates on trades made on your behalf. Also, ask whether or not the broker agreement includes a clause that automatically liquidates positions and closes out the account if and when losses exceed a predetermined amount.

Whatever you do, make sure the person or firm you deal with is registered with the Commodity Futures Trading Commission (CFTC), an independent regulatory agency of the U.S. government, and is a member of the National Futures Association (NFA), another self-regulatory agency. To confirm this information about a broker, call the NFA at (800) 621-3570.

The Price You Pay

Ira Epstein is president and CEO of Chicago-based Ira Epstein & Co., one of the largest discount futures brokerages in America. Today, his company—located right next door to the Chicago Board of Trade—celebrates 15 years as an innovator and leader in cutting-edge technology and expertise for a wide range of clients, from beginners to those running sophisticated, high-volume institutional accounts.

"I solidly recommend that at the beginning of each person's trading career," Epstein says, "they do not go out and try to do it all on their own. Initially, they should work one on one with a good retail broker. Shop around until you find one you're comfortable with. They won't manage your money, but you will get lots of valuable advice based on years of commodity futures trading and in buying options on futures.

> "The **typical person coming** from the **stock arena** thinks they just **walk over** and do **futures,** but **everything** is **different.**"

"The typical person coming from the stock arena thinks they just walk over and do futures," Epstein adds, "but everything is different. The leverage is different, the nuances are different…even the trading hours are different. *Nothing* is the same." That's why Epstein says, "You need to have experienced eyes and ears on tap for solid advice.

"If the commissions are fair and reasonable, you're way ahead. Consider it a small price to pay—tuition, if you will—to learn the ropes. Beginners are usually low-volume traders just getting the feel of things by trading one or two contracts at a time." Epstein succinctly drives home the point: "Typically, commissions won't break your account—but *losing* will.

"Later, the moment you're ready to start trading larger volumes, *then* maybe reconsider working with a retail one-on-one broker because commissions at that point can become prohibitive." When you feel you're ready, Epstein advises gradually working into doing your own trading.

"What you'll learn from a pro," Epstein points out, "is to handle each trade with risk in mind, not profits. Control risk, and profits will take care of themselves."

that trading your own account (opening an individual trading account and making decisions without the recommendations of a broker) is not the way to get started, no matter how extreme you think you are.

If you are attracted to currency trading, find a broker to whom you feel comfortable giving a written power of attorney to make decisions and execute trades, and then only get involved with money that you can afford to lose. You want to be able to sleep well at night.

"Or you can open an account with a professional commodity trading advisor, called a CTA," adds Jay De Bradley, director of asset management for Fox/ED&F Man International Inc., a global commodity brokerage firm in Chicago with headquarters in London.

"They'll do it all for you using systems that have a past performance history you can review before getting involved," Bradley says. "These are high-level pros who can be found by contacting commodity brokers and asking for information on managed accounts. Some of the largest commodity brokers are Merrill Lynch, Refco, Fox/ED&F Man International Inc, and Prudential Securities."

The Water's Fine!—Commodity Pools

To get your feet wet, become involved in the commodities market through the equivalent of a mutual fund, but one made specifically for commodities. Managed asset commodity futures pools commingle the funds of several investors in a limited partnership, or limited liability company. Most pools have minimum investment requirements—typically $10,000 and up—and offer great investment diversification and stability. Due to careful and experienced administrative management, pools historically perform well overall.

Not only does managed asset trading provide diversification while you're learning what you

commodity pool

need to know before you open an individual account, but through these pools, you won't be subject to margin calls, which occur if your account falls below a certain level—requiring that you send more money to cover a negative move in an individual issue or futures contract you hold. The commodity pool still trades futures contracts, and you get all the benefits of highly leveraged participation in sometimes-volatile markets, but with a greater degree of safety. With pools, make sure you are not responsible for losses in excess of your original investment (commodities carry with them the

Extreme Investor Resources

Commodity Futures Information

○ The Chicago Board of Trade's free publication, *Action in the Marketplace*, can be obtained by calling (800) THE-CBOT.

Industry Associations

○ Futures Industry Association, 2001 Pennsylvania Ave. NW, #600, Washington, DC 20006, (202) 466-5460, fax: (202) 296-3184

○ Managed Funds Association, 1200 19th St. NW, #300, Washington, DC 20036, (202) 828-6040, fax: (202) 828-6041

Regulatory Agencies

○ Commodity Futures Trading Commission, 3 Lafayette Centre, 1155 21st St. NW, Washington, DC 20581, (202) 418-5000, fax: (202) 418-5520, www.cftc.gov

○ National Futures Association, 200 W. Madison St., #1600, Chicago, IL 60606, (312) 781-1300, fax: (312) 781-1467, www.nfa.futures.org

Reporting Services (for listings of firms)

○ Barclay Trading Group Ltd., 508 N. Second St., #201, Fairfield, IA 52556, (515) 472-3456, fax: (515) 472-9514

○ Managed Account Reports, 220 Fifth Ave., 19th Fl., New York, NY 10001, (212) 213-6202, fax: (212) 213-1870

○ Tass Management Ltd., Corporate Center at Rye, 555 Theodore Fremd Ave., Ste. C-206, Rye, NY 10580, (914) 925-1145, fax: (914) 921-3499

Online Commodity Brokers

Here is a list of some online commodity brokers, with a brief description of the information and/or services they offer to novice commodity futures traders.

○ Alaron.com, (800) 929-9982: free trading booklets

○ Betterfutures.com, (800) 427-5550: features a "beginner's corner" link, plus trading advice and seminars

○ Fadc.com, (800) 984-9686: has a "free stuff" link

○ FoxInvestments.com, (888) 281-9570: free software, online trading, market news links, free charts and info

○ Futuresdiscountgroup.com, (800) USA-MORE: offers free cassette, "How Young Millionaires Trade Commodities"

○ Gpfo.com, (800) 847-4707: free starter kit with paper trading kit and introduction to options

○ Limitupllc.com, (888) LIMIT-UP: offers electronic paper trading (for learning)

○ Linkfutures.com, (888) 272-3009: home page has lots of goodies, including trade of the day

○ Netfutures.com, (800) 621-1414: offers an "eStarter Kit" to help people begin trading futures online

○ Optioncaddie.com, (800) 780-7001: education for traders

○ Tradecenterinc.com, (800) 894-8194: free online trading software, free indicators and trading systems

○ Tradersnetwork.com, (800) 521-0705: guarantee—will refund all commissions for first 30 days if not satisfied

○ Xpresstrade.com, (800) 947-6228: has a visitor center with a free demo

potential to obligate you past the amount you've invested), which is stated in the disclosure document that must be sent to you prior to investing.

Pools execute their trades through brokerage firms that are registered with the Commodity Futures Trading Commission (CFTC). See the resources on the facing page for many more sources that will lead you to commodity brokerage firms offering experienced commodity trading advisors (CTAs) who handle the actual trading of the firm's managed accounts.

There are an estimated 2,800 CTAs registered with the National Futures Association (whose address is provided on the facing page).

Choose a pool based on its trading philosophy and what types of contracts it trades. Choose one that parallels your interests and that trades actively on a daily basis if that's what you're interested in, or has a longer-term horizon if you prefer a slower pace.

Most important, choose a CTA with a performance history and demonstrable record of success that meets your individual requirements. The more you look and check, the better your odds for success.

Junk Bonds—
Not So
Junky
Anymore

nvesting in bonds is generally a low-risk proposition. Bond investors typically do not experience rapid increases in their investment capital, but they don't risk much, either. In fact, bond investing doesn't really qualify as an extreme form of investing.

However, within the overall landscape of bonds lies an infamous subset of bond investing that at least has a reputation as "extreme." That extreme facet of bond investing revolves around junk bonds. And while they do not represent a fully blossomed opportunity for extreme investors yet, online junk bond trading is on the horizon.

To understand junk bonds, you first need to understand bonds in general, a valuable addition to any investor's portfolio of knowledge.

When you buy a bond, you are lending money to whoever issued that bond. Basically, all bonds are just sophisticated IOUs.

To raise operating funds, bonds are issued by the federal government, municipalities (you've no doubt heard of municipal bonds) and foreign governments. Bonds are also issued by corporations that need money to conduct or expand their businesses.

In return for the loan, the bond issuer promises to pay a predetermined rate of return during the life of the bond (usually semiannually) and later pays back the original principal when the bond matures. A bond's stated maturity date tells you when you'll get your principal back and how long you can anticipate receiving interest payments.

The Bond
That Got A Bad Rap

Perhaps one of the most talked about, most colorful and most misunderstood segments of the bond spectrum are the instruments that are offered with a higher risk factor—better known as junk bonds.

Junk bonds have carried a vague, negative connotation for some time. The mere mention of them conjures up distant memories of Ivan Boesky, Drexel Burnham Lambert, Michael Milken and the financial scandals of the 1980s.

> **"Junk bonds** are **misunderstood** as **investment vehicles."**

In part because of this stigma, junk bonds are often misunderstood as investment vehicles. In truth, they are an interesting option for the extreme investor, as long as risk management techniques, such as diversification, are employed—as usual.

It may surprise you to know that many of the high-yield junk bond issues in the '80s were good investments back then, and many are still good investments today. Junk bonds are a legitimate form of investing that can reward the extreme investor with higher-than-normal bond yields.

Fund managers have learned that the higher interest payments associated with junk

high-yield securities

bonds can readily make up for the occasional and anticipated losses that are part of the inherent risk when investing in these high-yield securities. With this in mind, let's take a closer look at the realm of bonds in general.

Return, Visibility
And Renewed Potential

Because principal and interest payments are set in advance, bond trading is sometimes referred to as the *fixed-income market.*

However, some bonds have variable interest rates that are adjusted periodically according to an index tied to short-term money markets or Treasury bills (somewhat like variable-rate mortgages). Bonds with variable rates generally have yields that are lower than those of fixed-rate issues with the same maturity.

Other bonds pay no interest at all (the interest is referred to as *coupon* in this context) and are called *zero-coupon bonds.* But junk bonds generally don't fall into either of these categories; they pay interest over time and redeem the principal at some point.

Bond trading has lagged behind stock trading lately due to a lack of *transparency*, a term used to describe the ease and efficiency with which an investor or trader can see the bond activity and the overall bond marketplace to make trades. Unlike the stock market, the bond market didn't grow up with a tracking and reporting system that enabled investors to see what's going on out there.

While today's stock trader has access to all kinds of up-to-the-second quoting and trading mechanisms, bond traders still have to contact a dealer who then buys or sells the bonds for them. Only recently has it been possible for bond traders to get their hands on something similar to what equity stock traders have come to expect as routine—online trading.

It's not because bond trading represents a mere drop in the vast ocean of financial investments. Bond trading represents hundreds of billions of dollars of trading *per day*. But compared to what it could be, the volume is limited. To take advantage of this market potential, various companies have developed Internet-based electronic cross-matching systems so traders have access to information that displays bond market activity.

This recent entrance into the electronic age, coupled with the inherent risk and volatility of the junk bond market, requalifies junk bond trading as a true form of extreme investing—albeit a form of investing that lacks the instant rush and exhilaration that accompanies the potential gigantic gains available with stocks and options.

The Internet genie is now truly out of the bottle, and online bond trading is upon us. As a result, investing in junk bonds may become an integral strategy in the extreme investor's arsenal.

Uncle Sam Wants (IO)U

U.S. Treasury bills (T-bills) are short-term U.S. government obligations with an initial maturity of one year or less. They are issued and traded at a discount from their face value. A discount from face value means that when they mature, they're worth whatever their face value is, but until the specified maturity date, they trade at a lower, discounted price.

> **Unlike T-bills, Treasury notes** (T-notes) have a **maturity** of **between** two and **10 years**, and **Treasury bonds** (T-bonds) have a **maturity** of **more** than **10 years.**

You make money based on the difference between the discounted price you pay and the face value, which is the amount you eventually get; so you might pay $90 today for a bond that will be worth $100 one year from now.

Unlike T-bills, Treasury notes (T-notes) have a maturity of between two and 10 years, and Treasury bonds (T-bonds) have a maturity of more than 10 years. Neither is traded at a discount, like T-bills are, but instead have a stated rate of interest (the *coupon*) that pays semiannual interest to whoever holds the note or bond.

A *zero-coupon bond* is one in which the principal and the interest are separated into two components, which are then sold separately. Zero-coupon bonds therefore make no interest payments and instead are sold at a discount from their face value (like T-bills).

One
Man's Junk...

All bonds, including high-yield bonds (aka junk bonds), are rated. The rating depends on credit analysis and the financial health of the issuer. Credit analysis is similar to fundamental analysis done on equities in that it concentrates on the overall picture of the issuer.

The analysis and reporting for bonds helps investors predict the potential risk of a default. Issuers with really good financial track records and a low risk of default get high ratings. Issuers with less-than-perfect histories and greater risk of experiencing a default on their bonds get lower ratings.

A junk bond is simply a bond that doesn't qualify as *investment-grade*. That means a big bond rating agency, like Moody's or Standard & Poor's, has rated that particular bond as *speculative-grade*.

A bond rating of "AAA" is a rating only assigned to companies that are in perfect financial condition. "C" and "D" ratings are not so hot, and a bond issuer with either of these ratings is not nearly as credit worthy as one rated "AAA." The lower the grade, the more likely the company behind it might have difficulty making its monthly interest payments, or may have problems repaying principal.

Standard & Poor's ratings go sequentially as follows: AAA, AA, A, BBB, BB, B, CCC, CC, C, D.

Moody's ratings go sequentially like this: AAA, Aaa, Aa, Baa, Ba, B, Caa, Ca, C.

Bonds that are rated *below* BBB (S&P) or Baa (Moody's) are below investment-grade and thus are euphemistically dubbed "junk."

What's Junky—
What's Junqué?

Institutional investors (e.g., mutual funds, pension funds, banks and insurance companies) have to stick with investment-grade bonds. Not surprisingly, institutional investors are responsible for most of the investment bond trading activity. This is exemplified by the fact that until recently, less than 5 percent of all high-grade corporate bonds were held by individuals.

Speculative-grade bonds are more lucrative than investment-grade bonds and are perfect for individuals and mutual fund managers who are willing to accept the risk of owning these less-than-rock-solid financial instruments in exchange for higher yields.

As an aside, it is interesting to note that during the junk bond heyday of the '80s, the top of the uppermost tier of highly speculative bonds—those rated just under the coveted S&P BBB and Moody's Baa cutoff points—were then referred to as *"Junqué* bonds."* The *crème de la crème* of speculative-grade bonds.

The weaker a company's financial condition, the more it has to pay to float its bond (i.e., borrow money). While the borrowers may have less-than-stellar credit, as long as they pay a high interest rate, there's potential for the lender (an extreme investor, for example) to realize exceptional gains.

Of course, there's always the risk that they'll default and leave you hanging, too. To compensate for this potential instability, money mangers establish portfolios of high-yield bonds that are diversified by industry group and issue type, thus creat-

The Ups And Downs And Ups Again Of Interest Rates

When interest rates rise, bonds tend to go down in value. That's because as interest rates increase, new bonds are sold on the market paying a higher interest rate than the older bonds, which makes the older, lower-rate bonds less attractive.

Conversely, when interest rates go down, new bond issues come out with lower yields than yesterday's bonds, which results in the older bonds paying more, so their values go up.

Interest rates are closely tied to inflation, which generally rises during times of prosperity and economic growth. By contrast, economic downturns usually bring falling interest rates.

Current interest rates help determine what your bond is actually worth at that point in time should you choose to sell it before maturity.

ing a "basket" of junk bonds that will remain healthy even if a few of them develop flu symptoms.

Due to the high minimum size of bond trades and the credit knowledge required, it used to be that individual investors could only safely invest in junk bonds through high-yield junk bond mutual funds. However, this could be changing.

High-Yield Vs.
Investment-Grade Bonds

Investment-grade bonds provide stronger returns during times of financial volatility, such as recessions, because as interest rates fall, the price of these bonds goes up. High-yield bonds don't necessarily follow this trend because events that negatively effect the overall financial picture of a company tend to forecast a greater inability to repay interest and/or principal.

speculative-grade junk bonds

High-yield, speculative-grade junk bonds often trade like stock equities, frequently depreciating or appreciating along with company earnings. Extreme investors who trade high-yield bonds usually track the financial condition of the issuing company and make decisions to buy or sell based on the economic picture that emerges when looking forward.

High-yield bonds often perform better than investment-grade bonds when the economic outlook is stable. That's because when interest rates are tame, holders of high-yield bonds can concentrate on things like the issuer's earnings and market potential rather than on how interest rate hikes might threaten the company's short-term outlook. When it comes to servicing its debt (paying back the interest and principal), a string of good financial results might even move the bond's rating up a notch or two.

While the value of junk bonds often mirrors the value of the company's underlying stock, the overall return on the junk bond is usually less volatile than the price of the company's stock. The total return is made up of the change in value of the bond plus the interest income for the time period involved (e.g., buy a bond for $10, sell it for $12, and make $3 in interest income for a total gain of $5). This income can offset declines in the price of the bond, and if the company does well, the value of the bond can go up, too.

> Because **junk bonds trade** more like **stocks** than **investment-grade** bonds, **investor psychology** can be **influential** in sending the **overall trend** of the **junk bond** market **either up** or **down.**

For example, in 1991, the average value on the principal of junk bonds went up about 30 percent, income (interest) on those bonds hit about 14 percent, and the overall return approached 44 percent. In 1998, however, the overall return was dismal, coming in at less than 1 percent. In fact, in August of that year, the average bond return was not only negative, but worse than the devastating return rates of the horrific savings and loan crisis era.

Market Swings
And Low Liquidity

Because junk bonds trade more like stocks than investment-grade bonds, it's important to keep in mind that investor psychology can be influential in sending the overall trend of the junk bond market either up or down. Like the stock market, the high-yield bond market can take much wider swings than can the investment-grade bond market.

Junk bonds also cost more to trade than investment-grade bonds because junk bonds are much less liquid. As with stocks, liquidity is vital for trading, and the greater the liquidity, the tighter the price range. When there are only a few people in the market

overall return

who want to buy or sell a particular bond, the spread between the bid and the ask prices increases.

That means if you want to sell a bond, you might have to sell it for what a lonely buyer wants to pay, and if there aren't many buyers out there, you might get stuck with an undesirable price. But with investment-grade bonds, more people (and dealers) want to buy and sell them, so the price range tightens, and buyers and sellers have a better opportunity to get the prices they want.

Yelling "Fire!" In A
Crowded (Financial) Theater

The junk bond mess of the late 1980s was the result of some large high-yield bond issuers defaulting, which was exacerbated by a lack of liquidity. Junk bond mutual funds were hit with large-scale redemption requests, which was followed by the savings and loan mess, and then bonds tanked. Yields between junk bonds and investment-grade bonds widened even more.

The *bad* news was that lack of liquidity only made the rush for the door a bigger disaster. When demand is low and liquidity is limited, prices tend to drop really quickly. The *good* news was that in the 1990s, the bond market went up again and investors found that low liquidity coupled with high demand made bond prices zoom higher, a benefit to extreme investors.

Some junk bonds can go up as the result of companies repurchasing their debt (bonds) while prices are really low. Buying back their own debt improves their balance sheets and can positively influence their actual credit ratings, and thus the ratings of their bonds.

Till Death
Due Us Part?

There is a possibility that the issuer of a bond could default. That means the issuer of the bond simply can't pay the interest at the moment.

But when this happens, it doesn't mean the value of the bond falls all the way down to zero. In fact, that rarely happens—and only in the worst of cases.

Junk bonds that are subject to default go down in value, and foregone interest on the bond may be postponed or lost, but often a default is not the result of insolvency. Sometimes there are extenuating circumstances that just mean there's been a financial hiccup in the course of the servicing of this debt.

Good companies with great products and management some-times suffer temporary setbacks due to short-term competitive pressures, temporarily weak market demands or changes in the overall financial picture of a company's primary customer. It's important to know what's behind a default before hitting the panic button.

Many junk bonds are issued by hot companies—Internet companies, telecommunications start-ups and biotech compa-nies—that need cash now to turn a winning product or idea into big business down the road. The junk bond market today is not as fragile as it was a decade ago when leveraged buyouts inun-dated the news.

Today, there are far more bond issues rated B or above than ever before. And the lower-rated bonds still have a recent default rate of just over 1 percent. In fact, the historical average for defaults is only around 3 percent.

Extreme investors who trade junk bonds have done so recently in an eco-nomic environment that's been free of the signs of a recession. Recessions go hand in hand with bond defaults. The good news is that these days, it would be hard for a recession to sneak up overnight.

Extreme investors must carefully watch the financial statements that are put forth by the issuers of the junk bonds they trade. Revenues are important, but cash flow is vital. Asset values must also be watched very closely. Sometimes financial downturns can be hidden until the very last moment before a quarterly report, thus making it wise for the extreme investor to be always on the lookout when trading the highest-risk junk bonds.

It also pays to be well-diversified with several bond issues to compensate for a possible loss on any one of them. Extreme investors frequently use a risk management strategy that only allows them to invest in junk bonds with money that makes up a small percentage of their total investment portfolio (10 percent or less).

Thoroughly
Modern Bond Trading

Years ago, individual traders couldn't access the bond market to see real-time prices. Nor could they buy bonds online. But through many new Internet-based accounts, you can now buy and sell bonds online.

Jim L. of Redondo Beach, California, uses bonds as part of his strategy to diversify his investment portfolio. To buy bonds, he used to go to his financial advisor at Citibank, who in turn made money on each of Jim's trades through markups on the bonds he wanted to buy. But when E*TRADE began offering bonds over the Internet, he downloaded an application and mailed it in with a check to establish an opening balance for trading. Then he began the business of buying bonds over the Internet—just like he did stocks.

Here's how Jim went about buying an investment-grade corporate bond to add to his portfolio: First, he looked at the list of bonds that were offered for sale. He knew he wanted a bond that was safe and had an interest rate of around 6.5 percent. Initially, he went to the "Quick Picks" option offered on the E*TRADE bond Web site and looked through a "Focus List" of pre-selected bonds.

There he found a Bear Stearns bond maturing in August 2002 with a 6.45 percent coupon (interest rate) rated by Moody's/S&P at Aa/A. The price was listed at 97.601 for the bid and 99.103 for the ask. He clicked on the "Buy" button and was shown a page of information regarding the Bear Stearns bond. There he saw the yield and a place to enter the number of bonds he wanted to buy.

Jim then typed in his trading password and was provided a screen that showed exactly what his order entailed. Ten bonds had a face value of $10,000; it showed the product type as a corporate bond; the CUSIP number (the unique I.D. assigned to each bond), the coupon, the maturity, the coupons per year (number of times interest is paid); and the amount he was going to be charged for the total order.

But he didn't buy that bond just yet. He wanted to do a little more research.

Jim did some comparison shopping for bonds and found that for the investment-grade bonds he was looking at, E*TRADE offered a lot of choices, and the prices were very competitive.

Other Internet brokerages offered the same bond at virtually the same price, though in some cases the yield and the offering prices varied fractionally. His broker at Citibank told him that the transparency offered through the Internet (where it's easy to see current trade and quote information) was forcing better prices throughout the industry, but he insisted that buying through Citibank was also a wise choice for those who didn't have the time or inclination to do the necessary search to find the right bond.

> **Junk bonds** are **issued** by lots of **solid companies.**

But Jim liked doing the research and got a charge out of the learning process, which eventually led him to junk bonds as one of his preferred forms of extreme investing.

Junk Bonds Don't Necessarily Mean Poor Quality

Companies that issue high-yield bonds are not necessarily desperate, nor are they necessarily faltering companies. In fact, junk bonds are issued by lots of solid companies. Small companies, for example, may not have the track record or financial backing (this is probably why they need to float the bond issue in the first place) but are often totally viable companies with products and management poised for success.

The company Jim had his eye on was solid, and its bond issue looked promising. He knew from following business news reports that the few flat quarters the company experienced were simply due to one of its big customers taking part of its business in-house. The company issuing the junk bond, however, was in the process of signing up another big (replacement) customer.

Jim decided to pursue this speculation-grade bond with a maturity date of 2005, a coupon of 6.5 percent, and at a price of $90. Interest rates were in the process of going down at the time. If he bought the bond and held it for a year and then sold it, he felt sure he'd receive a higher price for the bond than he paid for it—because new bonds coming out on the market for sale by other issuers would be offered with lower interest rates.

He was mainly concerned with the *yield to maturity* on the bond, which represented the total return he'd get if he held the bond until maturity. The yield to maturity let him compare bonds with other maturities and coupons so he could compare apples to apples.

Calculating Risk And Forecasting

The bond Jim eventually chose had a *call provision*, which meant that the company issuing the bond retained the right to buy it back (redeem it) before the date of maturity. This is good for the company issuing the bond when interest rates go down. In that case, it can buy its debt instrument back and then float a new bond issue with a lower interest rate.

Jim knew this meant he risked losing the bond altogether at some point in the future, but it also meant this particular bond paid a higher yield to get investors to buy its call-provisioned bond. So in the worst case, the issuing company could call Jim's bond back the next month and Jim would have to find another bond to invest in.

This particular bond, however, had a *three-year call protection* built in, which meant that even though the bond *was* callable, it couldn't be called for three years. That was Jim's time horizon on this investment, and

three-year call protection

he wanted to invest in it, but at the last minute he changed his mind. Here's why:

Even though the interest rate was far better than for a CD, and Jim knew he would likely profit on his original investment in the bond itself (the principal), he felt uneasy about interest rates and decided to put his money into a junk bond fund instead (meaning that rather than investing in an individual junk bond, he decided to invest in a basket full of funds so that he would be diversified). In the meantime, he anticipates dividends of 10 percent for the next few years.

Jim has been busily gathering all the tools and information he will need so that he will be ready to invest in individual junk bonds after interest rates turn around and start heading downward, which he expects to happen as soon as 2002. Maybe he's dreaming.

But the good news for Jim is that he plans to put only a small percentage of his portfolio into bonds anyway. And if and when the momentum changes, he'll be up to speed on how to trade online and ready to take the junk plunge.

World-Class Junk Bonds

A while back, Dow Jones reported that underwriters were preparing a $295 million junk bond deal to help Mexico finance the acquisition of three private fixed satellites to be launched into space, with a countdown price tag of $950 million.

By nature, all junk bonds are risky.

A consortium led by Telefonica Autrey SA of Mexico and Loral Space now owns the satellites, with the involvement of Loral expected to boost the junk bond offering. Loral is expected to contribute about $370 million to the project, with some equity also coming from the Mexican government as a move to retain minority ownership in the satellites.

This is an example of a junk bond that appears to be not very junky—it has big-name backers (Loral and the Mexican government), even though the bond itself is not investment-grade.

By nature, all junk bonds are risky, but through your chosen bond broker or online research, you can locate this and other financial information in your pursuit of safer junk bond investing.

Let Your Fingers
Do The (Cyber) Walking

In 1999, the National Association of Securities Dealers Inc. (NASD) made a proposal to the Securities and Exchange Commission seeking permission to form a new trade reporting and transaction dissemination system for corporate bonds. If the SEC approves the measure, the NASD will begin reporting all over-the-counter transactions involving eligible corporate bonds in an effort to increase transparency.

Initially, transactions will be sent to a reporting system within one hour of execution. However, after the new system is introduced, the time frame will be reduced and the NASD will convey transaction information to the public almost instantaneously, boosting investor confidence in the trend toward increasing bond liquidity.

As mentioned earlier, E*TRADE also allows you to search online for bonds by type (corporate, municipal, government, etc.) and by industry, rating, coupon and maturity. If you know the bond you're interested in, you can search by CUSIP number. If in doubt, you can just flip through all kinds of offerings and let the software do all the calculations. E*TRADE will tell you what the call schedules are and figure the yield-to-worst call for bonds with more than one call date.

LimiTrader Securities (www.limitrader.com) and Trading Edge (www.tradingedge.com) have electronic cross-matching systems for bond trading over the Internet as well. LimiTrader allows prospective buyers and sellers to negotiate trades anonymously and privately in a real-time chat environment. BondLink, the electronic system developed by Trading Edge, matches institutional investors and bond dealers in a transparent and anonymous environment that streamlines junk bond trading.

The number of electronic bond trading systems has more than doubled in the past year, and it appears that the old electronic methodology of operating over private networks, or Bloomberg terminals, is giving way to trading over the Internet.

Another service, Instinet (www.instinet.com), primarily known for its after-hours stock trading platform and as a plat-

CUSIP number

Junk Bonds—Not So Junky Anymore

form for institutions, is also exploring the possibility of pursuing the electronic bond trading market.

The Future Of Extreme Bond Trading

While electronic junk bond trading has not hit the big time yet, it may soon be a perfect fit for the extreme investor. In early 1999, for example, junk bonds outperformed every other fixed-income security out there.

Some bond investment strategists recommend looking into and trading asset-backed securities. Securities backed by home mortgages, and others based on credit card receivables and auto loans, trade like bonds based on price and yield. They, too, may become extreme investment opportunities soon, available for trading over the Internet as simply as stocks are today. Stay tuned.

Better yet, remain alert. Because by now, you know the extreme investor spends as much time hunting the next opportunity as he does actually investing in it.

Wait, There's More! Tips From The Top

xtreme is in the eye of the beholder. What constitutes extreme behavior is somewhat relative, and degrees of extreme vary from person to person and situation to situation.

In the previous pages, we have observed the extreme investor to see what makes him tick. We have found many recurring themes, such as the profound impact the Internet is having on virtually every sector of the financial world and investing. And we have gleaned the importance of managing risk rather than simply focusing on making money.

We've seen how important analysis, patience and diversification are. And we've toured some of the venues and financial arenas that make up the world of today's extreme investor.

Following are insights from some pros in the major arenas of extreme investing we've explored throughout this book. We've also included some bird's-eye views from folks who are investing in areas that are somewhat off the beaten path—from mutual funds, real estate and fine art to rare coins and offshore investments.

Information From
The Front Lines

New technology and concepts in the world of Level II Direct Access trading are being developed at warp speed. To this end, entrepreneurs and day traders alike seek events such as the Online Trading Expo—considered *the* conference for direct access and Internet traders—to share information and to keep abreast of what's new in their world.

Tim Bourquin, co-owner and founder
Online Trading Expo, Mission Viejo, California

"I was a stockbroker for four years after I graduated from college," says Bourquin. "Eventually, I started one of the largest day trading clubs, called the World Day Traders of Orange County. At one point, we had a meeting on futures, and my now-partner Jim Sugarman came in to make a presentation to our group. Afterward, he and I began discussing taking our club concept to a national level.

"So we put on the first national conference and expo in Ontario, California, in September 1999. We had just under 100 exhibitors and 2,500 attendees. We have since done two others—one in New York City (with 130 exhibitors and 5,200 in attendance) and a smaller regional show in Dallas (with 35 exhibitors and 1,000 attendees) with two more planned in Ft. Lauderdale, Florida, and Ontario, California.

"Our goal is to do two major shows a year—East Coast and West Coast—featuring the things companies have to offer online traders—from broker and advisory services to software and data feed—as well as providing a wide range of informative seminars from technical analysis to the psychological aspects of trading."

warp speed

cutting edge

Extreme Investor: *What are the cutting-edge investment trends in day trading?*

Extreme Investor: *What are the cutting-edge investment trends in day trading?*

Tim Bourquin: New and better software that gives individual traders faster and improved access to markets. ECNs (electronic communications networks) are allowing individual traders to be able to avoid the regular Internet broker's fees for order flow. Executions now tend to be much faster, and traders are getting the price they intended to get rather than getting a one-quarter or one-half point away from where they wanted to be. While it may never be exactly like having a seat on the floor of the exchange, it's getting closer and closer to that. Spreads are getting narrower, and individuals have better access than they ever did before.

The cutting edge is also represented in the growth of the industry itself. Internet trading now represents the fastest and most dynamic element of online investing. According to a recent report from Forrester Research, by 2001 there will be 12.7 million investors trading online. That's up nearly 150 percent from 1999.

EI: What are the emerging opportunities in day trading?

Bourquin: There are more and more educational opportunities than ever before. Now, via the Internet, online training schools and a wide range of books on this subject have opened up this opportunity to a greater number of people. And events such as the Online Trading Expo make it even easier to pull all these things together, in one location, where both experienced traders and beginners can meet offline and face to face to explore new technologies, enhance techniques and exchange or obtain the latest information. It's a great starting place and probably one of the best ways to find out if day trading is really for you.

EI: Where might investors look for up-to-the-minute information on day trading?

> "While **it** may **never** be **exactly** **like** having a **seat** on the **floor** of the **exchange**, it's getting **closer** and **closer** to that. **Spreads** are getting **narrower**, and **individuals** have **better** **access** than they ever did **before.**"

Wait, There's More! Tips From The Top

Bourquin: I would certainly seek out the latest and most up-to-date book titles and use the Internet to find Web sites of local groups in your area that trade. Check out www.daytradersusa.com, and if there isn't a chapter in your area, you can go on to the day trader network and find the names and addresses of others near you interested in forming a chapter. You can also access our site—www.onlinetradingexpo.com—for both conference information and announcements of many new products and services, or call (888) 411-EXPO.

> ## "The **best defense** against **losing** or **making** mistakes is **getting** a **good education.**"

EI: What do you see ahead for day trading?

Bourquin: I see 24-hours-a-day/ 7-days-a-week computerized trading. Not too far down the line, I think you'll be able to trade currency, like Japanese yen, on the same platform as Amazon or IBM stock. You'll be able to trade any commodity or stock on one worldwide exchange around the clock—and without a spread. If it's trading at 120, that's what it is. Pure and simple. It may take a while, but I think it's inevitable.

EI: Words of wisdom?

Bourquin: The best defense against losing or making mistakes is getting a good education.

Hitting
The Books

From the brokerages and software system providers to day traders themselves, if there is a single recurring theme all throughout the rapidly changing Level II Direct Access arena, it is *education*. Period.

John O'Donnell, CEO
Online Trading Academy, Irvine, California

"I've been investing in the stock market since 1968 and have been heavily involved in direct access trading for the last two years," says O'Donnell. "Today our school is considered the leading direct access education entity in the world. We host classes in Irvine and—including the mobile boot-camp classes we take to various major metropolitan areas all over the world—I'd say we've trained more than 1,500 students to date, and we will soon be opening permanent licensed training facilities in many more cities worldwide."

EI: What are the cutting-edge trends in day trading education?

John O'Donnell: It is the transfer of the active stock trader—or extreme investor/trader—to the Level II DAT [direct access trading] platform. Today, it is estimated that half the American population directly or indirectly owns stock, and of these 100 to 150 million or so people, about 12 million people (or roughly 10 percent) are trading online via conventional and discount Level I brokerages.

Of these, only about 50,000 are highly active or "extreme investors," averaging about 20 trades a day. This small group, however, represents 76 percent of all online trading volume. So in reality, less than one-half of 1 percent of the online trading community does more than three-quarters of the transaction volume. This is a huge development, and it has all happened in the past 24 to 36 months.

The trend is that the active trader—sometimes called the semiprofessional trader—has emerged, and via the Internet, access to decision support tools and trading systems has become readily available. And perhaps the most cutting-edge investment trend today is that the platform the general public has access to has become more fair and a more level playing field for everyone. And that is a mega-trend.

The other cutting-edge trend is that old financial institutions, like the New York Stock Exchange, are undergoing major transformation and literally reinventing themselves. Because of technology, their systems are becoming more transparent (more visible, with greater breadth and depth of information for the investor) and more like that of Level II Direct Access trading. Another major paradigm shift is that this trend is also global, whereby all stocks and markets are becoming connected through this Level II platform.

> **"Today**, it is **estimated** that **half** the **American population** directly or indirectly **owns stock.**"

EI: What are the emerging new opportunities?

O'Donnell: It is for the average individual to get an education and learn how to access more advanced professional decision support tools on a part-time basis, at their leisure. You can now enjoy similar trading benefits that professional traders and insiders have enjoyed for years that have never been available or affordable until now. You just have to take the time and initiative to go out and learn how to use these tools.

As an example, before PCs, who could afford computing power when all you had were huge mainframes? But once things opened up and became affordable, and you could quickly and easily learn how to use it, look how things changed.

EI: What should the average investor do to become a more extreme trader?

O'Donnell: As tools become better, faster and cheaper, average investors should invest in themselves and get a formal education in their use from a course or a mentor vs. trying to learn by trial and error.

EI: Where might potential extreme investors look for more information?

O'Donnell: Our Web site—www.tradingacademy.com—has a "Wow" section with more than 200 links to other informational Web sites on day trading and related topics. We also have a sample one-hour tutorial you can take free of charge over the Internet. Or contact us and we'll send you a free CD-ROM: Online Trading Academy, 4199 Campus Dr., Ste. G, Irvine, CA 92612, (888) 841-841, fax: (949) 854-4056.

EI: What do you see in the future?

O'Donnell: I see faster, cheaper, better—for larger and larger segments of the population—with DAT connecting all the markets of the world in the decade ahead.

EI: Words of wisdom?

O'Donnell: Take it slow and get some professional coaching.

The Direct
Approach

One of today's most successful broker-dealers dedicated to training, developing and serving the professional day trader looks at succeeding in today's fast-paced industry and ponders what may lie in store just beyond the horizon.

Marc Friedfertig, CEO and founder
Broadway Trading LLC, New York City

Co-author of the bestselling books *The Electronic Day Trader* and *Electronic Day Trader Secrets* (McGraw-Hill), written with George West

"I've been involved in the markets for 20 years and have traded full time since 1988," Friedfertig says. "I was a professional market maker, and I recognized that changes in technology and the regulatory environment now allowed people to apply the techniques and strategies I was using as a market maker—as a floor trader—from almost anywhere.

"I saw that as an opportunity, and what has happened as a result is that the category of professional day trader has gone from the professional floor trader—or someone with a seat on the exchange, or on a trading desk at a Goldman Sachs or Morgan Stanley—to now include virtually anyone anywhere who has the right tools, the right training and the right amount of capital behind them. Instant access and fast, low-cost executions are the key.

"In 1995, I began setting up a business to take advantage of this and in 1997 opened Broadway Trading as a broker-dealer specializing in direct access training and day trading. I'd say at least 2,000 people have taken our training program. Today, we have about 800 active customers doing about 100,000 or more transactions a day—which typically represents from 1 to 1 1/2 percent of NASDAQ's total trading volume on any given day."

EI: What are the cutting-edge trends in day trading?

Marc Friedfertig: We built our business on the premise that individual investors can now access the market in a manner similar to Wall Street professionals—and the pros have historically always made money. Therefore, if we teach individuals the same strategies and tech-

> "The **category** of **professional** day **trader** has **gone** from the **professional** floor **trader** to **now** include **virtually anyone anywhere** who **has** the **right tools**, the **right training** and the **right amount** of **capital.**"

instant access

Wait, There's More! Tips From The Top

niques these pros use, they should be able to make money, too. And I think we have proved that premise to be true. The cutting-edge

> ## "NASDAQ is forming **alliances** with **Canada** and **Europe**, which **sets** the **stage** for **around-the-clock trading** and **cross-marketization.**"

trends that come out of that are the broadening of the professional trader market and the growing number of those who can now partake as a result of new technology and regulatory changes.

Also, the markets—NASDAQ in particular—are becoming more open and accessible where customers are trading with other customers as opposed to trading strictly with market makers. ECNs are making this possible—providing more liquidity, cutting out the middleman—and they put investors closer to the price they want vs. getting caught in the spread.

Narrowing spreads and the coming decimalization [prices in dollars and cents rather than fractions such as one-eighth/one-quarter/one-half] are another emerging trend that will surface fairly soon. Another is the fact that markets are becoming more global. NASDAQ is forming alliances with Canada and Europe, which sets the stage for around-the-clock trading and cross-marketization, such as for both stocks and commodities under one umbrella. You'll be able to access markets worldwide just like the big boys do...and do it online around the clock.

Cost is, and was, perhaps the final frontier. In 1975, commissions on trades were as high as $500; three years ago, it was down to $120, and that transition took almost 25 years. Now, a few years later, it's dropped to $12...and in some cases $9.95! Trading commissions are now rock-bottom, which means cost is no longer a consideration for the average investor.

EI: What can average investors do to take advantage of this and to become more extreme?

Friedfertig: Extreme investors are demanding better and better technology, and they recognize that to be successful, [they need to understand] how to use this great new technology. I think education will end up being the prevailing theme for extreme investors in the years ahead. People will recognize that if you don't know what you're doing, these tools can be dangerous. You absolutely, positively need to go out and educate

global

yourself about this business before putting your money at risk. You also need to be in position to function as a self-contained/self-sustained entrepreneur for a period of time before you start actually making money.

EI: Where might investors look for more information on direct access day trading?

Friedfertig: I think a good place to start is by reading, and there are two valuable Web sites for printed information—one is www.traderslibrary.com, and the other is www.traders press.com. Both offer books exclusively on day trading. And of course, there is my book, *The Electronic Day Trader*, that teaches *my* particular style of trading.

I think you should also go out and visit day trading broker-dealers to get a feeling for their style and operation. Look specifically for those that are doing well, and talk directly with some of their customers. You can also contact us at www.broadwaytrading.com, or contact our main office at Broadway Trading LLC, 50 Broad St., 2nd Fl., New York, NY 10004, (212) 328-3555, fax: (212) 584-0803.

EI: What do you see ahead?

Friedfertig: The professional trader market is just going to keep expanding; we've only just begun. I think this is evidenced by Charles Schwab's recent commitment to also start offering a DAT [direct access trading] system to its customers. The result is that professional-level trading systems will become even more mainstream—and education on their usage will become even more important in the years ahead.

What
It Takes

A day trading professional reveals the foundations and principles that allowed him to trade only five or six months last year while earning an impressive, six-figure, 600 percent return on investment using only 20 percent of his financial assets for trading.

Michael P. McMahon, professional day trader/trading instructor
Huntington Beach, California

"Over the past 20 years, I've been involved in the markets in a variety of ways," McMahon says, "first as a beginning investor, then as semiprofessional stock/options trader and even a stint in trading commodity futures—specifically precious metals in Chicago.

"In the early '90s, I left the corporate world and went back to equities. Today, I am considered a professional electronic day trader, and I am a professional educator in this area as well.

"I trade strictly for myself these days. I can therefore stretch my limits without guilt or reprisal. Generally, I only trade about four to five months out of the year, which provides me with enough money to cover my basic needs. As a DAT stock trader, I use only about 18 to 20 percent of my financial assets at any given time in the market. With this small amount, I returned a healthy six figures with a profitability rate of 600 percent for 1999. Again, I only traded for about five months last year. Some money goes back into my trading account, while some allows me to do underwater photography in places like Papua, New Guinea for a month or so at a time. Obviously, some goes to living expenses, and the leftovers are aimed at my long-term portfolio.

> **"I** have **learned** to **trade** for **fun**. If **I need** a **new car**, I **look** at the **auto stocks."**

"I have learned to trade for fun. If I need a new car, I look at the auto stocks. If I need a new suit, well, this February I traded SUIT [the trading symbol for Men's Wearhouse—a men's clothing retailer—was changed recently to MENS] on the NASDAQ to cover my year 2000 wardrobe, and I still had few bucks left over for accessories like belts, socks and ties."

EI: What are the cutting-edge investment trends in professional day trading?

Michael McMahon: There is no doubt that the American investor/trader is becoming more aware of this new financial arena; however, most seem to be far behind the power curve of knowledge and technology. Most still live off the meager tidbits and crumbs of the money gurus, news sound bites from CNBC and, now, the lure of online trading.

The greatest advancement in the past five

or six years has been the development of ECNs, their acceptance and the transparency they bring to the market. DAT allows us to use that transparency to its best advantage and empowers the educated trader to place trades into the market directly—that is to say, without a broker and a trade desk manipulating you to their advantage. This single tool has made the flattest, fairest playing field ever imagined. And it is opening the world.

EI: What are the emerging new opportunities in day trading?

McMahon: Globalization of the marketplace will allow us all to intermix. While I do not foresee the general investor "playing" the foreign markets, I do see tremendous liquidity and growth as the outside enables us to work better inside our markets. The simple horsepower of having more globally derived money available will provide incredible new opportunities for the enlightened trader.

EI: Specifically, what are extreme investors doing to take advantage or to participate?

McMahon: Mostly, the route is in education. The new tools of the trade require an education in their use and interpretation. To most, Level II and DAT is a swirl of confusing numbers and colors on the computer screen. The bottom line is that you have to fully understand what to do with the information to make it profitable.

There are three basic ways to learn—trial and error (and error is very costly), the self-study method (still a lot of error and extremely time-consuming) or a formal education in the fundamentals of trading with a healthy dose of new technology. The latter is obviously the best method in that it cuts costs, shortens the learning curve and thus saves time.

EI: What should the average investor do to become more extreme in day trading?

> "The **only way** the **average investor** is going to **break** the **mold** and **become** more **extreme** is to **face** the much higher **risks** of **trading** on a **bigger** scale."

McMahon: If extreme is what you want, then you have to involve yourself with the trading world in the DAT matrix. The only way the average investor is going to break the mold and become more extreme is to face the much higher risks of trading on a bigger scale intelligently. In my estimation, that requires knowledge, skill and experience. The knowledge can be taught and the skill can be developed, but experience only comes with time. Without education, few last long enough in the fight to gain any profitable experience.

EI: Where might investors look for more information on the trends and emerging opportunities you noted?

McMahon: There are many avenues to this new, emerging process. The Web delivers many simply by searching "day trading." A few stand out, such as www.onlinetradingacademy.com, www.MarketWise.com and several DAT broker-dealers who offer their own schools. A few books I've read and recommend are: *The New Market Wizards* (HarperBusiness) by Jack Schwager and *The Art of War* (Oxford University Press) by Sun Tzu.

knowledge, skill and experience

These, coupled with the ability to mine info from the Web, give the investor the turbo-boost to step up into DAT trading, assuming you have the heart and drive to learn new tricks and tools. Most don't, and even more don't understand the risks involved.

EI: What do you see ahead?

McMahon: Again, the market is expanding globally. The NASDAQ has raised the bar several times this year alone. Europe, Canada and Japan now *must* meet the challenge of an open market or lose market share. It is that simple. The ECN for your garage stuff is eBay, and it will only expand as the technology and knowledge races around the world. I foresee ECNs filling many roles, including the ability to buy and sell your household energy, heating oils, fuels, electricity—all on a bid/ask platform. Who will have the best skills at using them? Those who start learning early. Hopefully you.

> "I foresee **ECNs filling** many roles, **all** on a **bid/ask platform. Who** will have the **best skills** at **using** them? **Those** who start learning **early**. **Hopefully** you."

EI: Words of wisdom?

McMahon: Risk is equal to re-ward and vice versa. It is understanding and managing that balance that is imperative in good trading—conventional or DAT. Education is the first step in helping the average investor "see" the clear path. It is the understanding and development of skills in evaluation of the stock, the reward, the risk, and ultimately the execution that allows you to be profitable. Learn and prosper—learn and earn.

Back To
The Futures

Following are insider insights and tips on new trends that are (or will be) impacting and/or revving up the derivatives market from the founder of one of America's largest discount futures brokerages located within shouting distance of the Chicago Board of Trade.

Ira Epstein, president and CEO
Ira Epstein & Co., Chicago

"Today we're celebrating 16 years of innovation and growth," Epstein says, "and our new suite of high-tech offices has been designed for total computerization to handle our business of commodity futures and options on commodity futures."

EI: What are the cutting-edge trends in commodity futures?

Ira Epstein: The cutting edge is obviously the technology revolution that's been taking place in nearly every sector of almost everything in the world. And at the forefront has been the Internet, and for the first time, in our arena, you need not necessarily attend seminars in person—rather, you can begin learning strategy on the Internet. As an example, on our Web site, every week we offer a new and different market technique—such as different option studies, support resistance lines, swing lines, etc., with a verbal tutorial by myself supported by various illustrations and examples.

While this is certainly state-of-the-art and still quite new, I think the real cutting edge lies even beyond Web sites, going online and the Internet. We're now focusing on voice-activated order entry.

I believe we'll be the first in the country to release this. We've already experimented with it, and we've introduced a product called "Commodity

> "We **don't feel** that in this **highly technological** age **people** should **have** to **use touch-tone phones** just to get **limited information.**"

Fone." It works with touch-tone dialing, and you can call in and program the phone (with your account number and password) to set up your own personalized quote file, and in real time, you'll get quotes back.

Basically, we don't feel that in this highly technological age people should have to use touch-tone phones just to get limited information. They should be able to buy and sell over the phone, not talking to anyone, and have their order scanned, their account checked to make sure there is enough money available when the order is placed, place the order automatically, etc.

My company already automatically reports all fills [completed order transactions] via the phone, by which I mean our computer electronically picks up off the exchange the fill for a client. Then, in a voice we've animated like a human, it calls the client each day with his fills. When the client gets the message, he hits a tone, and the computer doesn't call him with that fill again. The next level we've added is not having to talk to anyone and still have your order done…and to do it all without waiting, all with voice technology. I don't know anyone else who's doing it today.

EI: What are emerging new opportunities in commodities?

Epstein: For 12 years, the world has taught stock traders about investing online in the stock market. In the past four or five years, we've witnessed a revolution in technology stocks—and extreme investors became extreme because of the new IPOs and fabulous ups and downs of NASDAQ tech stocks that can shoot up 300 percent one day and then plummet 200 percent the next. What has taken place is this extreme investor has now been educated to what the futures market has always been about.

The difference between stocks and futures is largely leverage. By that I mean it costs 5 percent to leverage futures, while it's 50 percent to leverage stocks. That means you get 10 times as much leverage for your investment capital. People who have been used to trading NASDAQ stocks have suddenly discovered indices on stock futures. And they have been coming over to that market in droves, as evidenced by the volume and open interest in those contracts. What those traders need to be taught is how to trade in the futures market, where with 95 percent leverage you have to be right both with momentum *and* timing.

And we do this in two ways: First, you must learn how to take the futures market and apply it to your portfolio. And second, and most important, you must learn how to slow things down to better control the volatility and risk so you can handle it. And options on futures are absolutely one of the best ways to do this.

EI: What should the average investor do to become more extreme in commodity futures?

Epstein: One of the things we're doing is developing much more of an options presence in the futures market than we have in the past. We feel the risk factor can be controlled better by slowing the game down a bit, even if you ultimately sacrifice some potential profit in the process. Successful extreme investing lies in the delicate balance of first taking and then controlling risks, and we feel that options strategies for commodities futures accomplish that objective. It's not a new concept, but one that is certainly coming to the fore with savvy extreme investors.

> **"Start** by **reading everything** you can get your hands on. **Cruise** the **Internet**, visit related **Web sites**, **learn** options…and then, when you're ready, **walk— don't run."**

EI: Where might investors look for more information on the trends and opportunities you noted?

Epstein: There are many great Web sites for information—such as www.ino.com—that are very dedicated to the futures market. They have an extensive library that spans decades of information, and they teach different strategies as well. We also recommend www.trifectatrading.com, for options strategies, and for futures trading, www.wizkid-trading.com, Floyd Upperman & Associates' Web site. Investors can also visit our Web site at www.iepstein.com, or contact us at Ira Epstein & Co., 223 W. Jackson Blvd., 7th Fl., Chicago, IL 60606, (800) 284-6000, fax: (312) 697-8778.

EI: Words of wisdom?

Epstein: Compared to stocks, commodities futures are an extremely limited universe—I'd bet there are only 500,000 traders in the whole world. But it can serve the extreme investor very well in many ways. Start by reading everything you can get your hands on. Cruise the Internet, visit related Web sites, learn options…and then, when you're ready, walk—don't run.

Mutual
Attraction

New ideas and indices take mutual funds from just being tired old conventional mainstays to the realm of extreme investments with growing numbers of "smart" exchange traded products.

Cliff Goldstein, president
TransNations Investments LLC, New York City

"I got into this business because I like the challenge of developing a new product when there are already 11,000 on the market," says Goldstein. "That's referring to the number of SEC-registered '40-act' [1940 Securities Act] mutual funds available today. I was originally an attorney but was intrigued by the idea of finding new opportunities emerging within these 11,000 existing funds. I rule out all sorts of ideas for niche mutual funds, and when I find one I can't rule out, I roll it out.

"We look for different exposure than anything else being offered by anyone else. In essence, we group and repackage things in what we believe to be a more efficient wrapper. For example, if you and I were to say we felt satellites in outer space were likely to be prominent in the future, the question would then be: 'Why don't we coordinate a global satellite mutual fund?' Instead of focusing on telecommunications or aerospace or whatever else satellites might have been previously classified as, we're going to isolate them and create a fund solely focused on this technology alone.

"For example, markets around the world are developing—and consumers are purchasing—goods in countries like China, the former Soviet Union and India. After they purchase the basics, what would be the next item they want to purchase? We might very well speculate that it would be cosmetics. So we in turn create a global cosmetics index that isolates these products from their current positions in everything from retail chain operations to pharmaceutical companies into a true cosmetics grouping instead."

EI: What are the cutting-edge investment trends in mutual funds?

Cliff Goldstein: The most exciting new concept and thing of the future is the *exchange-traded* mutual funds—and it's the last time mutual funds will be viewed as just another version of Dad's ancient Oldsmobile. Up until now, they've been slow, lethargic and conservative...and because they *pool* stocks, people perceive them as being mundane, mediocre and average. I disagree. I think there are opportunities to use these staid, conservative vehicles in a different sort of way.

Today, day trading is king, and the opportunity has now arisen to trade mutual funds as well. And rather than getting into a mutual fund for five or 10 years and listening to the pitches about long-term growth, you can leverage your mutual fund investment; you can hedge them, margin them and day-trade them. Right now it's an extremely small, limited opportunity with very few products available on the American Stock Exchange (AMEX). But in the next 10 years, you're going to see hundreds of these products rolled out.

exchange-traded mutual funds

AMEX is the sponsor of products called Spiders (SPY) and Diamonds (DIA), etc.—and there are 57 index-based exchange trade mutual funds coming out this summer from Barclay's. Then there are 12 more from someone else right behind that and then everybody's going to be doing it.

EI: What should the average investor do to become more extreme in mutual funds?

Goldstein: The entry point is the Spiders and Diamonds I mentioned, and people should become familiar with holding index-based exchange-traded mutual funds such as these in their portfolios, either because they're interested in the fact that they can be margined, leveraged and day-traded or because it's simply the most cost-effective way to purchase that index. It's cheaper to buy a SPY than it is to buy anybody's best regular mutual fund. This is only stage one. The trick is, as these things roll out, to move away from basic industries like the Dow and the S&P.

In stage two, the more extreme investor will be looking for more aggressive indices and will move away from things like the S&P 500 and seek out an emerging market-

> **"Today,** day trading is **king,** and the **opportunity** has now **arisen** to **trade mutual funds** as well."

Wait, There's More! Tips From The Top

based index, a single-country index or sector index instead. Here is an example from the recent past. A few years ago, *Red Herring* became a very popular magazine, and it came out with its own index. When things like this happen, you should perk up and take a look at what it is they've packaged—and if

> **"Late-comers** have **missed** the **curve**, and **they're never going** to **improve** on the original **idea."**

it's different from any other package or grouping out there, then it should be considered for diversification.

In the future, the bottom line is if a fund product is being offered by 10 different mutual fund companies, don't buy it. It's done. Ten years ago, there was only one Internet fund—called "the Internet fund"—an excellent move, and it should have been bought six years ago. Today, there are 50 or 60 Internet funds and probably 100 more in registration. These latecomers have missed the curve, and they're never going to improve on the original idea. In essence, it's done. Why buy it?

EI: Where might investors look for more information on the trends and opportunities you noted?

Goldstein: There are new niche Web sites that cater to investors looking for mutual funds without tickers. So you understand, when you open up the newspaper and you see mutual funds listed or you go to your financial info Web site and type in a symbol, what you'll find by definition are larger, older mutual funds—because to get a ticker symbol you need 1,000 investors or $25 million under management, and to get listed in the newspaper it's about the same standard. So there are hundreds, maybe thousands over the next few years, of these new mutual funds that are too new or too small to have tickers or be in the newspaper—and there are more niche Web sites devoted to index investors. You can find them through careful searches, or you can contact me at TransNations Investments LLC, 26 Broadway, #741, New York, NY 10004, (212) 425-0650, fax: (212) 425-0634, e-mail: cgoldstein@amidex.com.

You should also watch the financial news for new indices and new mutual funds. Generally, greater numbers of newer mutual funds often perform better than older monstrous mutual funds. Mutual funds have to file with the SEC, and by searching through the EDGAR system online [see Chapter 7], you can view new mutual fund filings and get as much as three to nine months lead on new offerings. Then contact the listed attorney for more information. It's a parallel to the IPO market. It's really a question of who knows about it and when it's going to happen. It's like an IPO for mutual funds in that regard.

However, there is a day one to mutual funds, and many believe getting in on the ground floor, during the subscription period, betters your chance for future growth. This may or may not be true; however, it may take a year or more for a new fund to get around to your broker, so he or she is not always a good source for these new mutual funds and indexes.

We are also offering two new mutual fund indices: AMIDEX, which is all Israeli stocks (Why? Because no one has done it before) and the ISDAQ, which is the 20 largest Israeli companies traded on the NASDAQ (again for the same reason). I'd be happy to discuss these offerings with any interested investors.

EI: *What do you see ahead?*

Goldstein: The exchange-traded mutual funds mentioned earlier and leveraging, margining and day trading of mutual funds. It's the wave of the future—and it's here today.

EI: *Words of wisdom?*

Goldstein: If you purchase "smart" mutual funds, you have a distinct advantage over stock pickers.

It's
A Plan

There is growing interest in unique charitable trusts that can provide great financial horsepower for extreme investing without immediate recognition of any capital gains or ordinary income tax.

Jeffrey B. Horowitz, certified financial planner
Horowitz Associates, San Francisco

"I specialize in advanced financial and estate planning with high-networth individuals, mostly who are executives with Fortune 500/Dow 30

investment planning

companies," explains Horowitz. "The areas I am a specialist in include estate planning, business extension planning, charitable planning, executive benefits and asset protection."

EI: What are the cutting-edge investment trends in financial planning?

Jeffrey Horowitz: My feeling is the cutting edge as far as investments is a combination of both investments per se and tax planning. And the issue on the latter is in trying to reduce the alternative minimum tax (AMT) and convert it to long-term capital gains for people who exercise incentive stock options (ISOs) and nonstatutory stock options (NSOs) [two types of stock options issued by companies to their employees]. My focus is to try to shift the tax burden from being in the 39 percent bracket down to the 20 percent bracket—and I would say over half the strategy is not investment planning, but rather it's on the tax planning side instead.

And as far as investment planning is concerned, it's just getting people from having highly concentrated positions in one company to diversify into other industries within, say, the high-tech area—such as fiber optics and the infrastructure of the Internet, not just Internet companies.

First, it's dealing with the tax reduction of their position in stock options and second, it's diversifying out of a concentrated position.

EI: What are emerging new opportunities in financial planning?

Horowitz: The opportunities are all in developing more sophisticated tax strategies, which is always half the battle, and the other half is just finding what the next new hot area is for investment.

EI: What are investors doing to take advantage or to participate?

Horowitz: With tax strategies, it's creating a structure on how to invest. I look at the various investments as being gasoline fueling the planning engine. And the key to success is also in having a solid foundation that this engine sits upon. Which is, for instance, setting up a NIMCRUT—an acronym for Net Income Make-up Provision Charitable Remainder Uni Trust—a charitable trust in which a donor can contribute a highly appreciated stock and then make themselves trustee of this trust, so that if as trustee they want to sell the stock in the trust,

they can do so without recognition of any capital gains or ordinary income tax at that time.

As a result, they have the full principal to work with so that when they reinvest it, they can do so into anything—trading as much as they want—and there is no ordinary income tax, no AMT and no long-term capital gains. Basically, there is no tax *inside* this NIMCRUT—only on the distributions that are taken from the trust. So what many people do is use it as a trading account so that they can liquidate their position and have the full principal and then trade as much as possible without taking the distribution. And then at some future point, they turn it on like a water faucet and make up the distribution they didn't take—and they take it when they need it.

Basically, it functions as a trading account and an asset protection strategy because it's an irrevocable trust [a trust that can't be changed or canceled without the consent of the beneficiary]. It's been developing more and more, but I'd say over the past two or three years, it's become a great vehicle to fulfill profit goals and, in essence, bulletproof assets from creditors, bankruptcy and divorce—and to eliminate and defer any tax position on highly appreciated assets.

> "**Be** a **leader** and do not **follow** the **pack**, not **necessarily looking** for **companies** that have done **well** with a **product**, but rather **ferreting** out those with a **lasting technology.**"

The only stipulation is that the IRS sets a rule that there has to be a 10 percent residual that goes to charity upon the donor's death. It's completely legal, fairly widespread and growing in popularity. I would consider this a tax structure that provides extra gasoline, if you will, to fuel your profit goals to even greater heights at a faster rate.

EI: What should the average investor do to become more extreme in financial planning?

Horowitz: One [thing investors shouldn't do] is join the herd *after* it's already running—and just *before* it goes over the cliff. Be a leader and do not follow the pack, not necessarily looking for companies that have done well with a product, but rather ferreting out those with a lasting technology that has a greater chance of going on and on. A strong technology allows [a company] to spin off lots of different products and promotes potential longevity.

I think it's important to listen to really bright people, accumulate diverse but highly experienced strategies, develop your own opinions and invest in [emerging] technologies that you feel are going to be the future—and then don't hesitate.

EI: Where might investors look for more information on the trends and opportunities you noted?

Horowitz: The *Gilder Technology Report* by George Gilder is a great resource for new technology information. His Web site is www.gildertechnology.com. He's heavily focused on all the different developing communication technologies. It's also always important to follow the Fed through vehicles like *The Wall Street Journal.* For some tax advice and information, I think the weekly *Kiplinger Report* is very helpful. Also, read *Forbes* magazine.

Should extreme investors wish to find out more about NIMCRUTs, the place to start is with an estate planning attorney who specializes in charitable work. And you can probably pick up a lot of information from large local charitable foundations and philanthropic trusts in your community or on the Internet.

Most major schools have very large endowments, and those are their charitable funds. If you simply write to some of the directors of these types of funds, they'll often provide you with lots of free information, up to and including the actual paperwork needed to set up a NIMCRUT. Obviously, they'd like to be the partial or complete designated recipient and beneficiary of the 10 percent donation requirement upon your death.

This type of information about NIMCRUTs is often available through public trusts such as museums and public television. And in many cases, the schools or the beneficiary actually draft the NIMCRUT document for free for the reason noted above.

EI: Words of wisdom?

Horowitz: Financial planning is a talent-driven business. Hire only the best.

You can contact Horowitz at Horowitz Associates, 303 Second Ave., #660, San Francisco, CA 94107, (415) 267-1060, jbhorowitz@lnc.com.

Going
Global

The world's leading authority and bestselling author on going global details the advantages and thinking behind offshore banking, investing and wealth-building in a tax-free environment.

Jerome Schneider, author and international financial planner Vancouver, British Columbia

Author of the bestselling book *The Complete Guide to Offshore Money Havens* **(McGraw-Hill)**

"Besides writing books on offshore tax havens and international investing," Schneider says, "I'm involved in providing one-on-one consultations and services to assist people in evaluating and determining whether offshore makes sense for them. I've been doing this for more than 25 years. Considering that I consult with an average of a dozen new clients a week, that equates to about 600 people a year or about 12,000 new clients during my quarter-century as an advisor.

"Originally, I was working as a stockbroker in New York City, and about 25 years ago, a client for whom I made an enormous amount of money decided to send me to the Cayman Islands in search of potential offshore investment opportunities and tax relief. This is how I became involved in this particular financial arena."

EI: What would be considered state of the art in offshore investing?

Jerome Schneider: Well, if you're a business, the objective is to maximize shareholder value. So whether you're a small, mom-and-pop business or General Motors, the idea is that if you have a company, you want to make certain that you're making the most amount of money possible. And if opportunity exists overseas where markets are more vibrant and offer more favorable conditions than in the United States, it's possible to use those markets—and in the process of doing so, it makes perfect sense to take the path of least resistance.

In other words, [it makes sense] to go to those countries and import or export and

tax-free enviroment

different rules

be able to invest in a way and in a place where you're not going to have any burdensome restrictions on your investments. And that manifests itself in several ways: no tax on the gains you make in the particular country you're investing in or no onerous investment restrictions. For example, a mutual fund in the United States is highly regulated and restricted from concentration rules, meaning mutual fund managers can't largely invest in one thing—they have to diversify and have a certain number of shareholders.

Offshore, the rules are entirely different. The rules for compensation, for example, allow investment managers to be compensated on the basis of performance (like a percentage of the profits), they can diversify into pretty much anything they want or concentrate in anything they want, and they get the huge benefit of compound growth from no taxation. So if they operate from offshore centers, the return on growth is completely tax-free.

Those are some of the various reasons you would want to do things offshore. From an individual perspective, most people are concerned that the Social Security system isn't going to accommodate the rush of baby boomers just around the corner seeking to retire after the year 2000. And for that reason, most people have sought to create private retirement accounts.

And those are essentially arrangements like 401(k)s and IRAs and things like profit-sharing plans or annuities that allow people to take a certain portion of their wealth and put it into an arrangement that makes it possible for it to grow completely free of tax until they need to use it. And the offshore world offers much more opportunity in that regard than any domestic option because the fundamental principle to private retirement and free growth is that if you put away $100,000 for 7.2 years at 10 percent, that $100,000 becomes $200,000.

Now that can be done in an IRA, but your restriction to the $2,500-a-year limit or, say, $30,000 in the 401(k) world slows things down a great deal. In the offshore world, if you have $100,000 to shelter, like with an inheritance or a windfall profit, you can immediately place it offshore in its entirety and allow it to start growing tax-free in a compound growth environment. It's great both for private retirement planning and for those concerned about the future of the U.S. economy. Not only can they experience rapid increases, but they can diversify geographically and politically as well.

As an example, with the recent NASDAQ correction, many people lost a great deal of money. Those who were involved in offshore mutual funds and various overseas markets didn't experience this at all. For the most part, their investment portfolios grew during that period of time. And not only did they grow, but they did so tax-free. Had those people who were heavily invested in high-tech stocks and the NASDAQ been more diversified to include offshore investments, they wouldn't have lost the lion's share of their earnings.

> **"Had** those **people** who were **heavily invested** in **high-tech stocks** and the **NASDAQ** been more **diversified** to include **offshore investments**, they **wouldn't** have **lost** the **lion's share** of their **earnings."**

EI: If a person had $100,000 to invest offshore, what would you recommend doing?

Schneider: I would set up a private retirement account, as noted earlier, that invested the money into what we call a private annuity, which would create an arrangement with an offshore bank or insurance company that would make it possible for the funds to get invested in a strategy you agreed with. Like maybe some NASDAQ, some global stocks, some offshore mutual funds— but it should be diversified enough to take advantage of a mix of both international and domestic markets. Most important, the growth of this arrangement would be completely tax-free. That's what I would do with $100,000 today.

EI: What are the cutting-edge trends in offshore investing?

Schneider: It's really taking advantage of entrepreneurial opportunities in new places. For example, 20 years ago, there were only 30 offshore financial centers. Today, there are about 50. And of the 20 or so that have come about in the past two decades, at a rate of about one new financial center per year, we've seen many new opportunities created along with them.

For example, some countries (like Bermuda) now offer highly favorable e-commerce laws with specific tax advantages. This makes it possible for you to set up or use a server in Bermuda that makes you virtually immune to any impending Internet taxation that may be imposed by the United States at a later date. Even though there is a temporary moratorium on that, it is still a big concern for many down the line—and countries like Bermuda have become a haven to offset any such eventuality. And other countries are expected to enact similar e-commerce protections soon.

That's just one of the new opportunities and only one example of the type of exciting and highly useful benefits that may be a part of newer financial centers coming online. And while the emphasis continually changes, the concept remains the same. What happened with ship registration many years ago is precisely why the major cruise lines still register their vessels in ports in, say, Panama today—to take advantage of the highly favorable laws in the countries.

Then, it was ships; today, it's the Internet. Regardless, the underlying reason for offshore registration or establishing a server in Bermuda remains exactly the same—a more favorable climate in which to operate tax-free.

Bottom line: The opportunity in offshore today lies in awareness and evaluation of emerging new financial centers.

EI: What should the average investor do and where might investors look for information on the offshore trends and opportunities you noted?

Schneider: The first thing they should do is educate themselves by reading a lot of material on what's involved, what people are doing, trying to get a handle on the experiences of people who have done things with successful results. Speak with a qualified financial advisor who's seasoned in offshore investments. And then taking some action, such as setting up a private retirement account, as mentioned, or a private trading account through an offshore platform, would be a good idea.

> "The **opportunity** in **offshore** today **lies** in **awareness** and **evaluation** of **emerging** new **financial** centers."

That's basically the same thing that would permit you to trade a stock portfolio using an offshore bank to have your money grow tax-free. That's certainly a positive thing to do—and something an average investor might consider doing to become more extreme.

If serious investors want more information, our Web site would be a good starting point—www.offshorewealth.com—and it will link you to many other sites, such as www.barclays.com, which is Barclay's Bank of London, and www.bankofbermuda.com. These are just a few examples of links to useful sources of information on offshore opportunities. I can also be contacted via e-mail at taxhavens@aol.com or by calling (604) 682-4000.

EI: What are the hottest offshore money havens today?

Schneider: I'd say Nevis (an island in the Caribbean near Antigua), the British Virgin Islands and Barbados are all good at this time. In the European theater, I'd say the Isle of Man and Cyprus (which is important because of the Russian connection, and it gives you a link to the Eastern bloc countries). In the Asian theater, I'd say Singapore would be good, and I would say Vanuatu in the Pacific and Fiji will be very big in the future. The Internet is a fantastic resource for making contact with countries and international offshore banks via their Web sites.

EI: Words of wisdom?

Schneider: Take your personal strategy as far as you can take it while minimizing risk as much as possible.

On The
House

As it has with almost every other area of investing and finance, the Internet has had a tremendous impact and influence on real estate transactions at every level. Today, there are roughly a half-million informational Web sites dedicated to buying, selling and financing residential real estate.

Jack Segner, author and senior manager
iProperty.com, Bloomington, Indiana

Author of *SAMS Teach Yourself Today: e-Real Estate* (SAMS Publishing)

"I've been in the mortgage business for seven years," Segner begins. "I'm a former mortgage banker with National City Mortgage, the seventh-largest mortgage lender in the nation. Before that, I had 12 years as a small-business owner in a computer software company and was with IBM for four years before that. Along the way, I invested in residential real estate as well. Currently, I'm with iProperty.com, the leading developer of Web-based transaction management for the real estate industry."

EI: What are the cutting-edge investment trends in real estate today?

Jack Segner: I think using the Internet to find and transact real estate investment opportunities is the cutting edge. A vast range of Web sites—covering every aspect imaginable—now makes it easier than ever to find real estate investment bargains, including bank REOs (real estate-owned) and other foreclosures and discounted mortgage notes. The banks and agencies—like Fannie Mae, FHA and HUD—are putting all of their real estate-owned (repossessed properties) on the Internet to broaden the market. Before the Internet, they had to just list properties with individual brokers, which limited their exposure. You can find and buy foreclosed property everywhere now. Most newspapers have their classifieds online. Another good resource is the *Bates Foreclosure Report*, which you can find at www.brucebates.com. There are all sorts of analytical sites out there that you can use to plan and execute real estate investments as well.

> **"I** think **using** the **Internet** to find and **transact** real **estate investment opportunities** is the **cutting edge."**

EI: What are the emerging new opportunities in real estate?

Segner: What's really different about real estate investing today is that you've got all these online resources where before you had to deal in hard copy and/or exert a lot of firsthand physical effort in sourcing and viewing potential properties. Online auctions of investment properties is in its infancy but holds promise as a new opportunity for real estate investors. You can get to the government auctions on the Internet now, too—such as Treasury Department-, Customs- or DEA-seized properties—and all kinds of lucrative things are online now that weren't readily available before.

EI: What are investors doing to take advantage or to participate?

Segner: I think the more extreme side of real estate investing lies in using the Internet to explore the emerging note-buying industry. Essentially, you buy mortgages and receive the interest payments just like a lender. Purchasing owner-financed, first-mortgage notes at discounts can produce high yields at low risk. There are niches where private investors can buy discounted residential mortgage notes that institutional investors avoid or ignore. It's easier than buying property, and the yield is in the 18 to 30 percent range. While it's lucrative, the trick has always been in finding note sellers out there. Now, the whole note brokerage industry has a good online presence, making it easier to deal in this arena.

Two good resources I recommend in this area are www.noteworthyusa.com and www.papersourceonline.com.

EI: Where might investors look for more information on the trends and opportunities you noted?

Segner: There are probably over a half-million active Web sites serving the real estate industry today, and specialized searches produce amazing results. Also, my book, *SAMS Teach Yourself Today: e-Real Estate*, has a section on Internet resources for real estate investors and also covers the note-buying business in greater detail with informational Web site references. I can also be contacted by e-mail at jrsmtgbnkr@aol.com.

EI: Words of wisdom?

Segner: If you buy a single-family home that's priced under the market—because it's a distressed situation—and you buy it with a 90 or 95 percent investor loan and turn that property around and sell it yourself, you don't pay a real estate commission—and you can realize up to a 40 percent annual yield on your investment. Considering the volatility of the stock market, real estate investing merits consideration—and the Internet is broadening options, reducing costs, adding speed and bringing velocity to the process.

Going
For The Gold

International numismatists and antiquity speculators operate in the intrigue-filled world of old coins, treasure hunts and intricate strategies to bring hoards of rare artifacts to dealers and collectors worldwide. In this arena, numerous opportunities lie waiting for those extreme investors who choose to glean profits from the ever-shifting sands of time.

John Saunders, senior numismatist and owner
London Coin Galleries, Newport Beach, California

"I've been collecting for 40 years and trading for 35. I've been a full-time professional rare coin dealer for 25 years," Saunders says. "I'm a former banker with American Express International Banking and worked in Manila, London and New York. My current specialty, in addition to operating four retail stores here in Southern California, is in supplying direct-mail companies and shop-at-home television stations with large quantities of coins for promotions."

Saunders also got into buying ancient coins when he lived in London, and he is known internationally for investing in large quantities of various antiquities as they become available, ranging from volumes of rare documents to recovered sunken treasure.

"We bought a deal from Sotheby's, a one-lot auction, for $750,000 for 80,000 Civil War Confederate Bond Certificates," he says. "We've also purchased 12,000 Comstock Load Newspapers circa mid-1800s, 4,000 oil lamps from Palestine, 40,000 Roman bronze coins at $2 apiece, and 10,000 Civil War bullets for 25 cents to $1 apiece, which we resold wholesale to mass marketers at $1 to $4 for ultimate retail sale at as much $10 to $50 each."

Saunders was also a major player in marketing more than 500,000 sunken treasure coins recovered from the *Admiral Gardner* off the coast of England, which he purchased for as little as 13 cents apiece and that now sell retail around the world for anywhere from $20 to $100 apiece.

Today, most of those coins in better condition have been sold wholesale and/or distributed to dealers, packaged for presentation and sold retail to collectors. As supply dwindles, demand increases and the price begins its climb. "I'd pay a dollar or more apiece to buy them back now," Saunders says. "In five or 10 years, I'd expect to have to pay $5 or $10 apiece to buy them back wholesale once they're all dispersed."

EI: What is your basic philosophy for making money in rare coins and collectibles?

John Saunders: Basically, speculators such as myself look for items that would normally be expensive and/or desirable that suddenly drop in price because a large quantity has just been found. I like to step in, buy 'em up, take them to promoters and disperse them—which ultimately builds the price back up again through their innovative packaging, clever presentation and broad promotion. In fact, mass marketers will often pay a premium because I can offer large numbers of a given item. For some things, like U.S. Mint coin Proof sets, I have to go to as many as 300 to 400 smaller U.S. dealers to accumulate a substantial offering that my customers need.

EI: What are the cutting-edge trends in rare coins and collectibles?

awakening of a sleeping giant

Saunders: The coin market is undergoing a dramatic shift. Everything that's been sold as investments in the past 20 or 30 years is usually the finest-grade and highest-priced coins—which performed wonderfully until about 1989 or 1990. But, like many trends where prices got way ahead of themselves, they reached a point above what investors were willing to pay, and current prices have cooled off to anywhere from 10 to 50 percent of values only 10 years ago.

But what has happened in the interim is the awakening of a sleeping giant in the form of vast numbers of new, young coin collectors, thanks to the heavily promoted and widely advertised 50 States Quarters Program now being offered by the United States Mint.

This has created both immediate investment opportunities within the State Quarters Program itself and related opportunities through widespread renewed interest in collecting items like common U.S. Mint Proof sets and lower-end collectible coins.

EI: What are emerging opportunities for extreme investing?

Saunders: Based on this resurgence of average collectors, if you bought and put away any of the 1960 to 1990 U.S. Mint coin Proof sets—especially some years in particular—you would most likely see a dramatic rise in prices in the near future. Things of interest to

> **"Basically, speculators** such as **myself look** for **items** that **would normally** be **expensive** and/or **desirable** that **suddenly drop** in **price** because a **large quantity** has just been **found."**

beginning and intermediate collectors are now coming to life pricewise—and your best bet is in obtaining and holding quantities for a period of time. A good example of this is evidenced in how many have invested in and profited from the 50 States Quarters Program.

EI: What can the average investor do to become more extreme in this area?

Saunders: Simply go down to your bank and buy some of the new state quarters and put them away.

EI: Quarters? Is this really extreme investor material?

Saunders: Right now, for a $1,000 bag of Delaware or Pennsylvania quarters, I'd pay you $5,000. This time last year, you could have gotten as many as you want from your bank for face value. That's a 500 percent profit in 12 months or less.

[*Note:* What John Saunders is referring to are brand new coins direct from the U.S. Mint that are stored and never circulated. These are held until the 10-week production-and-release cycle is finished. When completed, while most of that state's commemorative quarters have been put into general circulation, only those originally purchased and put aside in "mint condition" are called "BU"—or "Brilliant Uncirculated," making them a collectible commodity. Then, the sheer numbers available and supply and demand take over, and the price per quarter begins to rise.]

As of this writing, a $1,000 bag of Pennsylvania quarters is worth $5,000. That's $1.25 for each quarter—and that's wholesale, or what I'd pay for them, not what they'd sell for retail, which is much higher than that. New Jersey is worth $2,000 to $3,000 per $1,000 bag (200 percent to 300 percent profit in about 11 months), Georgia is worth $1,200 to $1,500 (20 percent to 50 percent profit in eight months), and Connecticut is worth about $1,200 (20 percent in just the past five months or so).

[*Note:* For what it's worth, Saunders purchases at least $100,000 worth of each issue upon release. Considering the fact that the first issue of Maryland State Quarters returned 500 percent in less than 12 months, this certainly qualifies as extreme.]

EI: Are you suggesting the extreme investor should put some away?

Saunders: It's hot today, and it's a very low-risk investment. Subsequent releases may not go up in value as much as the first issues did, but collector interest keeps growing. Who knows? And as more people get wise to this investment and start putting them away, it'll increase the supply and lower the return. But then again, I've been fooled before. Just when you think everybody's into it and it's run its course, everyone starts thinking the same thing, figuring the other guy is buying, and then less people buy and the whole thing starts over again.

EI: Where might investors look for more information?

Saunders: Certainly go to the United States Mint Web site (www.usmint.com) to keep up with new programs and current releases, and get on its mailing list. Most of its offerings are not necessarily good from an investment standpoint. However, if you establish communication with a good coin dealer who's followed this for 20 or 30 years, he or she will be able to tell you which ones are winners. You'll also find the window of opportunity is usually fairly small and doesn't last too long. As an example, the U.S. Mint Silver Proof sets with State Quarters recently came out at about $34, and I'd pay you $55 for them today. I think it's going to go as high as $100, $150— maybe even $200. That's a nice profit. How many would you like to have been holding?

The Internet has opened up the entire world for specialty collectors, too. You can now go to auctions anywhere and deal in French Revolutionary coins, Danish Medieval or coins of the Vatican or whatever, and you can communicate with just about every dealer anywhere in the world. When I was just getting started as a kid in Lexington, Kentucky, if I was interested in ancient coins, I was out of luck. Dealers may have had two or three in their stock at best, and most knew very little about them. Today, the entire world is at your fingertips. It's an exciting time in the world of rare coins and collectibles.

But investors need experienced advice. A good way is to spend a little money with a reputable dealer to develop a relationship first and then discuss broader investment strategies. That way, they'll know you're serious—not just a wanna-be collector type. Also read industry publications like *Coin World*, consider joining the American Numismatic Association in Colorado Springs, Colorado, and go to local coin shows to meet dealers and other serious investor/collectors. Big coin shows and expos, like Long Beach Coin and Collectibles Expo in Long Beach, California, are the best.

Current cheap prices are most likely only a temporary luxury for investors. The trick lies in keeping an eye on what's coming up—and thinking ahead. Buying entire hoards or major portions thereof at insider prices are great deals and another example of today's extreme investment opportunity in rare coins.

[If you would like to discuss current investment opportunities and strategies with John Saunders, contact him at London Coin Galleries, 2525-A MacArthur Blvd., Newport Beach, CA 92660, (949) 251-0375, fax: (949) 251-0888.]

EI: What do you see ahead?

Saunders: For the next six or seven years, I think the 50 State Quarters Program is just going to get better and better, with more and more collectors. I think the return on Proof sets and Mint sets in going to be wonderful (it could be 50 percent to 100 percent in five years or less). I think BU coins will remain good—and remember what I said about people tuning in and out of this at different points in time. So I'd hold some of each issue. Sooner or later, you'll probably get a big hit as others lose interest due to declining profits. It's just the old ebb and flow of coins.

With precious metals, such as gold, it tends to just drift along for extended periods of time. Then, for various economic reasons, it soars quickly. Right now, it's at bargain prices. I suggest that high-asset investors keep a small percentage in their portfolios (2 percent to 5 percent) in the form of easily tradable 1-ounce gold coins—Maple Leafs (Canadian), Krugerrands (South African) and American Eagles (United States).

EI: Words of wisdom?

Saunders: I go along with Will Rogers, who said, 'I'm more concerned with the return *of* my money than the return *on* my money.' That's what makes using the release of new U.S. money issues (like the 50 States Quarters Program) as an investment vehicle so attractive. You can't lose because it's always worth face value.

Extreme Investor—As Advertised

As we said at the outset, rather than being a how-to book, *Extreme Investor* introduces you to the principles and personalities that are forcing the norm to outer extremes.

More so, it is intended to be a portal where doors are opened for you, and you decide where you want to go. To that end, we have provided hundreds of entry points that will lead you to literally thousands of opportunities on Web sites that exist in the vast global world of the extreme investor.

We told you earlier that after meeting the experts and extreme investors, and after hearing their viewpoints and experiences, you would never see investing in the same way again.

Remember that the next time you hear a financial news broadcast. Or when you read a newspaper or even take a shiny new state quarter out of your pocket. Every bit of information and activity out there is an opportunity to study and seize the day. And, if you're smart, you'll figure out how to leverage your own insights and instincts and make a profit. How extreme of you!

Glossary

Stock Terms

advance/decline line: the number of stocks that advanced divided by the number of stocks that declined during a specified period of time, usually charted or used in technical analysis. If the resulting quotient is greater than 1, it's considered bullish, and if the quotient is less than 1, it's considered bearish.

annual report: a document required by the Securities and Exchange Commission (SEC) at the end of each fiscal year of all publicly traded companies that reports the financial results of the year, including balance sheet and income statement, and a commentary on the outlook for the future of the company

arbitrage: making simultaneous opposite trades with two identical or similar financial instruments in different markets, or in different forms, to profit by exploiting price differences (in other words, if two markets have two identical or similar financial instruments, but one of them is cheaper, arbitrageurs will sell the expensive one and buy the cheaper one)

Bollinger Bands: a form of technical analysis that shows where prices can expect to meet upward resistance as marked by an upper band, and downward support marked by a lower band on a chart that displays price change over time

broker-dealer: an individual or firm (other than a bank) in the business of trading securities for their own account or for others

contrarian: an investor who acts in opposition to the prevailing trend or market wisdom, for example buying pharmaceutical stocks when the majority of investors are dumping them

correction: a drop in price of a stock or an index after a recent price rise

diamonds (DIA—Dow Jones Industrial Average): a basket of 30 stocks you can invest in as a group, just like a stock (trading symbol DIA), without investing in each company individually

direct access trading (DAT): the process of trading directly with other traders on your computer without needing a broker as a middleman

electronic communications network (ECN): an independent system set up by broker-dealers to match stock orders so that traders can quote a bid or ask price on a stock the way market makers do

earnings: the income of a company, which is calculated by taking revenues (money received based on sales, mostly) and subtracting the cost of doing business (cost of sales, operating expenses and taxes)

earnings per share (EPS): earnings divided by the number of shares outstanding

EDGAR: Electronic Data Gathering, Analysis and Retrieval, a system employed by the SEC to coordinate quarterly and annual reports and S-1 filings, and other filing and disclosure information required by the SEC

Elliott Wave Theory: a form of technical analysis established by Ralph Elliott based upon his theory that markets follow a pattern of five waves up and three waves down in a bull market, and three up and five down in a bear market (the theory gets a lot deeper than this, but that's it in a nutshell)

fundamental analysis: a method of analyzing a company and its stock based on financials and operations (e.g., profit and loss, earnings growth potential, revenue growth and management)

hedge: the act of entering into a transaction that offsets another opposite position as a means of limiting loss

high-tech stocks: stocks within the information technology sector, such as telecommunications, software, semiconductors, networking and biotechnology

illiquid: stocks or other financial instruments that cannot be easily or quickly converted to cash. Although not as illiquid as real estate, some traded securities take time to match buyers and sellers because there aren't enough of either, and thus those securities are illiquid.

income: same as earnings, calculated by taking revenues (money received based on sales, mostly) and subtracting the cost of doing business (cost of sales, operating expenses and taxes)

index fund: a mutual fund that mirrors the performance of a particular index, like the S&P 500. These funds are passively managed, meaning they simply own all the stocks in a particular index.

Instinet: short for Institutional Networks Corporation, a computerized service that allows subscribers to see and display bid and ask quotes and make trades directly, without the intervention of a broker

institutional investor: investment companies, mutual funds, insurance companies, brokerages and other large, professional investment entities

limit order: an order to buy a specified quantity of a stock at or below a specified price, or to sell a specified quantity of stock at or above a specified price

listed security: any stock that is traded on a major exchange, which narrows it down to the NYSE. The American Stock Exchange used to be considered a major exchange that traded listed securities, but it merged with the NASDAQ, which now deals in listed securities, so this particular nomenclature is outdated.

margin: using money borrowed form a broker-dealer to purchase securities for one's account

market maker: a security broker, or bank, that maintains a firm bid and ask price for specific securities and who may actively buy and sell that same security for their own account, and for this privilege must avail themselves to buy those specific securities for which he is a market maker when there are no other buyers, and sell them when there are no other sellers for the purpose of maintaining market liquidity

market order: a buy or sell order that instructs the broker to execute the order according to the best price currently available

NASD: National Association of Securities Dealers, a self-regulatory organization responsible for the operation and regulation of the NASDAQ stock market

NASDAQ: National Association of Securities Dealers Automated Quotation system, the computerized system that facilitates trading by providing broker-dealers with the current bid and ask price quotes on over-the-counter stocks

NYSE: New York Stock Exchange, the oldest and largest U.S. stock exchange, located on Wall Street in New York City, responsible for overseeing the policy and activities of stocks called "listed securities"; also known as "the Big Board"

over-the-counter stock: a stock that is not traded on a large exchange, usually due to the underlying company's inability to meet listing requirements required by the NYSE, though this term is rather outdated since the NASDAQ has totally kicked butt over the traditionally more respected NYSE, which has yet to join the electronic age

Securities and Exchange Commission: the primary federal regulatory agency for the securities industry, established to protect investors against fraud and malpractice in the securities markets

short: the act of borrowing securities from a broker and selling them (say, at $100) in anticipation of buying those shares back again later on the open market for less (say, at $95), allowing the trader to profit from the difference (in this case, $5)

spiders (SPDRs—Standard & Poor's Depositary Receipts): a basket of stocks designed to mirror the performance of the S&P 500, which you can invest in as a group, just like a stock (trading symbol SPY), without investing in each company individually

stochastics: a form of technical analysis that shows overbought and over-sold conditions using two oscillating lines on a chart

split: an increase in the number of outstanding shares of a company's stock without increasing total shareholder equity. In other words, 100 shares of a stock that trades at $100 could be split 2-for-1, resulting in the holder now owning 200 shares of that same stock, but each share is now worth $50. The number of shares doubled, but the value of each share was divided in half. This means no net change in value to the holder, just more shares available for trading on the open market at a price that appears more attractive to the average investor.

trend: the current general direction that prices or investor sentiment appear to be headed at the moment

IPO Terms

aftermarket: a market where investors purchase stocks from other investors rather than the original investment bank that issued the stock for sale prior to the IPO in the primary market (same as the secondary market)

all or none: an offering that can be canceled by the lead underwriter if it is not completely subscribed (pre-sold to other institutions or brokers). Most *best-effort* deals are all or none.

allocation: a specific amount of stock in a new issue that is given to the client from the offering

best effort: a deal in which underwriters only agree to do their best to sell shares to the public. An IPO is more commonly done on a *bought* or *firm commitment* basis, in which the underwriters are obligated to sell the allotted shares. Best effort means if the underwriter can't pre-sell the entire allotment of shares, only the shares that have been prepaid prior to the offering are actually issued.

break issue: a term used to describe when an newly issued stock falls below its offering price

completion: when all trades in an IPO have been declared official, (making it complete). This usually happens about five days after a stock starts trading. Until completion, an IPO can be canceled with all money returned to investors.

dealer-broker: Dealers act as principals in the ownership of stock, buying and selling for their own accounts. Brokers act as intermediaries between buyers and sellers and generally charge a commission for these transactions.

direct public offering (DPO): a situation in which a company sells its shares directly to the public without the help of underwriters. This has been done by several Internet companies. Stock is sold, or in some cases even given away in minor quantities for conducting business through the company. Liquidity, which is the ability to sell shares on the open market, is extremely limited.

due diligence: research into a company, done as a reasonable investigation by the parties involved in preparing a disclosure document to form a basis for believing that the statements contained in it are true and that no facts were left out

flipping: the act of buying and then quickly selling shares, as when an investor buys an IPO at the offering price and then sells it immediately for a quick profit right after it starts trading on the open market. Flipping is widely discouraged by underwriters and can negatively affect an investor's relationship with brokers, and thus other underwriters, regarding future participation in IPOs.

greenshoe: part of the underwriting agreement that says the issuer will authorize additional shares—perhaps 15 percent of an IPO—for distribution to the underwriters if the IPO is extremely successful or popular

gross spread: also called the underwriting discount, this is the difference between an IPO's offering price and the price the members of the syndicate pay for the shares. It usually represents a discount of 8 percent, about half of which goes to the broker who sells the shares.

indications of interest: gathered by a lead underwriter from its investor clients before an IPO is priced to gauge demand for the stock issue; used to determine offering price

initial public offering (IPO): the first time a company sells stock to the public is called the initial public offering. Subsequent offerings are called secondary offerings. An IPO is the first offering, which occurs whenever a company sells new stock, and a secondary offering is the public sale of previously issued securities, often those held by insiders.

investment bank: usually a large institution that acts as an underwriter or agent for corporations (or municipalities) issuing securities. These banks, however, do not accept deposits or make any loans, unlike regular banks. Investment banks are often dealer-brokers.

lead underwriter: the investment bank in charge of setting the offering price of an IPO and allocating shares to other members of the syndicate

lock-up period: the time period after an IPO when insiders at the newly public company are restricted from selling their shares. The lead underwriter does not allow a company's directors and executives to sell any of their shares until after the lock-up period, which is typically six months after the IPO date.

new issue: see *initial public offering*

offering price: the price set by the lead underwriter that investors pay before the stock is actually released for trading on a stock exchange. This is not the same as the *opening price* (see following entry).

opening price: the first trading price of a new issue after it's traded on the open market on its first day

oversubscribed: a situation where investors ask for (subscribe for) more shares than are available, usually a sign that an IPO is highly anticipated and will open at a premium higher than the price established by the underwriters

premium: the difference between the offering price (the pricing) and opening price

pricing: the final price arrived at by the lead underwriter for the issue on the day of the IPO, or the night before the offering

pricing date: the date shares are assigned a price for sale to the general public. Companies and their lead underwriter generally set the price after the markets have closed in preparation for trading in the morning, but the price is often a moving target until the last minute.

primary market: the pre-public offering used by underwriters to allocate shares to large institutional investors and their best individual customers. The primary market represents all stock sales that occur before the company's stock is officially traded on a stock exchange, after which the stock is said to be trading in the secondary market.

prospectus: an official document that is an integral part of a company's S-1 filing, which is filed with the SEC as part of the process of going public. It defines the company's type of business and the risks involved, its strategy for future growth and how funds will be used to achieve that strategy, the competitive environment, lots of financial data on anticipated and existing revenues and earnings, if any, and a complete listing of corporate officers and board members. A preliminary prospectus is also called a *red herring*. There are two stories behind this terminology: 1) red herring means "to draw attention away from the central issue," implying that the information in the prospectus is secondary to the real business at hand, and 2) information such as share price and share amounts are printed in red as an indication that this information is subject to change.

quiet period: a period that starts once a company has filed its S-1 or SB-2 form with the SEC, extending 25 days after the company's stock has started trading on the open market. During this time, the company and its legal representatives are prohibited from making any statements that aren't already part of the prospectus. The lead underwriter and all officers of the company may not say anything that might hype the company in an attempt to influence the stock's price.

road show: aka dog-and-pony show, where officers of the company go on tour to make presentations to attract interest in the deal and otherwise prepare professional investors for an IPO. Only institutional investors, financial analysts and professional money managers may attend, by invitation only, and road shows are off-limits to the press.

secondary market: the actual stock market, as opposed to the primary market, which represents sales of an issue occurring before the company's stock is traded publicly.

S-1: an official document filed with the SEC announcing a company's intent to go public. It includes the prospectus and is also called the registration statement.

spinning: the action made by investment banks of distributing shares to certain special clients, such as venture capitalists and executives, as a means of increasing future chance of obtaining their business in the future

venture capital: funding obtained during the pre-IPO process, primarily as seed money or start-up financing for companies

withdrawal/postponement: when a company or lead underwriter decides that market conditions are not conducive to a successful IPO, the offering can be postponed or even withdrawn altogether. A down market is often one of the situations that prevents a scheduled offering.

Bond Terms

accreted value: the price a bond would sell for if interest rates remain at current levels

accrual bond: see *zero-coupon bond*

accrued interest: interest due on a bond since the last interest payment was made. This can occur for bonds purchased on the secondary market (since bonds generally pay interest every six months). The interest is accrued by the bondholders every month so that when a bond is sold, the buyer pays the seller the market price of the bond plus accrued interest, for which the buyer is reimbursed at the end of the six-month period. Zero-coupon bonds trade without accrued interest, as do bonds in default.

agency bonds: securities issued by U.S. government-sponsored agencies, created to help sectors of the economy reduce borrowing costs. These agencies include Fannie Mae (the Federal National Mortgage Association), Freddie Mac (the Federal Home Loan Mortgage Corporation), and Sallie Mae (the Student Loan Marketing Association). Proceeds from agency bonds are lent to banks, who in turn lend the money to individuals seeking financing.

agency trade: a trade in which the broker-dealer acts as an agent, meaning that the broker-dealer will disclose any markup/markdown in the transaction. Agents are not owners of—nor do they have control of—the securities.

callable bond: a bond that can be redeemed by the issuer (they can buy the bond back) prior to maturity within a specific time and for a predetermined price

call protection: a period of time in which the bond cannot not be called by the issuer, serving as protection for the buyer

convertible bond: a bond that allows the issuer to convert the bond into shares of the issuer's common stock at a fixed exchange ratio

corporate bonds: bonds issued by companies in the private sector, as opposed to government bonds

current yield: the return on a bond calculated by dividing the annual interest of the bond by the market price of the bond. Current yield represents the actual income rate, or the yield to maturity, as opposed to the coupon rate, assuming that the bond was not purchased at par value. For example, a bond with 9 percent coupon (interest rate) and a par value (face value) of $1,000 is bought at a market price of $900. The annual income on the bond is $90, but since $900 was paid for the bond, the current yield is $90 divided by $900, or 10 percent.

CUSIP: an identification number assigned to a bond by the Committee on Uniform Securities Identification Procedures (CUSIP)

dollar price: a fixed-income security's price, stated as a percentage of the security's face value, not including accrued interest

face value: the principal amount of a bond (also called *par value*)

financial sector bonds: bonds issued by financial companies such as banks, savings and loans, insurance companies and brokers

first call date: the first date at which an issuer of a bond has the right to redeem that bond before its maturity date. The first call date is usually listed along with a schedule of subsequent call dates and prices at which the bond can be called.

general obligation bonds: voter-approved bonds backed by the taxing power of the issuing entity

government bonds: bonds issued by governments or agencies of governments, which may include foreign as well as U.S. governments

insolvent: the state of being unable to meet debt obligations, as in bankrupt

insured bond: Some municipal bonds are backed with municipal bond insurance, which reduces investment risk. In the event of a default, the insurance company guarantees payment of principal and interest to the investor.

listed bond: a bond that is listed and traded over the major exchanges: NYSE, AMEX and NASDAQ

maturity date: the date upon which the principal amount of a security becomes due and payable

Moody's: a private company that assigns credit ratings to bonds to indicate their relative quality, or the strength of the ability to pay a bond's obligation

municipal bonds: fixed-income securities (bonds) issued by state and local governments or their agencies

noncallable: a bond that cannot be called for redemption (purchased back) by the issuer prior to the specified maturity date of the bond

par value: the face value of a bond, generally $1,000 for corporate bonds, $5,000 for municipal bonds and $10,000 for federal bonds

principal: the amount owed or the face value of a bond debt

principal trade: the mechanism by which a broker of a bond trade is compensated, such that he earns based solely on the markup or spread established through purchasing a bond, as compensation for holding it in inventory and reselling the bond at market rates

Standard & Poor's: a private company that assigns credit ratings to bonds to indicate their relative quality, or the strength of the ability to pay a bond's obligation

special assessment bond: a bond secured by a special tax

Treasury bill: a U.S. government security with a maturity of one year or less. T-bills are purchased at a discount from the full face value and the investor receives the full value when they mature. The difference or "discount" is the interest earned. In other words, you might buy a $100 bond for $90 (the discount rate), but it's not worth $100 until one year from now (the full face value upon maturity).

Treasury bond: a bond representing a long-term obligation of the U.S. Treasury that matures in 10 to 30 years. Interest is paid semiannually, and T-bonds can be purchased in minimum denominations of $1,000 or multiples thereof.

Treasury note: a U.S. government obligation available for terms of 1 to 10 years. Interest is paid twice a year, and T-notes can be purchased in denominations of $1,000 or multiples thereof.

Treasury strips: STRIPS (Separate Trading of Registered Interest and Principal of Securities) are U.S. Treasury zero-coupon bonds sold at a discount, and they are redeemed for their full face value at maturity. They are offered in amounts of $1,000 or more and pay no interest (the interest is reinvested over the life of the security).

yield: a measure of the income generated by a bond (generally the amount of interest paid on a bond divided by the price of the bond)

yield to maturity: the return based on a bond if it is held until the maturity date

yield to par call: the same as yield to maturity, but with the maturity date replaced by the par call date

yield to worst: the lower of either the yield to maturity or the yield to call

zero-coupon bond: a bond that pays no coupons (interest) and that is sold at a discount to its face value, and redeemable for face value upon maturity

Options And Futures Terms

arbitrage: the simultaneous purchase and sale of identical or equivalent financial instruments of commodity futures resulting in a benefit to the trader based on a discrepancy in their price relationships

assignment: the receipt of an exercise notice by the person who writes an option (the seller) that obligates him to sell or purchase (for a call or a put, respectively) the underlying security at the specified strike price

at the money: an option with a strike price that is equal to the market price of the underlying security

Black and Scholes Pricing Model: a pricing model used to assign a value to an option by comparing the price of the underlying stock, the strike price of the option, the expiration date of the option, and a standard deviation of that particular stock (standard deviation is a measure of the historical volatility based on the extent to which stock prices spread around its average)

call: an option contract that gives the holder the right, but not the obligation, to buy the underlying security at a specified price for a fixed period of time

closing sale: a sale of an option or futures contract that eliminates a short position

contract: the basic unit of trading used for commodity futures

covered call writing: a strategy whereby the investor sells call options while simultaneously owning the underlying security, or where he sells a put option and simultaneously shorts an equivalent position in the underlying security

delta: the change in price of a call option for every one-point move in the price of the underlying stock

derivative: a financial instrument whose value is derived from the characteristics of the underlying security. Futures and options are examples of derivatives.

exercise: the act of implementing the conditions under which the holder of an option is entitled, such as buying a security as in the case of a call, or as in selling a security, as in the case of a put

exercise settlement amount: the difference between the exercise price of an option and the settlement value (see entry) of the index on the day an exercise notice is given, multiplied by the index multiplier (see entry under the "Commodity Terms" section)

expiration cycle: the dates upon which options for an underlying security expire, assigned as either the January cycle, the February cycle or the March cycle

expiration date: the date upon which an option and the right to exercise it expire

futures: contracts for the purchase or sale of commodities or financial instruments over an exchange

gamma: a measurement of how fast the delta changes, based upon a unit change in the underlying futures price

in the money: a call option with a strike price that is less than the market price of the underlying security. For a put option, the strike price must be greater than the market price of the underlying security.

index option: an option based upon an entire index, such as the S&P 500, and if exercised, settlement is paid in cash since physical delivery of all the stocks in the index is not practical

intrinsic value: the amount that an option is in the money

LEAPS (long-term equity anticipation securities) : long-term stock or index options with an expiration date up to three years in the future

open interest: the number of futures contracts, or options, that have not been fulfilled or delivered, used as an indication of the depth and liquidity of an instrument or market

out of the money: a call option with a strike price that is more than the market price of the underlying security. For a put option, the strike price must be less than the market price of the underlying security.

premium: options have intrinsic value (the amount that an option is in the money) and time value (a value assigned to an option based on the time left before expiration—the longer, the greater the value), both of which make up the premium, or the amount the buyer of an option pays to the seller

put: an option giving the holder the right, but not the obligation, to sell an underlying stock to the purchaser of the put at a specific price for a fixed period of time

settlement value: the price calculated at the close of a trading session used to calculate gains and losses on futures prices

underlying security: the stock upon which an option contract is based

Commodities Terms

actuals: the physical or cash commodity, as opposed to a commodity futures contract

assignable contract: a contract that allows the holder to convey his rights to a third party

backwardation: a situation where the futures prices are progressively lower the further into the future the delivery months go (e.g., gold quoted in May is at $390 per ounce, and in June it's quoted at $380 per ounce). This word is just as weird as its counterpart, "contango," which is where prices in succeeding delivery months are progressively higher. Both terms are so novel, they had to be mentioned.

basis: the difference between the cash price of a commodity and the price of the closest futures contract for the same commodity

cash market: the market for the cash commodity, as opposed to the futures market

commodity pool operator: individuals or firms in the business of investing in commodity futures contracts using funds obtained from investors that are pooled to make purchases

commodity price index: an index or average of selected commodity prices used to represent the market in general, or a specific subset of commodities

contract: a unit of trading for commodity futures that describes the amount and grade of the commodity and the date on which the contract matures and becomes deliverable

corn-hog ratio: the relationship between the cost of feeding the hogs, expressed as a ratio, to the sale price of the hogs

delivery instrument: a document that indicates delivery on a futures contract, such as a warehouse receipt or shipping papers

index multiplier: part of a calculation associated with a specific index used in arriving at the value of stocks in settling gains or losses for index futures trading

GLOBEX: the international electronic trading system for futures and options that allows exchanges to list their contracts and derivatives for sale after normal trading hours

spot market: a market in which commodities like grain, crude oil and RAM chips are bought and sold for cash and delivered immediately (also called cash market)

Index

About The Authors

Randy Rodman started his professional career in marketing in the financial and computer industries, for clients ranging from Apple Computer and Ashton-Tate to Epson America and Hewlett-Packard. Randy left the world of marketing to write professionally on marketing and business, the Internet, investing and health, among other subjects. He lives in Los Angeles and has been an avid day trader for several years.

Don Logay boasts 17 years experience as a journalist. He is a contributing writer to hundreds of magazines and newspapers and is a three-time winner of the Business Press Association award for Excellence in Journalism. Logay is also a writer/producer/director of live business theater and multimedia presentations for Fortune 500 companies. He lives near San Diego.

About Entrepreneur

Entrepreneur Media Inc., founded in 1973, is the nation's leading authority on small and entrepreneurial businesses.

Anchored by *Entrepreneur* magazine, which is read by more than 2 million people monthly, Entrepreneur Media boasts a stable of magazines, including *Entrepreneur's Start-ups*, *Entrepreneur's Be Your Own Boss*, *Entrepreneur's Home Office* e-zine, *Entrepreneur's Franchise Zone* e-zine, and *Entrepreneur Mexico*. But Entrepreneur Media is more than just magazines. Entrepreneur.com is the world's largest Web site devoted to small business and features smallbizsearch.com, a search engine targeting small-business topics.

Entrepreneur Press, started in 1998, publishes books to inspire and inform readers. For information about a customized version of this book, contact Christie Barnes Stafford at (949) 261-2325 or e-mail her at cstafford@entrepreneurmag.com.

Current titles from Entrepreneur Press:

Benjamin Franklin's 12 Rules Of Management:
The Founding Father of American Business Solves Your Toughest Problems

Business Plans Made Easy:
It's Not as Hard as You Think

Creative Selling:
Boost Your B2B Sales

Financial Fitness in 45 Days:
The Complete Guide to Shaping Up Your Finances

Get Smart:
365 Tips to Boost Your Entrepreneurial IQ

Knock-Out Marketing:
Powerful Strategies to Punch Up Your Sales

Radicals & Visionaries:
Entrepreneurs Who Revolutionized the 20th Century

Start Your Own Business:
The Only Start-up Book You'll Ever Need

Success for Less:
100 Low-Cost Businesses You Can Start Today

303 Marketing Tips
Guaranteed to Boost Your Business

Young Millionaires:
Inspiring Stories to Ignite Your Entrepreneurial Dreams

Where's The Money?
Sure-Fire Financial Solutions for Your Small Business

Forthcoming titles from Entrepreneur Press:

How to be a Teenage Millionaire:
Start Your Own Business, Make Your Own Money and Run Your Own Life

How to Dotcom:
A Step-by-Step Guide to E-Commerce

Grow Your Business

"Mandatory reading for any small-business owner who is serious about success."

— *Jay Conrad Levinson, author, Guerrilla Marketing series of books*

ISBN 1-891984-04-7
$19.95
paperback
296 pages
(price subject
to change)

Powerhouse Marketing Tactics for Making Big Profits

Written for both new and established small-business owners, this nuts-and-bolts guide gives you the marketing firepower you need to satisfy customers, attract prospects, boost your profits and blast the competition.

Packed with proven techniques, tips and advice, this easy-to-read guide covers every aspect of marketing, including:

- How to think like a marketer
- How to select the best markets for your products and services
- 4 common marketing mistakes and how to avoid them
- Tips for writing your marketing plan
- Sure-fire selling tactics that get results
- Building your presence on the internet

Available at **www.smallbizbooks.com** and at local and online bookstores

The Secrets and Lives of the 20th Century's Most Influential Innovators and Trailblazers

The 20th Century marked an era of unprecedented progress, growth and ingenuity. *RADICALS AND VISIONARIES* reveals the complete stories of over 70 legendary masters of enterprise and the unsung entrepreneurial heroes who charted the course of business throughout the century. You'll discover little-known facts and learn the success secrets of such movers and shakers as:

- *Former cabaret singer Coco Chanel who thumbed her nose at the suffocating styles of the 19th century and sparked a fashion revolution that still influences designers today*

- *Ron Popeil, a part-time carnival huckster and cutlery salesman whose late-night TV commercials for kitchen gadgets kicked off the infomercial phenomenon*

- *A.P. Giannini, the greengrocer with no financial experience who took on "the suits" and founded the world's largest bank*

RADICALS & VISIONARIES is a lively, revealing, and often astonishing chronicle of the lives and accomplishments of the most influential entrepreneurs of the past 100 years.

ISBN 1-891984-13-6 $17.95   paperback   460 pages   72 b & w photos   (Price subject to change)

Available at **www.smallbizbooks.com**
and at local and online bookstores

Entrepreneur Press